Identification
Guide
to the
Trees
of
Canada

Identification Guide to the Trees of Canada

Jean Lauriault
National Museum of Natural Sciences

Illustrations
Marcel Jomphe
Susan Laurie-Bourque

Published by
Fitzhenry & Whiteside

© 1989 National Museum of Natural Sciences, Ottawa

Published by
Fitzhenry & Whiteside
195 Allstate Parkway, Markham, Ontario L3R 4T8

Editor: Glenys Popper
Translator: Translation coordinated by the Office of the Secretary of State
Illustrations: Marcel Jomphe and Susan Laurie-Bourque
Typesetter: Rowsell Typesetting

Written, typeset, and assembled in Canada
Printed and bound in the United States of America

Canadian Cataloguing in Publication Data
Lauriault, Jean
   Identification guide to the trees of Canada

Translation of: Guide d'identification des arbres du Canada.
Co-published by the National Museum of Natural Sciences.
Includes bibliographical references.
ISBN 0-88902-564-9

1. Trees - Canada - Identification. I. National Museum of Natural Sciences (Canada). II. Title.

QK201.L3813 1989   582.160971   C89-094778-3

This book is dedicated to my wife, Ginette, and to my two sons, Eric and Nicholas.

Contents

Illustrations

Foreword

This book evolved from a series of workshops offered to the general public by the Interpretation and Extension Division of the National Museum of Natural Sciences in the fall of 1977.

The workshops, directed particularly towards families, aimed to help people to recognize and become familiar with the trees of the Ottawa region with ease and enjoyment. A small guide book, herbarium sheets, fresh twigs, and exhibition pieces helped participants to learn more about the local trees.

Originally the guide contained only a few illustrations and a catalogue of codes. For each tree it gave the scientific name, the suggested English name and the suggested French name. But once we had seen how easily the uninitiated, particularly children, succeeded in identifying trees we decided to expand the guide to its present form.

Acknowledgments

I wish to thank the National Museum of Natural Sciences for making this book possible. The staff of the Botany Division, especially Mr Albert Dugal and Mr George Argus, offered invaluable advice and recommendations. I am grateful also to the Montreal Botanical Garden and Agriculture Canada Biosystematic Research Branch for providing specimens.

The information contained in this volume has been drawn from many pamphlets, brochures and publications produced by the Federal Departments of the Environment and Agriculture, the Provincial Ministries of Environment and Agriculture, and by the Provincial Museums. The following volumes were consulted regularly and are included in the Bibliography: Hosie's *Native Tress of Canada*; Marie-Victorin's *Flore laurentienne*; Roland and Smith's *The Flora of Nova Scotia*; Scoggan's *The Flora of Canada*; Moss's *The Flora of Alberta*; Budd's *Budd's Flora of the Canadian Prairie Provinces*; Lyon's *Trees, Shrubs and Flowers to Know in British Columbia*; Harlow and Harrar's *Textbook of Dendrology*; and Elias's *The Complete Trees of North America*.

The distribution maps by R.C. Hosie in the above-named book were of assistance in the drawing up of maps of the Canadian areas. Rousseau's *Géographie floristique du Quebéc-Labrador*, Soper and Heimburger's *Shrubs of Ontario*, Moss's *Flora*, and publications by the British Columbia Provincial Museum were also used as reference works. The *Atlas of Rare Vascular Plants of Ontario* and the Syllogeus series of rare vascular plants of the different provinces, both prepared by the National Museum of Natural Sciences, were invaluable sources of information that helped in the preparation of the distribution maps of trees rare in Canada. The research carried out by these authors has been instrumental in the clarificiation and/or confirmation of the ranges of Canada's native trees.

Information concerning the ranges of trees in the United States was taken principally from Little's *Atlas of United States Trees*. Elias's *The Complete Trees of North America* was consulted for those ranges not appearing in the *Atlas*. Other works were consulted to round out this information.

Maps of the forest regions are adapted from those in Rowe's *Forest Regions of Canada* and, for the areas in the United States, from Braun's *Deciduous Forests of Eastern North America* and Küchler's *Potential Natural Vegetation of the Conterminous United States*.

The scientific names given in this book have been taken largely from J.T. and R. Kartesz's *A Synonymized Checklist of the Vascular Flora of the United States, Canada, and Greenland*.

I am grateful to all authors of the above-named publications.

I would also like to thank Louise Leclair, Carol Campbell and Doug Hoy and all those, from near and far, who contributed to the realization of this book.

JEAN LAURIAULT

Introduction

This book is written for the general public and for all who are interested in our living world. Mechanization, industrialization and "progress" have produced concrete monsters, fatal clouds and increasingly hazy skies; and many people feel the need to seek out green places, breathe clean air and gaze at a clear sky. This book is intended for those people: for all who wish to enjoy, discover and appreciate the trees around them.

In addition to making tree identification easier, it is hoped that this guide will awaken in the reader a new interest in his environment. It is also intended as a starting point, designed to arouse the readers' curiosity and encourage the consultation of more advanced works. These works will in turn acquaint them even better with our Canadian tree flora and thus, perhaps, further its conservation.

With the help of an identification key, readers can use a visual approach based on examination of the leaf. Ambiguous specimens may require the use of our other senses. The more we use our senses to identify a tree, the better its characteristics will remain in our memory. Scientific language, invaluable as it is, often disheartens and discourages the uninitiated. Traditional dichotomous keys are sometimes long, complicated and filled with scientific terms and techniques hard to remember. In this guide, four easy-to-use leaf-identification tables replace the texts of traditional keys.

In a number of works, the morphological description of species is emphasized; in this guide, it is restricted to the tree's distinctive features. Descriptions of trees easily identifiable are succinct. Trees more difficult to identify have more elaborate descriptions. This volume highlights historical data; the past, present and future uses of trees; ecology; toxicity; diseases; and the origins of Latin, English and French names. Descriptions of some of the more frequently encountered ornamentals that are not native to Canada are also included.

In this book, two new species have been added to the native flora of Canada and one species has been omitted. The additions are the shumard oak (*Quercus shumardii* Buckl.) and the northern pin oak (*Quercus ellipsoidalis* E.J. Hill). The omission is the chestnut oak (*Quercus prinus* L.).

How This Book Is Organized

At first glance the manner in which the various species are treated may seem disorganized, but this seeming disorder masks an easy-to-use though unconventional approach: all trees with similar visual characteristics are grouped together, regardless of their genus, by way of a key consisting of the combination of a capital letter followed by three numbers placed in the guide *in alphabetical, then numerical, order*. For this reason some species are intermixed.

For each species will be found the assigned combination, the suggested English name, other English names, the suggested French name, and other French names, the scientific name, the family name, a distribution map, a list of the distinctive features, and facts of interest. An illustration of the leaf is also included.

Some tree-related activities are suggested: how to start up a leaf collection or herbarium, and how to determine the age of a tree.

It is recommended that the reader colour the illustrations to the guide according to the shades actually observed during trips. This will not only add a personal touch to the book but will create a permanent record of the reader's visual image of each species.

The Combination

A combination composed of a capital letter followed by three numbers, e.g., **G 572**, has been assigned to each species. These combinations were arrived at by applying the information set out in the identification system's four illustrated tables. The various species with the same combinations are represented by a lower-case letter placed at the end of the combination, e.g., **G 572a** and **G 572b**. The method by which each combination is obtained is described in detail in the following chapter—The Identification System.

Trees that are Rare in Canada

In addition to describing the trees' ranges, note is made of the species designated rare in Canada and catalogued as such in the National

3

Museum of Natural Sciences' Syllogeus collection (Numbers 14, 17, 18, 20, 23, 27, 28, 48, 50 and 59). At the end of the book is a list of rare trees of Canada and a list of rare trees grouped by province.

The Names of Trees

The English and French Names
The names of trees are handed down through generations. The first settlers brought a store of knowledge from their countries of origin. Sometimes, they mistook a native tree for a similar European species. For example, the arborvitae was erroneously called cedar; in fact true cedars of the genus *Cedrus* are found only in the Mediterranean and Himalayan regions.

In the individual entries, the first English name indicated for each tree is the recommended name, this is followed by the common English names. The French names follow. When no name exists for the species, the translation for the scientific name has been adopted. For instance, heart-leaved birch is used for *Betula cordifolia*.

Throughout this book, an attempt has been made to explain the origins and meanings of the colloquial English and French names. These names can reveal a great deal of information concerning the tree: its habitat; the texture, colour and smell of its leaves, twigs, bark, flowers and wood; and its uses and medicinal properties.

The Latin Name

The scientific name of each tree is given to establish the exact identity of the species and to serve as a reference for anyone wishing to learn more about it. The Latin name is very important because it is universally understood. To avoid any confusion arising from the diversity of common names existing for each tree, the Latin name should be noted and remembered.

Although the scientific names used in this book are largely taken from Kartesz and Kartesz (1980), some widely used synonyms have also been included.

The Latin name appears in italics and is made up of three parts: the generic name, e.g., *Populus* (always beginning with a capital letter); the specific name, e.g., *grandidentata* (always beginning with a lower-case letter); and the abbreviation of the name of the first person to have described the tree, e.g., Michx. (for Michaux). Thus, ***Populus*** *grandidentata* **Michx.** represents the scientific name for the large-toothed aspen.

As knowledge increases, it is often necessary to change the original classification of a plant. When this happens, the name of the author who first described the plant and gave it its original classification is bracketed, and the name of the author who renamed the plant follows. For example, *Abies lasiocarpa* **(Hook.) Nutt.** indicates that W.J. Hooker described this tree, a subalpine fir, for the first time as a pine (*Pinus lasiocarpa* Hook.) and that later T. Nuttall assigned it to the genus *Abies*.

The abbreviation **var.** stands for variety. The abbreviation **ssp.** stands for subspecies. The use of **ex** or **in** indicates that an author published a description provided by another author. Thus *Salix hookeriana* **Barr. ex Hook.** indicates that W.J. Hooker published (in *Flora boreali-americana*) a description that was afterwards published by J. Barratt.

In order to make these names more accessible and comprehensible to the general reader the author felt it important to deal with the etymology of each.

The Family Name

The family name is given for each species. This name is given in Latin and is not always very meaningful. Therefore, the family's main type is also mentioned. For example, Oleaceae is in this book referred to as the Olive family.

A list of trees by family appears at the end of the book.

Distribution Maps

Fifteen thousand years ago Canada was covered with a thick layer of ice. Vegetation appeared only after the glaciers retreated and the ground gradually dried out. The distribution of vegetation is such that there are recognizable bioclimatic or forest zones. These zones are most likely the product of altitude, climate, natural disturbances, soil and subsoil, wildlife and man's influence. The classification proposed by J.S. Rowe (1972) has been adopted in this guide. Canada's forests can be divided into eight forest regions plus the Grassland region. The trees we are interested in are located in these regions.

6

Forest Regions of Canada and Northern United States

Map 1
Boreal

Map 4
Coast

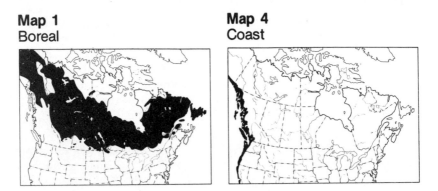

Map 2
Subalpine

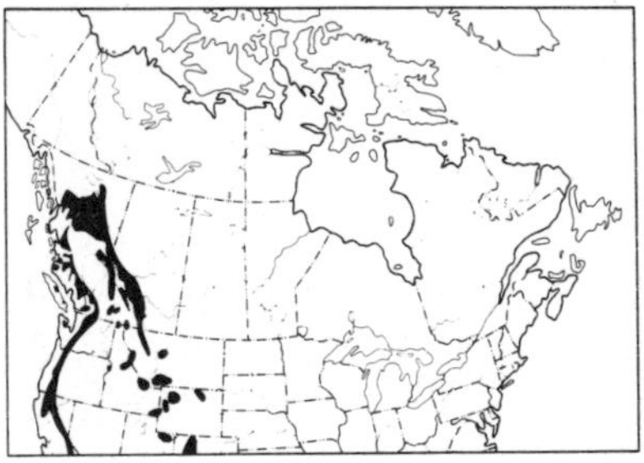

Map 5
Columbia

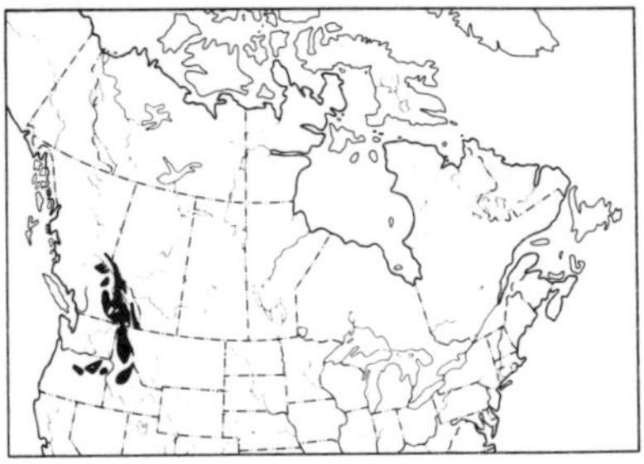

Map 3
Montane

Map 6
Deciduous

Adaptation from J.S. Rowe for Canada and
A.W. Küchler and E.L. Braun for U.S.

Map 7
Great Lakes – St Lawrence

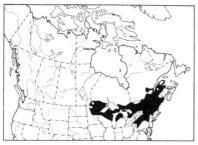

Map 8
Acadian

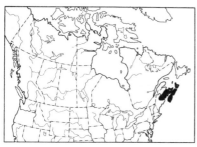

Map 9
Grassland

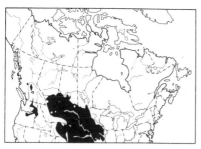

Interesting Facts

A synthesis of the author's readings is to be found in this section. Each tree is treated individually and the length of the text is related to the tree's abundance and past and present economic importance: some trees played a major role in a region's development, others played a prime role in the life of the North American Indians and that of the first settlers. The trees about which we know little and whose usefulness is not obvious, have not been treated at great length.

The etymology of the scientific, the English and the French names, historic details, facts concerning the economic importance, toxicity, medicinal properties, ecological situation and diseases of each tree are usually included.

In this section the reader should discover a wealth of information leading to a greater respect for, and knowledge and appreciation of, trees.

Illustrations

The illustrations were drawn using typical specimens from the Canadian National Herbarium and Agriculture Canada's Herbarium, as well as fresh specimens. The drawings illustrate, as much as possible, the variations in the shape and margin of leaves and leaflets that occur in specimens of the same species. Also illustrated are the characteristics of fruit, bark and silhouette that help to differentiate one species from another.

Distinctive Features

In this section the reader will not find a detailed morphological description of the species (these can be found in other, more specialized, works) but rather, the characteristics considered by the author to be the most obvious and easy to observe or detect. This is why the characteristic features of the tree are not systematically repeated for each species.

The list of distinctive features found in this book will help the reader confirm identification of a species. Details such as colour, smell and taste, provide information impossible to render in a drawing.

For purposes of comparison, height and diameter (expressed in metric units) have been added. These measurements represent averages for mature trees.

The Identification System

Each of the four leaf-identification tables deals with one of the most obvious characteristics of the leaf or leaflet: its arrangement on the twig, its shape, its margin and its veins. The grouping of these four characteristics normally enables us to identify the tree under observation. Although identification according to the tree's leaf enables us to choose between species, the use of the leaf-identification key (described in detail below) in conjunction with facts about the tree's silhouette, twigs, bark, flowers and fruits allows more precise identification.

How to use the Identification System

It is a good idea to become familiar with the illustrations in the *four tables* of the identification system, and with the illustrations accompanying the terminology pertaining to the tree, leaf or leaflet and twig.

Observing the Tree

Look closely at the tree you wish to identify. Use all of your senses in order to appreciate the tree in its entirety. Many of its secrets will be revealed this way. Study its silhouette, foliage, bark, twigs. Flowers, fruit and buds should also be studied, depending on the season. Does the silhouette have a specific shape? Is it flared, pyramid-shaped or slender? Is the trunk twisted or straight? Run your fingers along the bark. Is it smooth, rough, or in papery shreds? What colour is it? Is it covered with horizontal openings (called lenticels)? and are these large or small? Touch the twigs to determine the texture. Are they round or four-sided? Do they have needles? Are there several buds grouped at the tip? Is a smell released when you scratch the bark? Try to find the flowers, fruit or cones. Do they have a characteristic shape, texture or smell? The answers to these questions will give you clues that will make identification easier and help to confirm it.

9

Table I.   Arrangement of Leaves on Twigs.

Conifers

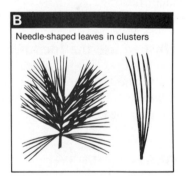

Deciduous (Flowering) Trees

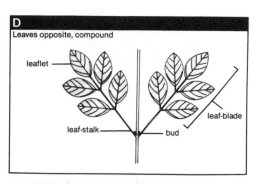

D
Leaves opposite, compound

leaflet

leaf-blade

leaf-stalk — bud

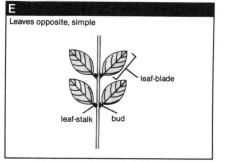

E
Leaves opposite, simple

leaf-blade

leaf-stalk   bud

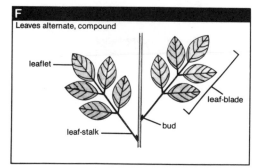

F
Leaves alternate, compound

leaflet

leaf-blade

leaf-stalk — bud

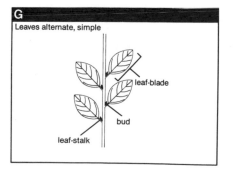

G
Leaves alternate, simple

leaf-blade

bud

leaf-stalk

12

Table II. Shape of Leaf or Leaflet.

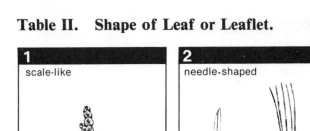

1 scale-like

2 needle-shaped

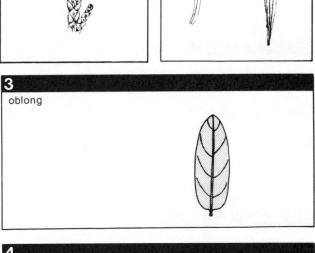

3 oblong

4 lanceolate or spear-shaped

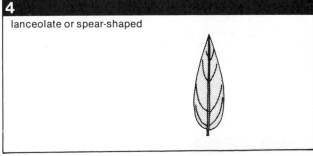

5 oval

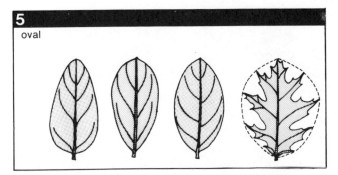

6
rounded

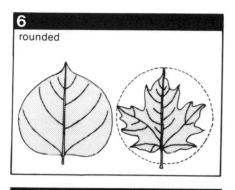

7
cordate or heart-shaped

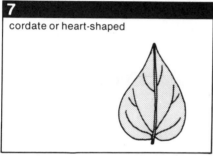

8
triangular

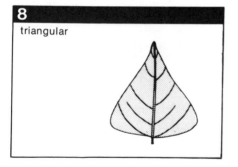

9
asymmetrical

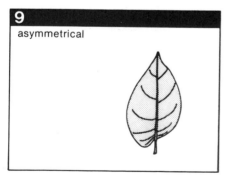

Table III.   Margin of Leaf or Leaflet.

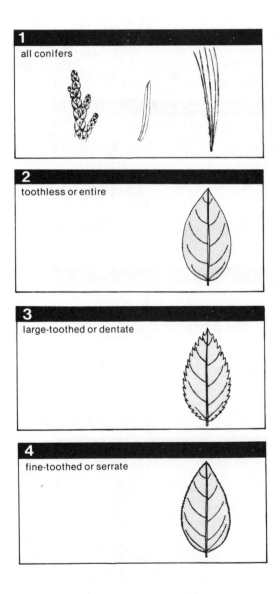

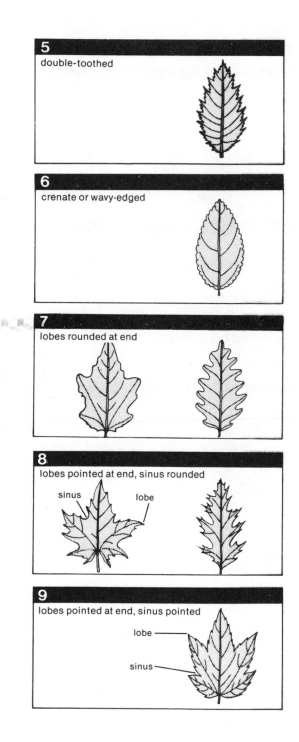

15

5

double-toothed

6

crenate or wavy-edged

7

lobes rounded at end

8

lobes pointed at end, sinus rounded

sinus   lobe

9

lobes pointed at end, sinus pointed

lobe —

sinus —

Table IV.   Arrangement of Veins of Leaf or Leaflet.

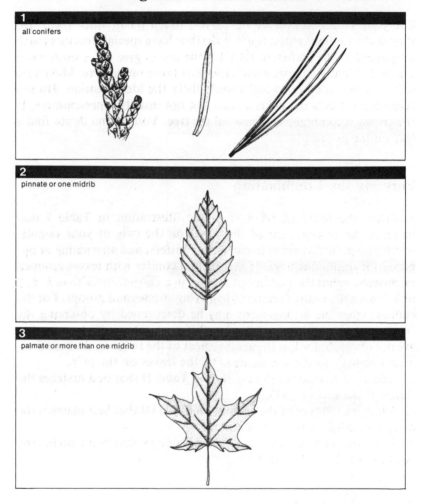

Observing the Leaf

Use your senses to observe the leaves; touch them, smell them. Do they shake in the slightest breeze? Do they have special structures such as glands? Is the leaf-stalk flat? Do the leaves give off a smell when crushed? Finally, choose a leaf typical of those on the tree. Make sure it is healthy—a diseased leaf could falsify the identification. Do not select base shoots or suckers, these are not usually representative. If the crown is too high, look around the tree. You will no doubt find a leaf on the ground.

Forming the Combination

a. Select the letter (**A-G**) next to the illustration in Table I that matches the arrangement of the leaves on the twig of your sample: overlapping, in clusters or isolated for conifers, and alternating or opposed for deciduous trees. If the tree is a conifer with leaves grouped in clusters, count the number of needles in a cluster: more than **5, 5, 3** or **2**. This will greatly facilitate identifying species and groups. For deciduous trees the arrangement may be determined by observing the current year's growth, usually of a different colour. If the branches are out of reach, look at the arrangement of the twigs on the branches; it corresponds to the arrangement of the leaves on the twig.
b. Select the number of the example in Table II that best matches the shape of the leaf or leaflet.
c. Select the number of the example in Table III that best matches the margin or edge of the leaf or leaflet.
d. Select the number of the example in Table IV that best matches the venation of the leaf or leaflet.

Discovering the Tree

a. Now combine the letter and the tree numbers. Let us assume that the result is **G 532**. The letter **G** means the tree is a deciduous one with alternate, simple leaves. The first number, **5**, corresponds to the leaf's oval shape and the number **3** describes the leaf's large-toothed margin. Finally, the number **2** indicates that the leaf has a single midrib. A combination has been assigned to each of 149 species described in this volume. They are arranged in **alphabetical order from A to G**, and in **numerical order from 111 to 962**. The combination is shown in the upper left-hand corner of the page. Once you have located the combination in the guide, you will obtain the name of the species you are observing.

b. Compare the leaf to the illustration and read about its distinctive features to confirm your identification. A combination might correspond to several species of trees. Possible choices are shown by a *lower-case letter* at the end of the combination (such as in **G 532a**). In this case, a choice must be made. It may also happen that certain species of trees have two different combinations because the shape and margin of the leaf or leaflet vary within the same species. This is the case with the large-toothed aspen: **G 532b** and **G 632**. The more common shape of leaf on this tree is oval, i.e. **5** (the first digit in the numerical portion), and the tree is located under the combination **G 532b**. Sometimes, however, the leaf is almost round, i.e. **6**, which produces the combination **G 632**. This combination is listed with a cross-reference to combination **G 532b**.

Problems of Identification

If you fail to identify a tree, it may be for one of the following reasons.

a. A mistake in selecting the combination.

b. The tree may be an introduced species not covered in this guide (due to limited space, it is not possible to cover all introduced species or all varieties).

c. The example may be a hybrid (most common among spruce, poplar, ash and willow).

d. Your specimen could be a shrub rather than a tree, according to the definition of a tree at the beginning of the guide.

Note on the genera *Crataegus* (hawthorn) and *Amelanchier* (serviceberry): Given the extreme plasticity of these two genera, the number of species varies considerably from one author to another. Identification of species is made enormously complicated by their very great capacity for hybridization. For this reason, both the hawthorn and serviceberry are treated here as genus only.

Sample Identification

To help the reader understand the identification system, two examples, a conifer (the red pine) and a deciduous tree (the American basswood), are identified below.

The Red Pine

1. Observing the tree and its leaves

Look closely at the tree to be identified. It is a conifer, located in a sandy field. Touch its foliage. Notice that the dark green needles are sharp, long, grow all around the twig and are grouped in twos. Next, run your finger over the bark: it is reddish and scaly. Smell your hand: you will probably detect a smell of resin. Now, try to find some cones. There should be some on the ground; if there are none, examine the crown, where you may spot some, either open or closed.

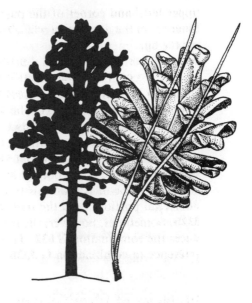

2. Forming the combination

a. Choose the letter next to the illustration in Table I that corresponds to the arrangement of the leaves on the twig: **B** (needle-shaped leaves in clusters).

B ---

b. Select the number of the illustration in Table II that best identifies the shape of the leaf: **2** (needle-shaped).

B 2--

c. Select the number of the illustration in Table III best identifying the margin of the leaf: **1** (all conifers).

B 21-

d. Select the number of the illustration in Table IV that identifies the venation of the leaf: **1** (all conifers).

B 211

3. Discovering the tree

a. The combination of the letter and the three numbers gives **B 211**. Look up **B 211** in the guide. Notice that the combination **B 211** corresponds to several species of trees. A lower-case letter at the end of the combination is now used to identify the species more precisely. In this example, there are 13 species of which 12 are native, giving **a** to **m**. This combination groups all conifers with needle-shaped leaves in clusters. In our example, there are two needles per cluster, of 10 to 15 cm in length. The name of the tree can be found simply by comparing the specimen to the illustrations.

b. Begin with **B 211a**. It is clear from the illustration that there are more than two needles per cluster. This is not what we are looking for. Only **B 211j**, **B 211k**, **B 211l** and **B 211m** have two needles in a cluster. Look at the three combinations **B 211k**, **B 211l** and **B 211m**. All three have two needles per cluster, but they are much too short. **B 211j**, however, has two *long* needles per cluster. Our choice is confirmed by reading about the distinctive features. The tree is called *red pine*; a map shows the range of the species, and the text provides several interesting facts about it.

The American Basswood in Early July

1. Observing the tree and its leaves

Look closely at the tree. It has a regular, slender silhouette, with dense foliage. The breeze carries the pleasant fragrance of its cream-coloured flowers. Look more closely and you will notice thousands of bees busy gathering honey from the flowers hanging from a sort of leaf. The greyish bark is scaly, but smooth to the touch on the large branches. The small branches form a zigzag pattern. Choose a typical leaf. It will be large and vary from 12 to 15 centimetres in width.

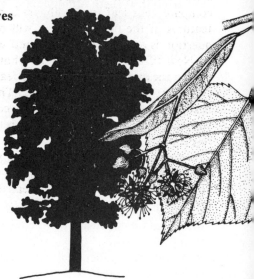

2. Forming the combination

a. Select the letter of the illustration in Table I that corresponds to the arrangement of the leaves on the twig: **G** (simple leaves that alternate on the twig).

G ---

b. Select the number of the illustration in Table II that corresponds to the shape of the leaf. Notice that the leaf is asymmetrical and heart-shaped. The drawings in Table II show both, but only **7** matches the heart shape.

G 7--

c. Select the number of the illustration in Table III to match the leaf's margin: **3** (large-toothed).

G 73–

d. Select a number of the illustration in Table IV that corresponds to the leaf's venation. Since more than one midrib starts at the base of the leaf-blade, the choice comes down to **3** (palmate). The arrangement of the ribs is not always clear in some leaves, so **2** may also be chosen.

G 732 and **G 733**

3. Discovering the tree

We now have two combinations: **G 732** and **G 733**.

a. Look up combination **G 732** in the guide. You must make a choice, since two species correspond to the same combination. When you compare your leaf to the illustrations and read about the distinctive features of the two species, it will become apparent that the tree in question is an American basswood with the combination **G 732a**.

b. Now take a moment to see what would have happened had you chosen the asymmetrically shaped leaf instead of the heart-shaped leaf (Table II), namely, **9** instead of **7**. The combinations would then have been **G 932** and **G 933**. Look these combinations up in the guide; you will find that they include cross-references to **G 732a** and **G 733a** respectively.

If you do not succeed in finding your specimen in the guide after following these steps, you may have made a mistake in arriving at your combination. Carefully repeat all steps of the identification process.

What Is a Native Tree of Canada?

Most of us think of a forest as a group of trees living on a piece of land. But we need only use our eyes and ears to realize that the forest is alive with intense activity, from its carpeted floor to its mature timbers. It is a complex community of living organisms composed of countless, extremely diversified populations of which the tree is the dominant species. Think of the forest as nature's city and the trees as its inhabitants.

Many definitions can apply to the tree but it is, above all, a living thing that is born, grows, reproduces and dies. Like all living organisms, trees are made up of cells, but they are unique in being composed principally (approximately 80 per cent) of dead cells: only a small portion of the tree is alive and these few living cells maintain its vital functions.

It is often said that trees are the giants of the forest, and this is particularly true of the redwood (*Sequoia sempervirens* (Lamb. ex D. Don) Endl.). Try to imagine a tree 90 metres in height, 10 metres in diameter and over 2000 years old. This giant, the largest living tree on earth, is a species native to California. But although the redwood wins the prize for greatest diameter, the Great Basin bristlecone pine (*Pinus longaeva* D.K. Bailey) can boast a 3000 to 5000-year lifespan. By way of comparison, the average eastern white pine specimen measures approximately 25 metres by 1 metre and lives for 400 years.

Canada has its own giants, for example, the Douglas fir (*Pseudotsuga menziesii* (Mirb.) Franco), a species native to the Pacific Coast Region. Some specimens may reach 90 metres in height, measure over 5 metres in diameter and live for 1200 years (the oldest known trees in Canada are located on Vancouver Island).

In this guide, a *native tree of Canada* is defined as a *perennial woody plant at least 5 metres in height and growing naturally in Canada, whose stem (trunk or bole), which supports a crown, does not divide below a certain distance from the ground.*

Some intermediate species, i.e. small trees or large shrubs, are included in the guide, along with several trees that have been introduced as ornamentals. *Shrubs*, or woody plants without a bole and under 5 metres in height at maturity, have been excluded.

The trees fall into two groups: *conifers*, or *gymnosperms*, and deciduous trees, or *angiosperms*.

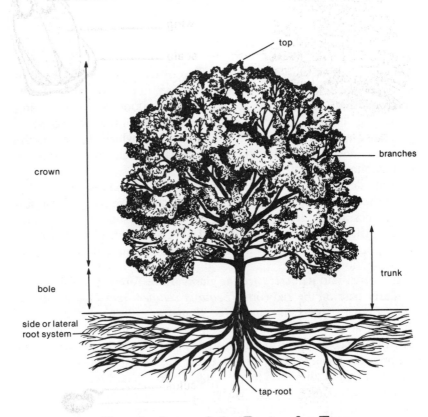

Figure 1.   Terminology of the Parts of a Tree.

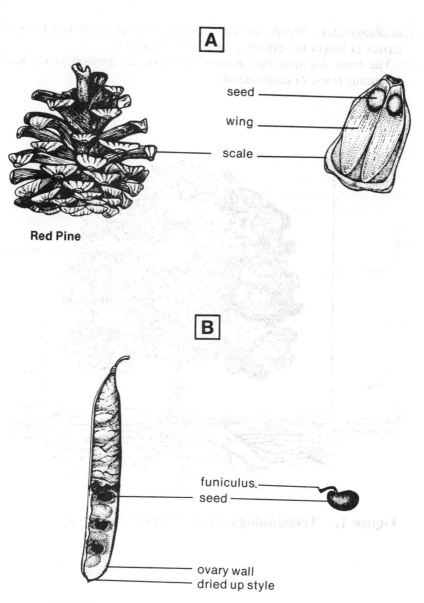

Figure 2. Gymnosperms and Angiosperms.
A) the Gymnosperms are plants with seeds naked on the cone-scales;
B) the Angiosperms are plants with seeds enclosed in the fruit.

Conifers

The conifers are associated with the gymnosperms. They are known as the softwoods and evergreens. Unlike the deciduous trees, most of which shed all their leaves in the autumn, conifers shed small numbers of leaves continuously remaining green and vigorous all year round. The only exception to the rule is the larches, which shed their needles every autumn.

Properly speaking, conifers do not have flowers. Nevertheless, the term flower is the common designation for the male and female organs of these trees. The seed-bearing organ is generally a cone, hence the origin of the term conifer. Although the conifers do not have fruit (a fertilized ovary at maturity), the term fruit is used in almost all reference works on botany.

As suggested by the etymology of the word gymnosperm, from Greek *gymnos* (naked) and *sperma* (sperm, or seed), the ovules and seeds are not enclosed respectively in ovary and fruit. The female cone, formed of scales, bears the seeds, which generally take two years to reach maturity. As a rule, coniferous trees are *monoecious*, i.e., they have both male and female organs on the same tree. The exceptions are the junipers and the yews, which are *dioecious*, i.e., the male and female organs are found on different trees.

Deciduous Trees

The angiosperms, or deciduous trees, include most of the native trees of Canada. They are known as hardwoods, and their leaves fall each year. The sole exception is the arbutus (*Arbutus menziesii* Pursh). It keeps its green foliage year-round and is the only evergreen deciduous tree in Canada.

The word angiosperm is derived from Greek *aggeion* (box, or envelope) and *sperma* (sperm, or seed), referring to plants in which either ovules are contained in an ovary or the seeds are enclosed in a fruit. These trees have true flowers and may be monoecious or dioecious.

What Is A Leaf?

The sun provides energy for all living organisms, but only green plants can capture and convert it into energy that can be assimilated by animals. This process is called photosynthesis. Chlorophyll, the pigment that gives plants their green colour, is the substance that intercepts the light energy. In the presence of solar energy channelled by the chlorophyll, simple elements such as water and carbon dioxide (carbonic gas) react to release complex, energy-rich chemical products such as sugars (carbohydrates) and oxygen. Plants, therefore, produce the energy necessary for the functioning of the vital processes of their consumers: animals. This is why plants are so important. This transformation of energy occurs in the marvellous factory that is the leaf.

The definition of a leaf is a plant organ attached to the stem by a *petiole*, or leaf-stalk, of varying length (*petiolated leaf*)—there may be no stalk (*sessile leaf*)—and most often supporting a thin blade that usually broadens out; this is called a *leaf-blade*. In some plant families, the leaf-blade is reduced to a needle or scale.

Simple and Compound Leaves

Leaves that are neither needles nor scales can be divided into two main categories: *simple leaves* and *compound leaves*. Simple leaves, such as those of the oak, birch or poplar, are best known; they consist of one part, whereas compound leaves have a leaf-blade divided into small leaves called *leaflets*.

Various characteristics allow us to differentiate between compound and simple leaves. A simple leaf is always attached to a woody, or ligneous, twig, whereas a leaflet is always attached to a fleshy principal or secondary leaf-stalk. Towards midsummer, buds appear at the leaf's axil, but there are no buds at the axil of a leaflet. Furthermore, in Canada, simple-leaved species are much more numerous (80 per cent) than compound-leaved species.

A compound leaf should not be confused with a group of simple

27

28

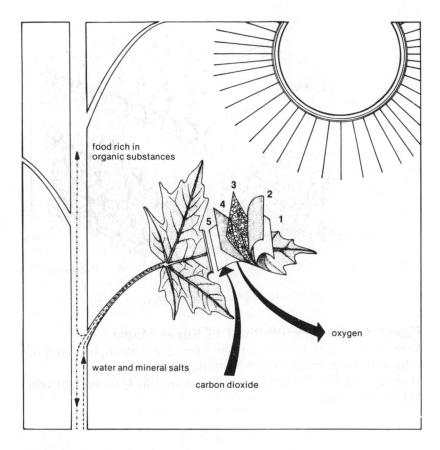

food rich in
organic substances

3

2

4

1

5

oxygen

water and mineral salts

carbon dioxide

Figure 3. Photosynthesis.

Photosynthesis is the transformation of solar energy into food usable
by plants. Water and mineral salts are carried to the leaves by xylem
vessels in the trunk and branches. Food produced in the leaves is redis-
tributed to the rest of the tree by phloem vessels. The tree breathes
through stomata, tiny holes in the epidermis, to exchange carbon
dioxide and oxygen.
1) upper epidermis 2) palisade cells 3) network of veins 4) spongy cells
5) lower epidermis.

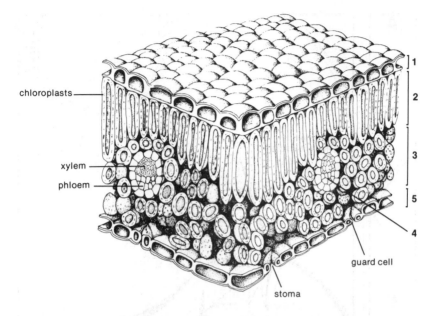

Figure 4. Perspective View of Sugar Maple Leaf.
Note the numerous chloroplasts, which contain chlorophyll, and the
veins with xylem and phloem-conducting cells.
1) upper epidermis 2) palisade cells 3) spongy cells 4) network of veins
5) lower epidermis

30

Opposite leaves

Alternate leaves

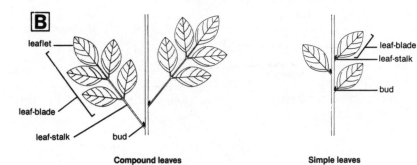

leaflet

leaf-blade

leaf-stalk   bud

Compound leaves

leaf-blade

leaf-stalk

bud

Simple leaves

Figure 5.   The Leaf
A) Leaf arrangement B) Leaf composition

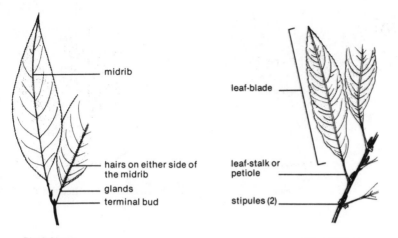

midrib

hairs on either side of
the midrib

glands

terminal bud

Black Cherry

leaf-blade

leaf-stalk or
petiole

stipules (2)

Pussy Willow

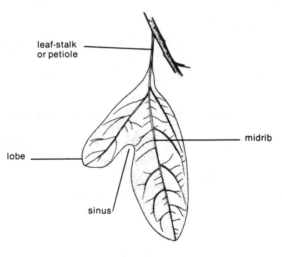

leaf-stalk
or petiole

midrib

lobe

sinus

Sassafras

Figure 6a.   Terminology of the Leaf.

32

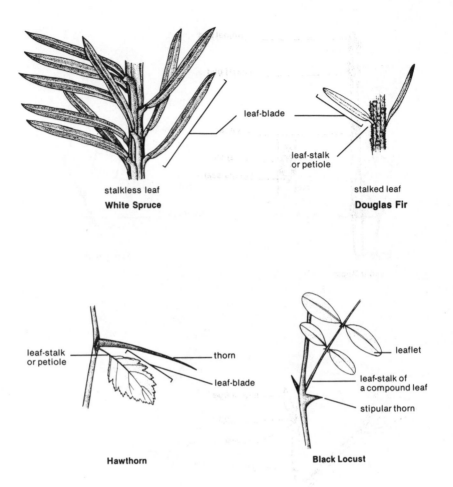

leaf-blade

leaf-stalk
or petiole

stalkless leaf
White Spruce

stalked leaf
Douglas Fir

leaf-stalk
or petiole

thorn

leaf-blade

leaflet

leaf-stalk of
a compound leaf

stipular thorn

Hawthorn

Black Locust

Figure 6b.   Terminology of the Leaf.

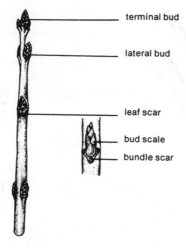

Sugar Maple

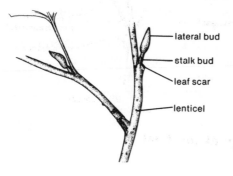

Speckled Alder

Figure 7. Terminology of the Twig.

leaves on a *shoot* (very short twig). These can be so close to one another that they seem to emerge from the same point. This feature can be observed in birch, larch, plum and apple trees.

If the leaflets are arranged either side of the midrib like the barbs of a feather, as in the ash and walnut, the leaves are called *pinnately compound*. If the leaflets are arranged like the fingers of a hand, as in the horsechestnut, they are called *palmately compound*.

Arrangement of Leaves on the Twig

Simple or compound leaves are attached to the stem or twig in one of two ways: *alternate* (in alternate positions), or *opposite* (at the same level). In some species, more than two leaves are found at the same level. These are called *verticillate* and in this work are considered opposite leaves.

Sometimes, when the crown is very high, it prevents the observer from seeing the arrangement of the leaves on the twigs. Since the buds are located at the axils of the leaves, and give birth to new twigs, the arrangement of the twigs on a branch reflects the way the leaf is attached.

At the leaf base of the leaf stalk two small foliar formations called *stipules* are sometimes found. There are also *winged leaf-stalks* or leaf-stalks with a *sheath* (nannyberry) and *glands* at the junction of the leaf-blade and the leaf-stalk (some willows, plum trees, cherry trees and poplars). Also, certain species have stipular thorns (black locust) or needles (hawthorn) on their twigs and in some species (e.g., honey-locust) even on their trunks. The presence or absence of such thorny bodies are other characteristics that can help identification.

Shape of the Leaf

The size and shape of leaves growing on the same tree may vary. Leaf characteristics are directly influenced by the habitat, age and size of the tree. Leaves also depend on the climate, and tree's health and their position in the crown (i.e., exposed to sunlight or not). For the best comparison, one should select leaves located in the same area in the crown and on twigs of equal size. The shape and size of the leaves of conifers are much more alike and regular than are those of deciduous trees.

Leaf Margin

The leaf's margin may vary in appearance. A leaf is designated *entire*, or *toothless*, when the edge is continuous, and *finely toothed*, or *serrate*, when the margin resembles the teeth of a saw. The term *largely toothed*, or *dentate*, applies when the margin has large teeth that are spaced apart and pointed. *Double-toothed*, refers to each tooth itself being finely toothed. If the margin has blunt or round-edged teeth, the leaf is called *crenate*, or *wavy-margined*. In maples and oaks, the notched leaf-blade forms relatively deep lobes, which may be rounded or pointed at the tip. The cleft between two lobes, called a *sinus*, may also be rounded or pointed.

Venation

Venation, the arrangement of veins on the leaf or leaflets caused by the vascular system, varies from one leaf to another.

As is the case for the leaflets in compound leaves, the veins may be arranged in one of two patterns: on either side of the midrib, like the barbs of a feather, in which case they are called *pinnate*; or arranged like the fingers of a hand, in which case they are called *palmate*.

Cones and Fruits

The seed-bearing organ, in the conifers called a *cone* and in the angiosperms called a *fruit*, is an important element in identifying the various species. The presence and type of cone or fruit often confirm the collector's identification. They are easier to find than the flowers since they usually remain on the tree longer or are found nearby.

The Cones of Conifers

Conifer seeds are borne on the scales of a cone. Most conifer cones have a woody consistency (lignified) except for the juniper which bears a fleshy fruit known as a berry; it is, nevertheless, a true cone whose scales become fleshy and then fuse together.

It is said that the exception confirms the rule, and sure enough, there are conifers that do not have cones. The western yew (*Taxus brevifolia* Nutt.) is a small western Canadian tree whose single, naked, dark-bluish seed is partly surrounded by a bright red fleshy body called an aril. Eastern Canada also has a yew: the Canada yew, or ground hemlock (*Taxus canadensis* Marsh.), a low-spreading shrub. Although its aril is edible, the pit and leaves contain poison that can be fatal to man and beast.

Flowers, Fruits and Seeds of Deciduous Trees

Angiosperms alone possess true flowers composed of four basic parts: the stamens, pistil, sepals and petals. The stamens (male) produce tiny grains of various colours and shapes called pollen. The *pistil* (female) consists of the ovary, which contains one or more ovules. The ovary, usually flask-shaped, may be one-celled (one carpel) or many-celled (many carpels). The *sepals*, normally green, are located at the base of each flower. Together the sepals make up the *calyx*. The *petals* are adjacent to the ovary and the stamens. Together the petals make up the

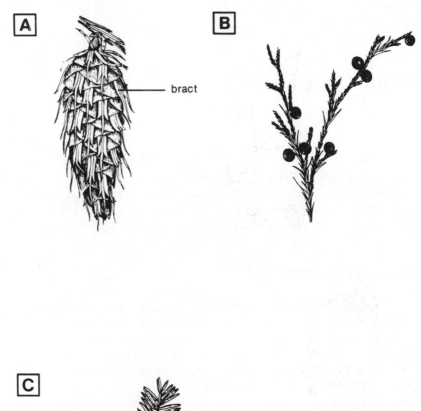

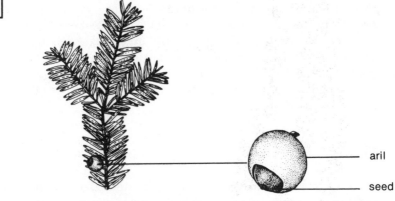

Figure 8.   Cones of Conifers.

A) woody cone of the Douglas fir B) fleshy cone of the red juniper
C) seed surround by aril of the western yew

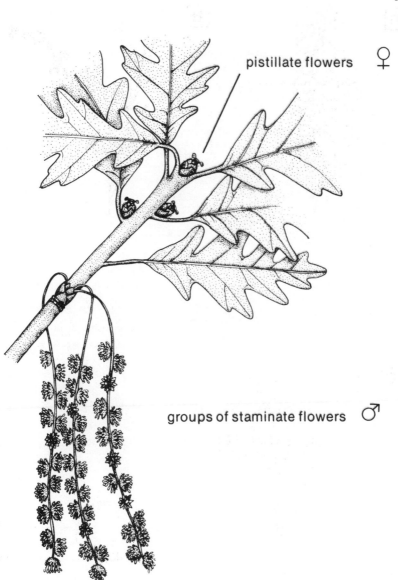

pistillate flowers ♀

groups of staminate flowers ♂

Figure 9.   Unisexual Flowers of the white oak.

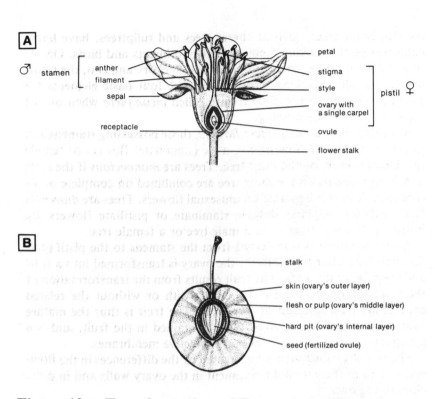

Figure 10. Transformation of Parts of the Flower to a Fruit.
A) parts of a complete flower B) parts of a plum (drupe)

corolla. Some trees, such as cherry trees and tuliptrees, have large, colourful petals, making them attractive to insects and birds. On the other hand, for other species, such as oak, hickory and elm, the petals are very small or lacking. Flowers with the four basic elements are called *complete flowers*. Flowers are called *incomplete* when one or more basic parts are missing.

Most trees bear either *perfect flowers*, those possessing stamens and pistils, or *unisexual flowers*, i.e. male (staminate) flowers or female (pistillate) flowers on the same tree. Trees are *monoecious* if the male and female organs on the same tree are combined on complete or incomplete flowers or separate on unisexual flowers. Trees are *dioecious* (e.g., willows, poplars) if their staminate or pistillate flowers are borne by different trees, i.e., a male tree or a female tree.

After the pollen is transferred from the stamens to the pistil (pollination), and after fertilization, the ovary is transformed into a fruit and the ovules into seeds. The fruit results from the transformation of the pistil, more specifically the ovary, with or without the related organs, after fertilization of the ovule. The fruit is thus the mature ovary. The seed is a fertilized ovule contained in the fruit, and is a mini-plant, with food reserves and protective membranes.

The fruits' various shapes are created by the differences in the flowers, as well as the varied development in the ovary walls and in parts close to the ovary.

The fruits of deciduous trees can be classified into two main groups. The first, the *simple fruits*, are those that come from a single ovary, e.g., that of the maple and oak. The second, *compound fruits*, are those that come from more than one ovary, e.g., the tuliptree. The simple fruits are divided into *fleshy fruits* or pulpy fruits, which become juicy and soft at maturity, and *dry fruits* or fruits with thin, dry walls.

Fleshy fruits are usually dispersed by animals or man, whereas the wind is the principal agent of distribution for dry fruits. Acorns or nuts (dry fruits), however, are usually disseminated by small mammals, especially rodents.

42

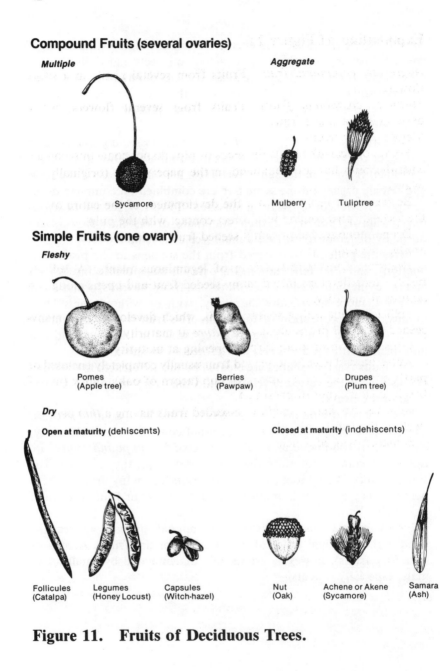

Compound Fruits (several ovaries)

Multiple *Aggregate*

Sycamore Mulberry Tuliptree

Simple Fruits (one ovary)

Fleshy

Pomes
(Apple tree) Berries
(Pawpaw) Drupes
(Plum tree)

Dry

Open at maturity (dehiscents) Closed at maturity (indehiscents)

Follicules
(Catalpa) Legumes
(Honey Locust) Capsules
(Witch-hazel) Nut
(Oak) Achene or Akene
(Sycamore) Samara
(Ash)

Figure 11. Fruits of Deciduous Trees.

Explanation of Figure 11

Aggregate, compound fruits. Fruits from several pistils in a single flower.

Multiple, compound fruits. Fruits from several flowers, which develop into a single fruit.

Simple, fleshy fruit

Pomes or pear-like fruit: the seeds or pips do not come into contact with the pulp but are contained in the papery core (originally the ovary).

Berries: fruit resulting from the development of the entire ovary, the seeds or pips coming into direct contact with the pulp.

Drupes: one-seeded or many-seeded fruit having a stone.

Simple dry fruit

Legumes: fruits characteristic of leguminous plants. A solitary pistil, which develops into a many-seeded fruit and opens along *two sutures* at maturity.

Follicles: fruit with a solitary pistil, which develops into a many-seeded fruit and opens along *one suture* at maturity.

Capsules: two or more carpels opening at maturity.

Nuts: hard-shelled, one-seeded fruit usually completely enclosed or partly surrounded by a capsule or cup (acorn of oak), shuck (nut of beech) or husk (nut of chestnut).

Achenes, or akenes: small, one-seeded fruits having a *thin pericarp* (wall of the fruit).

Samaras: winged achene.

The Bark

The bark, composed of several successive layers of cork, covers the trunk, branches and twigs. It forms an impermeable envelope that protects the tree's thin layer of living cells.

The bark protects the tree from insect attacks, fungi, forest fires and sudden temperature changes. Despite its impermeability, the bark must allow exchange of gases with the inner tissues. This is why the bark is dotted with openings, called lenticels, whose shapes vary according to the species. They are more or less apparent depending on the tree's age. In birch and cherry trees, among others, the lenticels are shaped like horizontal slits or lentils.

The bark is a characteristic that can be used year-round for identification. Although it is very distinctive for some species, like the paper birch and sycamore, identification using the bark may be difficult for a number of species. The colour, shape and texture can vary with the tree's age and growth rate.

This book contains illustrations of the most characteristic types of bark only.

lenticels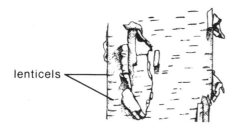

Paper Birch   **Sycamore**

Starting a Collection

At one time or another, most of us have collected objects. Whether they were natural objects or man-made (pebbles, or stamps, cards, etc.), this collection enabled us to discover a number of interesting things.

Putting together a leaf collection is an enjoyable, enriching activity enabling us to discover and appreciate the natural sciences while developing a sense of observation. A collection is also a learning tool to be consulted at any time. It is a unique, personal experience that no book can replace: you yourself collect a leaf in its habitat, examine it from all angles, and after turning it over and over, succeed in identifying the family to which it belongs, its genus and its species.

Before describing the different means of preserving the leaves of a tree, here are some recommendations: *avoid rare plants; adhere to the laws and rules of parks and reserves as well as the regional and provincial regulations; respect private property; do not damage the natural environment while gathering your specimens.*

There are various ways of putting together a leaf collection with ease. Start with a notebook or looseleaf folder.

Preservation Methods

The first method consists of *drying* the chosen specimens between two sheets of newspaper placed under a weight. After a few days, the specimens will be dry, flat, and ready to paste into the notebook. A second method consists of *sealing* the leaf by immersing it in soft paraffin wax. An alternative is to press the leaf onto wax paper. To do this, insert the leaf between two sheets of wax paper covered by a piece of fabric, and run a hot iron over it to melt the wax. Cut off the excess taking care to leave a border around the leaf. The *tracing* method requires you to take a rubbing of the specimen: place it on a flat surface and cover it with a sheet of paper; rub firmly with a pastel, coloured pencil crayon or lead pencil—the veins and margin will appear. You

may also use the *splattering* method: place the specimen to be repro-
duced on a sheet of paper and splatter it by means of a toothbrush or
paintbrush that has been dipped in gouache or water colours—you
will obtain the margin of the leaf. The advantage of these last two
methods is that one leaf can be used many times by a number of
people.

Every time a new leaf specimen is added to your collection, carefully describe its shape, colour, margin, veins, where it was gathered
and, if possible, the tree from which it came.

The leaves are not the only objects suitable for a collection. Dry
fruits, cones and bark tracings or prints in modelling clay can also be
used.

Starting a Herbarium

It is not necessary to grow your own arboretum in order to study trees. A good way to learn to recognize them is to collect their most representative parts : the twig with some leaves, the flower and the fruit. These can be preserved for a long time after having been pressed, dried and mounted on a herbarium sheet. You will need only a plant press, plastic bags, a knife, scissors, newspapers or felt, herbarium sheets and glue.

Collecting

To begin with, choose a mature tree that is as representative as possible of its species. Young trees often have different bark and lack the flowers and fruits sometimes very important to their identification.

The leaves should not have been attacked by insects or disease nor should the twigs to which they are attached be marred. It is not essential to have a piece of bark, although it is sometimes necessary for identification. Information such as habitat, location, the collector's name, the date the objects were gathered and useful comments (height, colour of flowers, abundance) should be noted and remain with the sample during the drying and mounting process. A specimen number should be assigned for reference purposes.

All samples should be dried immediately but may nevertheless be kept for a few hours (a maximum of 12 hours) in a plastic bag; if kept longer, the plants often wither, shrivel up and become discoloured. The moist environment of a closed plastic bag also promotes the development of mould and mildew.

Pressing and Drying

It is easy to build a durable plant press. To do so, you will need two wooden boards 1.3 centimetres thick and measuring 45 by 30 centi-

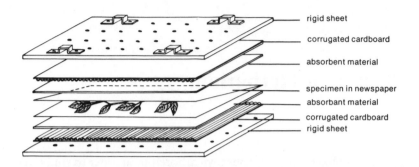

rigid sheet

corrugated cardboard

absorbent material

specimen in newspaper

absorbant material

corrugated cardboard

rigid sheet

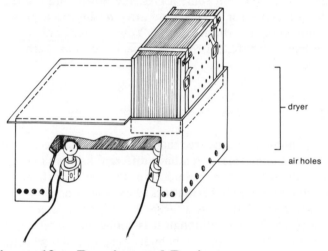

dryer

air holes

Figure 12. Pressing and Drying.
Exploded view of a plant press, and an assembled press on a portable dryer.

metres (plywood, fibreboard, or pressed wood), corrugated cardboard with the corrugations running widthwise, pieces of felt or sheets of newspaper.

For purposes of identification, the leaves attached to the twig must be dried flat and at least one of them should show the underside; the flowers should be arranged to clearly show all of their parts. All samples should then be inserted into a sheet of newspaper covered with felt on both sides. Each unit made up of newspaper and felt and containing the samples is separated by a piece of cardboard, thereby permitting better circulation of air to speed up the drying process.

Sheets of plastic foam (0.6 to 1.2 centimetres thick) may be used instead of the pieces of felt. They are much more porous than the felt pieces or layers of newspaper and give off moisture more quickly, taking the shape of the specimens easily. The result is much greener plants that are never crumpled. Plastic foam sheets are also lighter, an important factor when doing fieldwork, and do not require drying as do felt pieces and sheets of paper.

The successive layers are inserted between the two boards and the entire structure is held solidly together using straps. The press must then be placed in a warm, dry place or simply exposed to the sun. The felt pieces or the foam sheets must be replaced regularly to avoid blackening of the plants.

If you collect many specimens, a drier would be a very efficient, much appreciated accessory, since it can dry plants in only a few days. The drier can be made of a wooden box with no top or base and should be equipped with two electric cartridges with 60-watt bulbs. However, you must be careful to remove the specimens as soon as they are dry, or they will turn black; also, *this apparatus could become overheated and catch fire*. Another drying method is to force air on the plant press with an ordinary fan. The plants will dry quickly, but care must be taken not to overdo it, as excessive drying causes brittleness and thus complicates the mounting process.

Regardless of which drying method is used, the fastest one is the best, as it will keep the colour intact before fermentation occurs.

Mounting and Preservation

As soon as the specimens are dry, they can be mounted on a herbarium sheet, using a few drops of white glue or thin strips of gummed white linen. Avoid using adhesive tape, as it yellows, dries and in time curls up. The cardboard herbarium sheets are white in colour and measure 30 by 42 centimetres. Once mounting has been completed, these sheets should be placed in file folders and kept in an airtight box containing pieces of paradichlorobenzene (mothballs). Another method for protecting your specimens consists of freezing them at $-20\,°C$ for 48 hours. This will eliminate all insects.

Identification

Although the mounted specimen lends itself well to identification, it is often easier to identify a plant before mounting, since it can be handled and examined from all sides. It is also preferable to attach a permanent label on which are written the scientific name of the species, the family name and the common names. Stick this label on the herbarium sheet. You now have a dried "natural forest"!

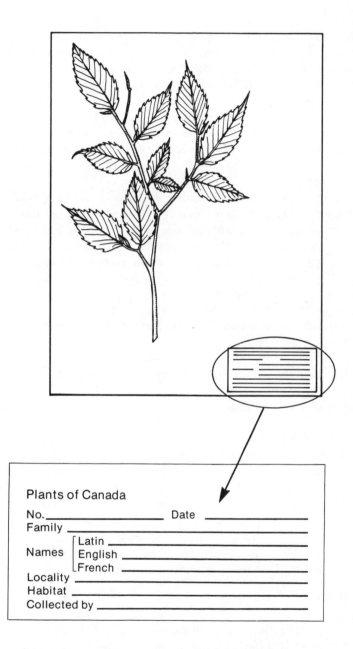

The label in the figure reads:

Plants of Canada

No._____ Date _____
Family _____
Names { Latin _____
English _____
French _____ }
Locality _____
Habitat _____
Collected by _____

Figure 13.   Mounting and Identification.
Specimen mounted on a herbarium sheet and the requisite information label in the lower right-hand corner.

How to Determine the Age of a Tree

Determining the age of a living tree requires a great deal of experience and a specific tool called an increment borer—an apparatus used to extract a cylindrical sample or core without endangering the life of the tree. It is easier to determine the age of a cut tree, billet or log. If you wish to try this technique, you can obtain a cross-section from a lumbering firm or by contacting a public or private pruning agency. Simply freshen up the cutting with sandpaper and count the number of concentric rings of a cross-section of the trunk. Each ring, called a *growth ring*, or *annual ring*, corresponds to one year. The circles are visible only in trees where the climatic conditions (winter or a dry season) cause growth to stop. The trees of tropical forests do not develop such rings.

In addition to revealing the tree's age, the growth rings recount its history. Their colour bears witness to the seasons. Springtime promotes rapid growth and the development of large-cavitied, thin-walled cells (conifers); this rather pale, tender zone is called *springwood* or *earlywood*. As the season progresses, growth slows down. The cells produced are small-cavitied and thick-walled; this darker, harder zone is called *summerwood*, or *latewood*. The alternating pattern of the pale springwood and dark summerwood enables us to see the growth rings better.

The structure of the wood of deciduous trees and coniferous trees differs in the presence of cells, called *vessels*, or *pores*. The pores in the wood may be concentrated in the springwood and are much larger than those of the summerwood. An example of this phenomenon is the wood of oak, ash and elm. The pores may also be dispersed uniformly throughout the growth layers and be of similar size. Birch, maple, poplar and the cherry tree possess this type of arrangement. In such woods, growth rings are difficult to distinguish. The problem can be solved by applying dye or ink; summerwood becomes a brighter colour than springwood.

In addition to discerning the growth rings, in some species a distinct difference may be seen between the sapwood and the heartwood.

54

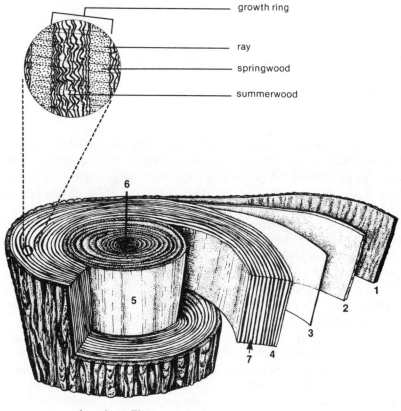

growth ring

ray

springwood

summerwood

American Elm

Figure 14. Wood; its Various Structures and an Enlargement of Rings.

1) bark: protects the tree from disease, insects and bad weather 2) liber or phloem: transports the food rich organic substances elaborated in the leaves towards the cambium 3) cambium: microscopic tissus generating new cells 4) sapwood: transports water and mineral salts from the roots to the leaves 5) heartwood or core: plays a support role, 4-5) wood or xylem 6) pith 7) growth ring

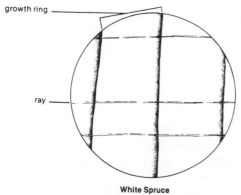

growth ring

ray

White Spruce

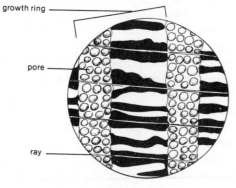

growth ring

pore

ray

Red Oak

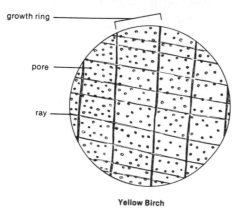

growth ring

pore

ray

Yellow Birch

Figure 15.   Enlargement of Rings, Seen with a Magnifying Glass.

These make up what is called the *wood*, or *xylem*, and constitute the dead part of the tree. Over the years, the old sapwood's layers of cells, located closer to the centre, cease their function of transporting water and mineral salts and are infiltrated by deposits of resin, tannin or other products of extraction. These substances darken the colour and harden the wood. The sapwood is thus transformed into heartwood. In some species, such as the white oak, the heartwood fills up with toxic substances that slow down the development of fungi, making the wood more resistant to decay. Devoid of physiological activity, the heartwood forms the tree's skeleton, playing the role of a support.

Unlike the heartwood, the *sapwood*, *phloem* and *cambium* make up the active portion of the tree. However, only the phloem and cambium possess living cells. The sapwood transports to the leaf, water and minerals drawn from the soil by the roots. The phloem (inner bark) transports the food materials produced in the leaves to the cambium. Cambium is not a conductive tissue, but one that generates new cells. It surrounds all parts of the tree with several layers of cells and is situated between the xylem and the phloem. It is responsible for growth in the tree's diameter.

Since the active region is situated at the tree's periphery, it is easy to understand why an old, hollow tree that has kept its conductive portion can turn green every spring for many years.

In addition to determining a tree's age by the number of concentric circles, the rings recreate climatic sequences. The study of growth rings, *dendrochronology*, is a very useful tool for climatologists. Analysis of growth rings is used, among other things, to date volcanic eruptions, earthquakes, forest fires, the former levels of lakes and rivers and climatic changes.

The pattern formed by the growth rings is also significant. A very wide ring indicates a year during which the tree enjoyed ample sun and moisture. A narrow ring corresponds to a difficult period in the tree's life: insects, disease, unusual climatic conditions, pollution and a change in light-intensity are some of the factors that could have hindered its growth.

System of Presentation for Each Tree: A Typical Entry

Combination assigned

G 572b

(G ---- table I: leaves alternate on twig
   5--- table II: oval-shaped leaf
     7-- table III: leaf with rounded lobe
       2- table IV: leaf with one midrib
         b more than one species of tree has this same combination)

Observation as to rarity (from species list, Rare Plant Series, *Syllogeus*, NMNS)   Rare in Quebec

Suggested English name   **White oak**

Other English name(s)   Stave oak

Suggested French name, other French name(s)   **Chêne blanc,** chêne de Québec

Scientific name (generic, specific and author)   *Quercus alba* L.

Name of family   Beech family (Fagaceae)

Regions where the species naturally grows

Distribution
Deciduous Forest Region and southern Great Lakes-St Lawrence Forest Region.

Species' most obvious features

Distinctive features
Leaves. 12-22 cm long; downy only when unfolding, then become hairless; 5-9 deeply cut lobes. **Twigs.** With no corky ridges. **Fruit.** Elongated acorn, edible and sweet-tasting kernel; 1.2-2 cm long, in shallow, knoblike cup without fringe along rim; matures in autumn of first year. **Bark.** Pale grey, scaly. **Size.** Height 15-30 m, diameter 60-100 cm.

Interesting facts

Coniferous Trees
Leaves Scale-like, Overlapping

A 111a

Eastern Arborvitae

American arborvitae, arborvitae, cedar, northern white
cedar, swamp-cedar, tree of life,
white arborvitae

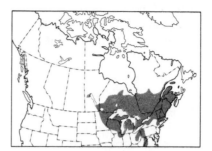

Thuya occidental, arborvitae,
balai, cèdre de l'est, cèdre, cèdre
blanc, thuya de l'est, thuya du
Canada

Rare in Nova Scotia

Thuja occidentalis L.

Cypress family (Cupressaceae).

SB 84

Distribution
Great Lakes-St Lawrence Forest Region, most of the Acadian Forest Region, central and eastern parts of the Boreal Forest Region.

Distinctive features
An eastern tree with highly aromatic wood and foliage.
Leaves. Scale-like, yellowish green, dull, with glandular spots. **Twigs.** Flat, fan-shaped, small, with opposing scales. **Cones.** Approximately 1 cm long, woody, oval, 10-12 scales. **Bark.** Reddish brown, fibrous, peeling off in narrow strips. **Size.** Height 15-20 m, diameter 50-100 cm.

The generic name *Thuja* comes from the Greek *thuon* or *thuia*, meaning odorous tree, the resin of which was used as incense in religious ceremonies. The specific name, *occidentalis*, means of the Occident. One of the first species of arborvitae discovered in North America was classified as *occidentalis* to distinguish it from the other known species, all of which were native to the Orient. The word cedar is a misnomer, since the true cedar, of the genus *Cedrus*, is native to Africa and Asia.

This historically renowned conifer, probably the first to be introduced into Europe (1536), saved Jacques Cartier's crew from certain death in the winter of 1535. Apparently the Iroquois along the St Lawrence River prepared a tea that was high in vitamin C. Called *annedda*, this decoction, made by boiling the bark and foliage of the eastern arborvitae, cured the sailors of scurvy, a disease caused by a deficiency of vitamin C in the diet. After this seemingly miraculous cure, Cartier named the tree arborvitae (tree of life).

French settlers used the foliage of the eastern arborvitae to make brooms (hence the French common name, balai); these gave off an odour, thus serving to deodorize as well as to sweep the house.

Eastern arborvitae grows in various habitats: in swampy areas, on river banks, and even on rocky surfaces. Since it grows best in moist soils that are limestone-based, neutral or alkaline, its presence is a good indication of the nature of the soil. A slow-growing tree even under the best conditions, it can live for two or three centuries.

In the early days of settlement, the eastern arborvitae was used to construct the stockades that protected the forts. Its wood is used wherever lightness, durability and resistance to rot are desired. Barn shingles, telephone poles and century-old fences all bear witness to this.

North American Indians long exploited these qualities. The timber, steamed into shape, provided the framework for bark canoes. They used its branches in sweat lodges to invigorate and purify themselves. The young leaves were used in herbal teas, decoctions, ointments and poultices to combat burns, bad coughs, headaches or toothache, and swelling of the hands or feet. The bark provided excellent kindling.

Essential oils are obtained from the branches or wood through distillation. Oil derived from the branches was formerly used in medicine. "Ceder oil", sold today in pharmacies and stores featuring natural products, is used in perfume-making and microscopy, and as an insect repellent and a deodorizer. But beware—it is for external use only, and ingesting a large amount could prove fatal.

Today the wood is used wherever there is a high risk of rot. It is also used for siding, panelling, wardrobes and chests. The seeds are an important part of the diet of crossbills, pine siskins and finches. It is the tree most widely used in eastern Canada for evergreen hedges.

A 111b

Giant Arborvitae

British Columbia cedar, British Columbia red cedar, giant-cedar, cedar, canoe-cedar, Pacific red cedar, shinglewood, western red cedar

Thuya géant, cèdre de l'Ouest, cèdre rouge de l'Ouest, cèdre

Thuja plicata Donn ex D. Don

Cypress family (Cupressaceae)

Distribution
Coast Forest Region and Columbia Forest Region as well as wet parts of the Montane Forest Region and the Subalpine Forest Region.

Distinctive features
A western tree with highly aromatic wood and foliage.
Leaves. Scale-like, yellowish green, shiny on upper surface, usually without glandular spots. **Twigs.** Flat, soft when brushed the wrong way, fan-shaped, small, with opposing scales. **Cones.** Approx. 1 cm long, woody, oval, 8-12 scales with short point at tip. **Bark.** Reddish brown, shiny, fibrous, peeling off in narrow strips. **Size.** Height 30-50 m (rarely reaching 65 m), diameter 120-260 cm.

The giant arborvitae, the largest of our two Canadian arborvitae, is a species characteristic of the wet forests of the Pacific coast (Pacific red cedar), as are the western hemlock, Sitka spruce, Douglas fir and Nootka false cypress. The term giant is very appropriate since the giant arborvitae can, under favourable conditions, reach gigantic proportions. Canada's largest trees are found on Vancouver Island. In 1948, a tree measuring more than 4 metres in diameter and close to 1000 years old was cut down. First discovered in 1791 during an expedition on Vancouver Island, the giant arborvitae is essentially a tree of the northwest Pacific coast. It can also be found in the wet valleys of the Interior, where it is rather stunted. At altitudes above 1400 metres it is reduced in size to a shrub. The conical mature tree generally has a wide base and long, drooping branches, giving it a very unique appearance.

The generic name *Thuja* comes from the Greek *thuon*, or *thuia*, the common name of an odorous African tree whose resin was used as incense in religious ceremonies. The specific name, *plicata*, from the Latin *plicare* (to fold), refers to the overlapping scales.

The name cedar is a misnomer, since the true cedar, of the genus *Cedrus*, belongs to the pine family and is native to Mediterranean regions and to the Himalayas. The common name western red cedar is inappropriate, since it creates a link with the red juniper—another species of the same family. The term red, found in a number of the common names, refers to the colour of the wood, which ranges from pale to dark red.

The giant arborvitae was as valuable a resource to the Indians of western Canada as was the paper birch to the indigenous people of eastern Canada: an invaluable source for products indispensable to the existence of a number of tribes. The coastal Indians preferred this light, non-resinous, strong and decay-resistant wood to all other species. From the hollowed-out trunk of this tree they made huge canoes more than 15 metres long, able to hold more than 60 people (hence the name canoe-cedar). They built houses with posts and split planks made from the wood, fashioned boxes of all types and constructed temporary shelters from the bark. Famous totem poles and death poles were carved from the wood of the giant arborvitae. The inner bark, or liber, was used to weave clothing, fishing nets, baskets, hats, rugs and mattresses. It was twisted to make rope, belts, collars, nets and a host of ceremonial objects. Frayed, the inner bark was used to make brooms, costumes, masks, bandages and even baby diapers.

The giant arborvitae is one of the four most important species of trees in British Columbia. Its wood is light, aromatic, with a straight grain and low shrinkage. Highly resistant to decay, the soft wood of the giant arborvitae is highly valued for the manufacturing of shingles, small boards, poles, greenhouse frames, exterior siding, panelling and woodwork. The wood of a fallen or cut tree remains intact for at least a century. This resistance to decay is due to the presence of powerful fungicides in the wood. British Columbia's shingle industry uses a large proportion of the giant arborvitae harvest and is the principal supplier of shingles to Canada and the United States.

Like the eastern arborvitae, the conical shape of the giant arborvitae lends itself very well to landscaping, but, unlike its eastern cousin, its foliage does not turn brown in winter.

A 111c

Nootka False Cypress

Alaska cedar, Alaska cypress, Alaska yellow cedar, Nootka cypress, Sitka cedar, Sitka cypress, stinking-cedar, yellow-cedar, yellow-cypress

Faux-cyprès de Nootka, cèdre jaune, cèdre de l'Alaska, cyprès de Nootka

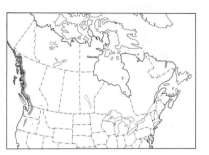

Chamaecyparis nootkatensis (D. Don) Spach

Cypress family (Cupressaceae)

Distribution
Coast Forest region and the coastal zone of the Subalpine Region. Inland, it is found near Slocan Lake and in southeastern British Columbia.

Distinctive features
A western tree with wood and foliage characterized by an acrid odour. **Leaves.** Scale-like, with tips often diverging from twig, glossy yellowish green, usually without glandular spots. **Twigs.** 4-sided but slightly flat; rough to the touch, fan-shaped; clearly drooping branchlets. **Cones.** Approx. 1 cm in diameter, spherical with uneven surface; resembling a greenish berry, covered with a whitish bloom the first year; woody the second year and reddish brown at maturity; scales with a long point at tip. **Bark.** Ash-brown, fibrous and intersecting; does not peel off in long narrow strips. **Size.** Height 15-30 m, diameter 30-120 cm.

The Nootka false cypress is easily recognized from a distance by its drooping crown, lacy foliage and greyish brown bark. At first glance its leaves may be confused with those of the giant arborvitae, which explains the inclusion of the word cedar in many of its names. But the twigs of the Nootka false cypress are rough and prickly whereas those of the giant arborvitae are soft to the touch.

The generic name *Chamaecyparis* is derived from the Greek *chamai* (ground) and *kuparissos* (cypress, or false cypress), because its cones, although smaller, resemble those of the true cypress (*Cupressus*). The specific name *nootkatensis* (of Nootka) refers to Nootka Sound, the area on the western side of Vancouver Island that was inhabited by a North American Indian tribe and where in 1791 both the Nootka false cypress and the giant arborvitae were discovered by the Irish naturalist Archibald Menzies who was accompanying Captain George Vancouver on an expedition. The yellow colour of its wood was the inspiration for many of its common names.

The Nootka false cypress grows best in the deep soil of the cool, wet coastal forests. The largest specimens once flourished on the northern B.C. islands of the coast of southwestern Alaska—hence the name Alaska cedar. It is known as the Sitka cypress, as it often grows in association with the Sitka spruce.

The Nootka false cypress, like the amabilis fir, is native to the Pacific coast but has also been found on several sites in the Interior. These isolated inland sites are the vestiges of a great forest of Nootka false cypress that existed at the time of the last glaciation. The tree grows slowly and has a lifespan sometimes exceeding 1000 years. Its longevity can be attributed to the toxic chemical compounds in the microscopic fungi concentrated in its heartwood.

North American Indians have long been aware of and exploited the properties of the Nootka false cypress. The wood is easy to work, very durable and does not splinter. From it they made hoop nets, bows to be used for bartering, decorative masks, oars and a wide variety of containers. Its inner bark, or liber, is similar to that of the giant arborvitae but is softer and finer in texture. Woven into cloth with down or goathair, it was valued for the making of clothing and blankets. Torn into pieces, it was used for bandages and washing babies.

Its wood is durable, decay-resistant and, because of its low shrinkage, very stable. These qualities make it ideal for boat building. It is also prized for cabinetmaking and woodcarving.

The Nootka false cypress is used as an ornamental in cool, wet climates.

A 111d

Red Juniper
Cedar, juniper, savin, eastern
red cedar

Genévrier rouge, bâton rouge,
cèdre rouge, cèdre rouge de
Virginie, genévrier aux crayons,
genévrier de Virginie

Juniperus virginiana L.

Cypress family (Cupressaceae)

Distribution
Great Lakes-St Lawrence Forest Region; grows sparingly in the Deciduous Forest Region.

Distinctive features
An eastern tree with aromatic wood.
Leaves. Of 2 types: needle-like on new growth and scale-like on older twigs. **Twigs.** Rounded, not forming sprays. **Cones.** Female tree: approx. 1 cm in diameter, round, resembling a blue berry, covered with a whitish bloom at maturity, maturing in one season. Male tree: miniscule pollen cones. **Bark.** Reddish brown, fibrous, separating into long, narrow strips. **Size.** Height 10-20 m, diameter 20-100 cm.

The generic name *Juniperus* is from the Latin and designates the European junipers, and the specific name *virginiana* is the latinized name of the state of Virginia, where the tree was first observed in 1564.

The name red cedar is a misnomer. This tree does not belong to the genus *Cedrus* (the true cedar), which is native to Africa and Asia. Baton Rouge, the capital of Louisiana, owes its name to this tree, which the early settlers referred to as the French equivalent of "red stick". Its reddish wood is highly prized for cabinetmaking.

This tree is found in dry, open spaces with sandy or rocky soil, generally of limestone origin. The male and female flowers are borne on different trees. Its dark blue fruit is found only on female trees.

The red juniper was used for the making of pencils until the supply of trees was exhausted. Incense cedar: (*Calocedrus decurrens* (Torr.) Florin) then became the main source of wood for pencils.

The Indians burnt the twigs for use as a nasal decongestant. A tea made from the leaves eased a persistent cough, and the oil extracted from the fruit combatted dysentery.

When European settlers arrived, they began to use the fragrant wood of the red juniper to make moth-resistant chests. The wood is still used for linen chests, as well as for the lining of cupboards and wardrobes. Its fragrant quality is also exploited by the perfume industry.

Gin takes its name from a related species, *Juniperus communis* L., whose cones or "berries" are used in the making of this drink, giving it its characteristic odour and taste. Juniper "berries", well known as a seasoning, can be used to make a coffee substitute or a refreshing tea.

Because of its longevity and slow growth the red juniper is considered an ideal ornamental. Several cultivars can be obtained from specialized nurseries.

Numerous small mammals and birds, including the cedar waxwing—so named because of this tree—feed on its small blue berries and are among the main agents of seed dispersal for the various species of Juniperus.

A 111e

Rocky Mountain Juniper
River juniper, Rocky Mountain red cedar, western juniper

Genévrier saxicole, genévrier des Rocheuses, genévrier des montagnes Rocheuses, genièvre des Rocheuses

Juniperus scopulorum Sarg.

Cypress family (Cupressaceae)

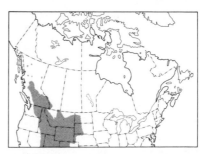

$B 86

Distribution
Montane Forest Region and the dry habitats of the Coast Forest
Region.

Distinctive features
A small western tree with aromatic wood.
Leaves. Of 2 types: needle-like on new growth; scale-like on older
twigs. **Twigs.** Rounded, not fan-like. **Cones.** Female tree: approx.
1 cm in diameter, round, resembling a blue berry, covered with a
whitish bloom at maturity, maturing in two seasons. Male tree: miniscule pollen cones. **Bark.** Ranging from reddish brown to greyish
brown, fibrous, shreddy, peeling off in narrow strips. **Size.** Shrub or
small tree in Canada, usually not more than 7 m in height and 30 cm in
diameter.

The Rocky Mountain juniper is so similar to the red juniper that Lewis
and Clark mistook it for that species during their western expedition
to the Rockies in 1804. For a long time it was classified as a variety of
red juniper. However, the fleshy cones of the Rocky Mountain juniper
take two seasons to mature whereas those of the eastern tree mature in
one year. Hybridization occurs in areas of the United States where the
Rocky Mountain juniper's range overlaps with that of other species,
producing offspring with intermediate characteristics.

The generic name *Juniperus* is the Latin name for European
junipers, and the specific name *scopulorum* designates plants that
grow among rocks (saxicolous plants), and refers to the dry, stony
habitat of this tree—hence its English names.

Like its eastern counterpart, the Rocky Mountain juniper was valued by the Indians for its fragrant properties and was used to purify
the air and chase away evil spirits after illness or death. An infusion
made from its needles was used to cure colds and heart problems.
Hunting arrows were soaked overnight in a strong decoction used to
stimulate blood clotting in wounded game, thus preventing the animal
from running too far. Its hard wood was used for making bows, snowshoe frames and spears. The foliage of all species may be used in infusions but can cause digestive problems if eaten.

Although its wood resembles that of the red juniper, it is of no commercial importance in Canada, often occurring as a small, scrubby,
multiple-stemmed tree. Nevertheless, a number of ornamental
varieties are currently being cultivated in different shapes and colours.

Coniferous Trees
Needle-shaped Leaves in Clusters

B 211a

Eastern Larch

Alaskan larch, American larch,
black larch, juniper (Maritimes),
larch hackmatack, red larch,
tamarack

Mélèze laricin, épinette rouge,
fausse épinette rouge, mélèze
d'Amérique, mélèze, tamarac,
violon

Larix laricina (Du Roi) K. Koch

Pine family (Pinaceae)

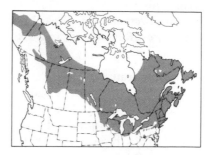

Distribution
Boreal Forest Region, Great Lakes-St Lawrence Forest Region, Acadian Forest Region and, to a lesser extent, Deciduous Forest Region.

Distinctive features
Leaves. Soft, flexible, 10-20 needles per cluster, 2-2.5 cm long, triangular in cross-section; light green turning attractive golden yellow before falling in autumn. **Twigs.** Small, flexible and hairless. **Cones.** Round, light brown, less than 2 cm long. **Size.** Height 15-20 m, diameter 40-60 cm.

The generic name *Larix* (fat), a reference to the resin of this tree, is the common Latin name for larch; *laricina* means resembling Larix—for this species was formerly considered to be a pine. The French name *mélèze* is probably derived from the word for honey (*miel*), in reference to the bittersweet natural honey, or galactan, that it secretes. Another possible derivation would be the Indo-European word *mel* or *mal*, meaning mountain, which suggests a mountain tree—the European larch (*Larix decidua* P. Mill.) is generally found in mountainous regions.

A trans-Canadian species characteristic of the boreal forest, the eastern larch, like the bald cypresses (*Taxodium*), loses its needles every autumn. They are arranged spirally in two different ways on different kinds of twigs: in clusters on a spike on older twigs and singly on new twigs.

When French settlers first came to Canada, they referred to this tree by the name *épinette* (spruce), used at that time for several species of conifers.

The eastern larch is intolerant of shade, growing on very wet soils, in swamps or bogs, or on dry plateaus or slopes.

Its resin and bark have been used to treat kidney and lung disorders and ulcers, and to dress burns; its leaves can be used to make a tea and an antiseptic. Its resin, when dried and ground, was used as a baking powder, and the Indians used its roots to sew together pieces of birch bark when making their canoes.

The wood of the eastern larch is hard, strong and rot-resistant even in water, and thus can be used for posts and poles. Its roots, which are curved, sometimes by as much as 90 degrees, were formerly used by builders of small ships.

Since the turn of this century, the eastern larch has been in decline as a result of forest fires, logging and the invasion of a sawfly.

The European larch is cultivated as an ornamental. It resembles the eastern larch, but may be distinguished by its larger cones with more numerous scales (40 to 50) and its longer needles.

B 211b

Western Larch
Hackmatack, larch, tamarack,
western tamarack

Mélèze occidental, mélèze de
l'Ouest

Larix occidentalis Nutt.

Pine family (Pinaceae)

Rare in Alberta

Distribution
Southern part of the Columbia Forest Region, on the wet slopes of the
Montane Forest Region and occasionally in southwestern Alberta.

Distinctive features
Leaves. Flexible, 15-30 needles per cluster, 2.5-4 cm in length, flat and triangular in cross-section; turn an attractive golden yellow before falling in autumn. **Twigs.** Thick, brittle, slightly downy at first but later becoming hairless (glabrous). **Cones.** Oval, yellowish brown at maturity, less than 4 cm long; small needles (bracts) extend beyond the scales. **Size.** Height 20-50 m, diameter 50-150 cm.

The most impressive of the Canadian larches, the western larch is also one of the most economically important trees in western Canada. Its hard wood is the strongest of any of the conifers marketed by Canada. It is a very rapid-growing, rapidly colonizing species. The older trees have very thick reddish bark that insulates them from damage caused by fire, and in this respect it is the most resistant species in the northwest.

Its resemblance to the eastern larch earned it the name tamarack. However, the western larch is a large tree that grows in dry, rocky soil, whereas the eastern larch is relatively small and prefers the wet soil of marshes and peat bogs.

The generic name *Larix* is the Latin name for the larch and refers to the sweet resin it exudes. The specific name *occidentalis* refers to its being a western North American species.

The honeyed resin, which hardens when exposed to air, was chewed by North American Indians. The "honey" was collected from tree cavities and boiled down to the consistency of molasses. The Indians also prepared a red powder by heating the resin, then grinding it. Blended with bear fat it was used as a cosmetic, and mixed with Balsam Poplar buds it was used as a red paint.

The western larch, with its long straight, knotless trunk, produces a very dense, solid wood similar in quality and used for the same purposes as that of the Douglas fir. It is used in construction and for making plywood, ties and pilings, interior finishing and flooring. It makes a beautiful, hardy ornamental and is used as such in many regions of Canada.

The needles of the western larch are a major source of food for the Blue and Spruce Grouses, and its seeds are eaten by mice, chipmunks and seed eaters such as the Red Crossbill.

Unfortunately, a small insect, the larch casebearer (*Coleophora laricella* Hbn.), devastates western larch populations; attempts are being made to introduce a parasite to control it. A further threat is posed by mistletoe (*Arceuthobium* Bieb.), a small parasite of conifers that can do serious damage to the western larch.

B 211c

Alpine Larch
Lyall's larch, mountain larch, subalpine larch

Mélèze subalpin, mélèze de Lyall

Larix lyallii Parl.

Pine family (Pinaceae)

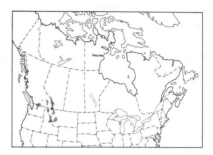

Distribution
Normally at altitudes of over 2000 metres in the southern parts of the Subalpine Forest Region.

Distinctive features
Small tree growing at high altitudes.
Leaves. Flexible, 30-40 needles per cluster, 2.5-4 cm long, quadrangular in cross-section; turn a beautiful golden yellow before falling in autumn. **Twigs.** Stout and tough; new growth covered with very fine white down. **Cones.** Oval, brown at maturity, 4-5 cm long, small needles (bracts) protrude between the scales. **Size.** Small tree. Height 8-10 m, diameter 30-60 cm.

To find the alpine larch it is usually necessary to climb high mountains, as did naturalist David Lyall in 1858. The generic name *Larix* is the Latin name for larches. The only species it can be confused with is the western larch. The latter, however, grows at lower altitudes. Nevertheless, these two species are sometimes found on the same site. They can be differentiated by the shape of the crown and the hairiness of the twigs: the western larch has a rather slender, regular crown and nearly smooth twigs; the alpine larch has a wide-spreading, irregular crown and densely hairy twigs.

Due to its general inaccessibility the alpine larch is not used for commercial purposes.

B 211d

Eastern White Pine

Cork pine, majestic pine, northern white pine, pattern pine, Quebec pine, sapling pine, Weymouth pine, white pine, yellow pine

Pin blanc, pin jaune, pin du Lord, pin strobus, pin de Weymouth

Pinus strobus L.

Pine family (Pinaceae)

Rare in Manitoba

Distribution
Great Lakes-St Lawrence Forest Region and adjacent regions.

Distinctive features
Leaves. 5 needles per cluster, 7-12 cm long, flexible and soft to the touch. **Cones.** Hanging, cylindrical, often curved, 8-20 cm long with a stalk approximately 1 cm long; green when closed, opening in September and falling in winter; flexible scales. **Size.** Height 30-40 m, diameter 100-150 cm.

The generic name *Pinus* is the Latin name for the pine, and the specific name *strobus*, from the Greek *strobilor* (top), or *strobos* (rolled around), refers to the cone.

The eastern white pine, now naturalized in Europe, was introduced into England in 1705 by Lord Weymouth. Large specimens usually contain a great deal of heartwood, the yellowish colour of which has earned this tree the name yellow pine. It differs from the other pines east of the Rockies in having clusters of five bluish-green needles, which are soft and flexible. It is the most tolerant of all pines in terms of light and moisture, but grows best on moist sandy or clayey soils. Its smooth bark is very thin, making the tree particularly vulnerable to forest fires.

The Iroquois venerated this tree, considering it to be the symbol of their invulnerability. It was used in some 20 medicinal preparations and was even used against illnesses caused by the spirits.

In the days of the great sailing ships, the eastern white pine soon became indispensable to the shipbuilding industry. Because of its size it quickly replaced the Scots pine (*Pinus sylvestris* L.) for use in the making of masts for British ships. In fact, a law was proclaimed reserving it solely for the use of the Royal Navy.

The eastern white pine has played an important role in our history. At the beginning of the nineteenth century, the demand for it made Quebec City the world's largest timber port. It was used for the first timber rafts that navigated the St Lawrence. On the Gatineau River the first timber raft of squared-pine made its downstream journey in 1806. These rafts travelled our major rivers for roughly a century.

Trees of large diameter became increasingly difficult to find. The lumber kings gradually ceased to harvest square timber and instead built sawmills for the processing of smaller trees. These sawmills began to appear along waterways, and around them arose towns and villages such as Hawkesbury, Ottawa and Hull.

Today, because of intensive logging, forest fires and various diseases, the eastern white pine is smaller and rarer than it was. It currently faces two dangers: blister rust, a serious parasitic disease; and an insect called the white pine weevil (*Pissodes strobi* (Peck)). Successive attacks by this insect deform the tree, reducing its commercial value. From an economic standpoint, blister rust is the most serious tree disease in Canada and the United States. All pines with 5-needle clusters, indigenous or cultivated, are vulnerable to it. It affects young and old trees alike, annually destroying nearly 6 million cubic metres of wood. It was introduced separately into eastern and western Canada at the turn of the century, via white pine seedlings from nurseries in France and Germany. Because white pine seedlings from Europe cost less than North American seedlings, their use in reforestation was more economical. We are, however, still suffering the consequences. Blister rust limits the suitability of eastern white pine for use in reforestation. The extent of the damage could be limited by destroying the gooseberries and wild or domestic currants (*Ribes* ssp.) that are essential intermediaries in the spread of this disease; but the ideal solution would be to develop a variety of eastern white pine resistant to it.

Eastern white pine is used in the making of planks and furniture. Its chips and sawdust are used in the manufacture of asphalt tile, tarpaper, disc brakes, distributor caps, telephones, and many other items.

B 211e

Western White Pine

Idaho white pine, mountain
Weymouth pine, mountain
white pine, silver pine, white
pine (B.C.)

Pin argenté, pin blanc de
l'Ouest, pin montagnard

Pinus monticola Dougl. ex D. Don

Pine family (Pinaceae)

Rare in Alberta

Distribution

Southern parts of the Coast and Columbia Forest Regions.

Distinctive features

Leaves. 5 needles per cluster, bluish green, 5-10 cm long, flexible and soft to the touch. **Cones.** Hanging, cylindrical, often curved, 10-25 cm long, with a stalk of approximately 2 cm long; green when closed, opening in September and falling in winter; flexible scales. **Bark.** Smooth, silver-grey in young trees, breaking into plates, becoming brown or black with age. **Size.** Height 30-40 m, diameter 100-150 cm.

The western white pine, like many western conifers, was discovered by the Irish botanist David Douglas. First sighted in 1831 on the banks of the Columbia River, it can be identified by the long cones hanging from its top, the rectangular plates furrowed into its bark and the carpet of dead needles and pine cones surrounding its trunk.

The specific name *monticola*, from the Latin *montis* (mountain) and *colere* (to dwell), refers to the habitat of the western white pine, which is largely mountainous. *Pinus* is the Latin name for the pine tree. The word white in its common names refers to the colour of its foliage.

The resemblance of the western white pine to the eastern white pine has been the inspiration for many of its common names in both English and French. The western tree, however, has longer needles and cones, and the ranges are so widely separated that they cannot be mistaken for one another. Western Canada has two other pine species with 5-needle clusters: whitebark pine and limber pine, but both have shorter, prickly needles and smaller cones than the western white pine.

All pines with 5-needle clusters, indigenous or cultivated, are vulnerable to blister rust. This serious disease (discussed on page 86) entered the West in 1910 in a single shipment of 1000 eastern white pine seedlings sent to Vancouver from a nursery in France. The disease spread through western stands and plantations of 5-needle cluster pines. The western white pine, like the eastern white pine, is also open to attack by the white pine weevil, a destructive insect known from coast to coast, which deforms the tree, thereby reducing the commercial value of its wood. Fires, even minor ones, pose yet another threat to the western white pine, for its thin bark offers little protection.

Although the wood of the western white pine is easy to work, the North American Indians seldom used it. They did use the bark to fashion baskets and build canoes, which they stitched with roots treated with pine resin to make them waterproof.

The western white pine would be a very important species were it more abundant. It sometimes forms pure stands but is usually found in small numbers mixed in with other species. Its wood resembles that of the eastern white pine and is used for the same purposes. Its dark knots make it a wood much in demand for panelling.

90

B 211f

Whitebark Pine

Alpine whitebark, creeping pine, scrub pine, white-stemmed pine

Pin albicaule, pin à blanche écorce

Pinus albicaulis Engelm.

Pine family (Pinaceae)

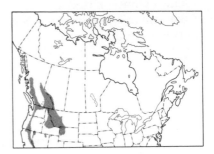

Distribution
Subalpine Forest Region beginning at altitudes of approximately 1000 metres.

Distinctive features
Leaves. 5 needles per cluster, slightly curved, 4-8 cm in length, stiff and prickly to the touch. **Bark.** Whitish, smooth at first, later becoming deeply furrowed and scaly. **Cones.** Oval, 3-7 cm in length, stalkless, purple; at maturity fall closed to the ground and gradually decay; thick cone-scales with pointed ends but no prickles; edible seeds. **Size.** Low-spreading shrub to small tree. Height 4-15 m, diameter 30-60 cm.

The specific name, white bark pine, along with many of the common names, stresses the colour of its bark. The Latin *albicaulis* breaks down into *alba* (white) and *caulis* (stem)—white-stemmed pine. The generic name *Pinus* is the Latin name for pine.

The whitebark pine grows near the timberline. It ranges in size from a small upright tree to a scrubby, low-spreading, twisted shrub (hence the names creeping pine, and scrub pine) depending on altitude and exposure. It forms pure stands or mixes with other species such as the western white pine. These two species with 5 needles per cluster are easy to distinguish: the western white pine has foliage soft to the touch, and large, hanging cones; the whitebark pine has prickly foliage clustered towards the ends of the branches, exposing the whitish twigs and small, erect, stalkless cones.

The range of the whitebark pine overlaps in some areas with the limber pine. They are readily distinguished, however, by their cones, for only the whitebark pine sheds its cones closed, to decay on the ground; a feature (unique in North America) because of which it is considered the most primitive of the native pines.

The large edible seeds can be eaten raw or roasted like the pine nuts of the pinyon tree to the south. The Indians gathered the nuts in autumn, eating them raw, roasting them, storing them for the winter, and grinding them into flour. The seeds are a source of food for rodents, and birds such as the Clark's nutcracker.

B 211g

Limber Pine
Limbertwig, Rocky Mountain
white pine

Pin flexible, pin souple

Pinus flexilis James

Pine family (Pinaceae)

Rare in B.C.

Distribution
Rocky Mountains of southern British Columbia and southern Alberta
beginning at altitudes of approximately 1000 metres.

Distinctive features
Leaves. 5 needles per cluster, slightly curved, 3-7 cm long, stiff and
prickly to the touch. **Bark.** Smooth and grey at first, becoming almost
black, deeply furrowed and scaly later. **Cones.** Cylindrical, 8-20 cm
long, with stalks less than 0.5 cm long; green when closed, changing to
light brown, reaching maturity in September, opening and falling in
winter; thick cone-scales; edible seeds. **Size.** Low-spreading shrub to
small tree. Height 4-15 m, diameter 30-60 cm.

The specific name *flexilis* (flexible) refers to the great suppleness of its
branches, and *Pinus* is the Latin name for pine. Limber pine was first
observed by Dr. Edwin James, an American army doctor associated
with an expedition to the Rocky Mountains in 1820.

Limber pine and whitebark pine are so similar they could almost
pass for two varieties of the same species, but because of the great difference in their cones, they are considered to be two distinct species.
The two species are difficult to distinguish. Both trees have branches
so supple that they can even be tied into knots. Like most alpine
species, both limber pine and whitebark pine can colonize exposed
slopes, due to highly developed root systems that anchor them firmly
into the ground.

The large edible seeds can be eaten raw or roasted like the pine nuts
of the pinyon tree to the south. The Indians gathered the nuts in
autumn, eating them raw, roasting them, storing them for the winter,
and grinding them into flour. The seeds are a source of food for
rodents, and birds such as the Clark's nutcracker.

B 211h

Pitch Pine
Hard pine, yellow pine

Pin rigide, pin des corbeaux, pin dur

Pinus rigida P. Mill.

Pine family (Pinaceae)

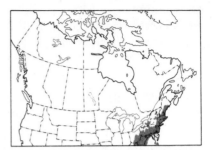

Rare in Quebec and Ontario

Distribution
Confined to the area between Kingston and Montreal, along the St Lawrence River.

Distinctive features
Leaves. 3 twisted needles per cluster, 4-12 cm long; yellowish green. **Cones.** Ovoid when closed, 4-8 cm long, stalkless; rigid cone-scales with a sharp prickle at tip; opening at maturity in autumn and remaining on the tree for many years. **Trunk.** Needle clusters present on trunk. **Size.** Height 10-15 m, diameter 30-40 cm.

The pitch pine is easily recognized by its triads of rigid, twisted, yellowish-green needles (hence the Latin name *rigida* and the popular name yellow pine), and by the tufts of needles on the trunk. The generic name *Pinus* is the Latin name for pine. This tree can grow on almost sterile soils: rocky or sandy. Ordinarily stunted, it has a contorted and neglected appearance.

Of all conifers, the pitch pine alone can produce suckers from the roots. Young suckers are often found at the base of the tree after a fire or after the tree is cut, which explains why the pitch pine is often the only tree to repopulate an area after a serious fire. In the United States it is used for reforestation in poor soil conditions. In Pennsylvania and New York, where it abounds, it is used in building construction. Its resin is the main ingredient in tar and pitch; hence its name.

The knots contain so much resin that they resist rot. In pioneer days, children gathered them and put them at the end of sticks to make torches, thus obtaining an inexpensive source of lighting. In Canada, the pitch pine is rare and is not exploited commercially. In 1977 the province of Quebec created the Pitch Pine Ecological Reserve, near Chateauguay.

Another pine with 3-needle clusters, the long-leaved pine (*Pinus palustris* P. Mill.), is found in the southeastern United States. It is from this pine that essence of turpentine, often used in oil-based paint, is obtained. (Essence of turpentine should not be confused with the turpentine or resin produced by conifers. The essence is obtained by distilling the resin.)

B 211i

Ponderosa Pine

Big pine, blackjack pine, British
Columbia soft pine, bull pine,
heavy pine, western yellow pine,
western pitch pine, yellow pine

Pin ponderosa, pin à bois lourd,
pin lourd

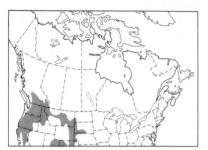

Pinus ponderosa Dougl. ex P. & C. Lawson

Pine family (Pinaceae)

Distribution
Southern part of the Montane Forest Region in British Columbia.

Distinctive features
Leaves. 2, usually 3, needles per cluster, 12-28 cm long; dark green, tightly clustered like the hairs of a paintbrush. **Cones.** Ovoid when closed, 7-15 cm long, stalkless, cone-scales tipped with rigid sharp prickles at tip; opening at maturity in autumn and falling during autumn and winter. **Bark.** Blackish, rough and furrowed in young trees; becoming yellowish brown and separating into large thick plates that in mature trees resemble puzzle pieces. **Size.** Height 18-45 m, diameter 60-180 cm.

Ponderosa pine reaches its northern limit in the dry regions of the Interior of southern British Columbia. It is the most abundant of all North American pines and has the widest range. Because it is so widespread it has developed in many forms that, depending on the latitude, vary in cone size and number and length of needles. It often grows in pure stands or forms characteristic park-like forests.

The ponderosa pine is a fast-growing species intolerant of shade and severe cold and incapable of regenerating under its own canopy. To propagate it requires that the forest be thinned out, whether by fire, man or some other means.

First sighted by Lewis and Clark during their 1804-1806 expedition, it was another 20 years before the Irish botanist David Douglas named this pine *ponderosa*. The specific name is derived from the Latin *pondus* (heavy, or imposing), a reference to the tree's massive size. The names blackjack pine and bull pine are given to specimens with blackish bark and wood whose quality is inferior to that of the large trees with yellowish-brown bark that are known as the western yellow pine. Like the pitch pine, the wood of the ponderosa pine contains pitch, hence the name western pitch pine. For reasons that are unclear, some tree stumps contain a high concentration of pitch. The pitch makes the stump wood decay-resistant and inflammable; it is used for fence posts and kindling.

The Indians made large canoes from the ponderosa pine by hollowing out the trunk, and they burned the cones, wood and bark as fuel. The fragrant branches were fashioned into a kind of mattress and were used as a floor covering. The cones were gathered for their seeds (eaten raw). From the pollen they made a yellow dye, and they chewed the resin as gum.

The seeds are a mainstay in the diets of many birds, including Clark's nutcracker, and small animals such as squirrels and chipmunks.

The ponderosa pine is exploited for its wood in North America and central Europe, where it has been introduced. Second only to the Douglas fir in importance as a lumber-producing tree, the ponderosa pine is also planted as an ornamental. Its wood varies from pale yellow to reddish brown and has a pleasant smell. It resembles eastern white pine in texture and quality and is used for the same purposes.

B 211j

Red Pine

Bull pine (Maritimes), Canadian red pine, Norway pine, yellow pine

Pin rouge, pin à résine, pin résineux, pin de Norvège

Pinus resinosa Ait.

Pine family (Pinaceae)   Rare in Manitoba, P.E.I. and Newfoundland

Distribution
From the Atlantic coast to southern Manitoba, Great Lakes-St Lawrence Forest Region.

Distinctive features
Leaves. Flexible needles, 2 per cluster, 10-15 cm long, breaking cleanly when bent; dark green. **Cones.** Ovoid when closed, 4-7 cm long, with a short stalk; cone-scales lack prickle at tip. **Size.** Height 20-30 m, diameter 50-150 cm.

The red pine's scientific name *resinosa* is perfectly suited, as it is the most resinous of our pines. The generic name *Pinus* is the Latin name for pine, and derives from the Sanskrit *pitu* via the Greek *pitus*.

The red pine takes its name from the reddish colour of its scaly bark, which cracks into flat, irregular-shaped plates. Its needles break cleanly, distinguishing it from the Scots pine and the Austrian pine (*Pinus nigra* Arnold), two introduced species.

The red pine, a native of North America, is also known as the Norway pine, as the early explorers confused it with the Norway spruce. The red pine was found in abundance near the town of Norway in Maine.

The red pine grows quickly when young, and is resistant to wind, drought, insect infestations and blister rust, thus ranking above all other pines as a reforestation tree. It is, however, vulnerable to the scleroderris pine canker (a fungus disease) and the tiny caterpillar of the European pine shoot moth (*Rhyacionia buoliana* (Schiff.)), and these can cause damage to young plantations. While it grows best on a soil that is light, sandy, well drained and slightly acid, it is found on a variety of soils, some of which are too poor for the eastern white pine. In a dense stand, its crown is symmetrical, three-fourths of its trunk is limbless, and the foliage seems to form dark green tufts at the ends of branches—creating the effect of a chimney sweep's brush. Its thick bark protects it well, and it is often the only survivor after a forest fire.

The Indians collected the pitch or resin of red pine, eastern white pine, balsam fir and spruce, then boiled it down. They then added suet, letting the mixture boil until it reached the consistency of raw molasses. This preparation was used to waterproof canoes and repair roofs and birch-bark containers.

In the nineteenth century, after intensive logging of the eastern white pine, our ancestors turned to the red pine, a tree that, through self-pruning, develops a trunk that is almost free of knots. Like the eastern white pine, it was used to build sailing ships and wharves. It is still used for the same purposes as eastern white pine. In addition, its bright red wood, heavier than that of eastern white pine, is used in construction and as pulpwood. It is also frequently used in reforestation. The Wampum Red Pine Ecological Reserve in Manitoba was established for the express purpose of protecting the population of red pine, a species rare in Manitoba.

B 211k

Jack Pine
Banksian pine, grey pine, pine, princess (or princy), scrub pine

Pin gris, cyprès, pin chétif, pin divariqué, pin des rochers, pin de Banks

Pinus banksiana Lamb.;
   syn. *Pinus divaricata* (Ait.) Dum.-Cours

Pine family (Pinaceae)   Rare in B.C. and P.E.I.

Distribution
Boreal Forest Region, introduced into Newfoundland.

Distinctive features
Leaves. Slightly twisted needles, 2 per cluster, stiff and spread apart, 2-4 cm long. **Cones.** Asymmetrical, curved strongly inward on the branch, pointing toward the end of the branch; 2.5-7.6 cm long, often persisting on tree. **Size.** Height 10-20 m, diameter 30-60 cm.

Banksiana is the latinized name of Banks, an English naturalist (1773-1820) and a companion of the famous British navigator, James Cook. The synonym of *banksiana*, *divaricata* (spread apart), refers to the two needles in the cluster, which extend in different directions. *Pinus* is the Latin name for pine.

In the West, where the jack pine's range overlaps that of the lodgepole pine, numerous hybrids occur that are difficult to distinguish.

The jack pine has low shade tolerance and on poor soil is a sorry-looking tree with a twisted trunk, thus earning the name scrub pine. Considered a pioneer species, it often grows in pure stands, a consequence of mild burnings that liberate the seeds from the loosely closed cones. The cones may remain on the tree for a number of years, not opening unless exposed to a temperature of at least 50°C.

Most natural stands of jack pine have sprung up following forest fires. Many pure stands in the Great Lakes Forest Region have replaced red pine and eastern white pine following intensive logging or forest fires, or as a result of poor soil conditions.

The jack pine is frequently used in plantations and for reforestation, as its extensive roots enable it to grow on poor soils. Its wood is most often used for pulp and for construction.

Early settlers believed that jack pines poisoned the land and attempted to destroy the trees with fire. One can imagine their chagrin when the burnt-over areas became positively infested with fresh jack pine.

B 211l

Lodgepole Pine

Black pine, cypress (in southern
Alberta and Saskatchewan),
jack pine (B.C. and Alberta),
western jack pine, shore pine,
scrub pine

Pin tordu, pin lodgepole, pin de
Murray

Pinus contorta Dougl. ex Loud.

Pine family (Pinaceae)

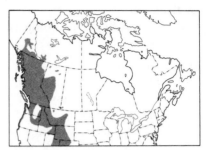

Rare in the N.W.T.

var. *contorta*   var. *latifolia*

Distribution
Essentially confined to the Rocky Mountains and British Columbia. East of the Rockies found only in the Cypress Hills of southern Alberta and Saskatchewan.

Distinctive features
Leaves. 2 needles per cluster, often spirally twisted, stiff and spread apart, 2.5-7.6 cm long. **Cones.** Often asymmetrical, cone-scale with prickle at tip; 2.5-5 cm long, persisting on tree. **Size.** Height 15-30 m, diameter up to 60 cm.

The lodgepole pine has two quite distinct forms: a crooked tree that grows along the Pacific coast (var. *contorta*), and a tall, slender tree that grows inland (var. *latifolia* Engelm.). The two forms were long considered as distinct species. The tall, slender form bore the name *Pinus murrayana* Balf., hence the French name *pin de Murray*. Today, after further study, it has been concluded that these trees differ only in their growth form and some botanists now consider them as two varieties of the same species. The generic name *Pinus* is the Latin name for pine, deriving from the Sanskrit word *pitu* by way of the Greek *pitus*. The species and variety name, *contorta*, comes from the Latin *con* (together) and *torquere* (twisted), in reference to the crooked appearance of the west coast tree. *Latifolia*, from the Latin *latus* (wide) and *folium* (leaf), refers to the needles, on average wider than those on the coastal tree.

The Indians used the flexible trunks of trees 12-14 cm in diameter to construct their lodges or teepees as well as their horse-drawn travois. They braided the roots to make rope. They used the resin for waterproofing canoes and baskets and as a glue.

The wood contains a great deal of pitch and burns even when freshly cut.

The lodgepole pine shares the following characteristics with the jack pine: needles paired and often twisted; the persistence of cones on the tree; and the need for heat to open them. It is also an aggressive colonizing species, forming huge pure stands after a forest fire or logging. Because of these very similarities, settlers moving westward mistook the lodgepole for the jack pine, which perhaps explains why it is also called jack pine (its most common name in B.C.) or western jack pine. Furthermore, in areas where the ranges of the two species overlap, numerous hybrids occur that are difficult to distinguish. Like the true jack pine, the lodgepole was also incorrectly called cypress.

But the true cypresses of the genus *Cupressus* are to be found only in the western United States, and their leaves are scale-like rather than needle-like.

In the West, the lodgepole pine plays a major economic role. It is used as structural timber, and for railroad ties, fence posts, mine supports and firewood; it is also used in the construction of log houses and in the pulp and paper industry.

For wildlife, the lodgepole pine offers food and shelter. Its seeds form a major part of the diet of pine grosbeaks and nutcrackers.

B 211m

Scots Pine
Scotch fir, scotch pine

Pin sylvestre, pin d'Écosse

Pinus sylvestris L.

Pine family (Pinaceae)

Distribution
A native of Europe and northern Asia, this species is often seen here in plantations and forests.

Distinctive features
Leaves. Needles in pairs, bluish green, twisted, 3.5-8 cm long. **Cones.**
Curved, 5-8 cm long, curving toward the base of the twig in second
year; falling in autumn or winter after two years. **Bark.** Orange-red
when young; shiny on upper part of tree; scaly. **Size.** Height 20-35 m,
diameter 20-50 cm.

In Europe, the Scots pine is highly valued as a natural forest species
and as a reforestation tree. Its specific name, *sylvestris*, is appropriate,
deriving from the Latin word *silva* (forest). The generic name *Pinus* is
the Latin name for pine.

The uses of the Scots pine in Europe correspond to those of the eastern white pine in North America. It was used for the masts of sailing
ships before the discovery of the giant eastern white pine. Its resin protected the mast against decay, a resistance increased by soaking the
mast in limewater.

The Scots pine was imported to North America in the early days of
settlement. It was first used as an ornamental, but was soon used in
reforestation, in hopes that it would provide a new source of timber.
Unfortunately it did not possess all the qualities of our native pines.
Due to the use of poor seed sources and the tree's proneness to a parasite disease, our ancestors quickly experienced the problems associated
with introducing a species into a new land. A number of plantation
projects were therefore abandoned. However, the Scots pine's rapid
growth as a young tree, its resistance to urban pollution and its tolerance of a variety of soils make it an ideal species for use as Christmas
trees and in erosion control.

Coniferous Trees
Needle-shaped Leaves Occurring Singly

C 211a

Balsam Fir

Balsam, Canadian fir, fir, var
(Maritimes), white fir

Sapin baumier, sapin, sapin
blanc, sapin rouge

Abies balsamea (L.) P. Mill.

Pine family (Pinaceae)

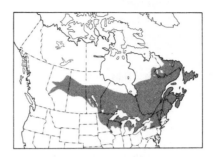

Distribution
Great Lakes-St Lawrence Forest Region, Acadian Forest Region, southern and central portion of the Boreal Forest Region.

Distinctive features
Leaves. Flat needles without stalks, arranged on either side of twig; 3-4 cm long; dark, shiny-green above with two white bands beneath; difficult to roll between thumb and forefinger. **Cones.** Cylindrical, standing erect on branches; 5-10 cm long, maturing in the autumn of the first season; cone-scales detach completely from the cone, leaving a central axis that remains on tree. **Bark.** Smooth, greyish, dotted with aromatic, raised resin blisters when young. **Size.** Height 10-15 m, diameter 30-80 cm.

The scientific name *Abies* means long-lived. *Balsamea*, Latin for balsam, aptly describes the tree's fragrant resin, known as Canada balsam or fir gum.

The balsam fir is one of our best-known conifers. Its pyramidal shape and lasting, fragrant foliage, made it the species most favoured as a Christmas tree. Today it is often replaced by Scots pine, Norway spruce, white spruce, and occasionally by eastern hemlock and red pine.

It can be distinguished from spruces by its flat needles and erect cones, and from hemlocks by the absence of stalks on its needles. Unlike other conifers, specimens of dried fir and yew (*Taxus*) retain their needles in a herbarium. Once its needles are removed, a fir twig is smooth with circular scars—this distinguishes it from hemlock and spruce twigs.

The balsam fir is essentially a boreal species that prefers moist, cool locations. The young trees can live for several decades under the cover of spruce trees. Like the black spruce, the balsam fir can multiply by layering; i.e., reproduction can occur when the tree's living lower branches take root in leaf litter.

Each year, many hectares of balsam fir are destroyed by the spruce budworm (*Choristoneura fumiferana* (Clem.)); the tiny caterpillar of a moth), which attacks and devours needles, and by the balsam woolly aphid (*Adelges piceae* (Ratz.)), which deforms or kills the tree. The spruce budworm is oddly named, for its preferred host is in fact the balsam fir. Of the two pests, the spruce budworm is the most harmful to fir and spruce.

The resin of the balsam fir is known throughout the world. Of all conifer resins, it was the most effective and widely used of French Canadian folk medicines. Its antiseptic quality was legendary for its effectiveness in the healing of burns and wounds. It was used in microscopy and in the making of soaps, glues, candles, perfumes and deodorizers.

Its wood is used by the pulp and paper industry and in the manufacture of boxes, doors and panelling.

C 211b

Alpine Fir
Balsam fir, caribou fir, mountain fir, Rocky Mountain fir, subalpine fir, sweet-pine, western balsam, white balsam fir

Sapin subalpin, sapin de l'Ouest, sapin des montagnes Rocheuses

Abies lasiocarpa (Hook.) Nutt.

Pine family (Pinaceae)

Rare in the N.W.T.

Distribution
Subalpine Forest Region and northwestern part of the Boreal Forest Region.

Distinctive features
Leaves. Flat needles, stalkless, extending in all directions like a brush; from 2.5-4.5 cm long, bluish green with white bands on both surfaces; difficult to roll between the thumb and forefinger. **Cones.** Cylindrical, erect, in clusters, purple, from 6-10 cm long, covered in resin, maturing in the autumn of the first season; shed cone-scales completely, leaving a central axis. **Bark.** Smooth, greyish, marked with raised aromatic resin blisters when young, later breaking vertically. **Size.** Height 15-45 m, diameter 30-130 cm. Occurs as a small shrub on exposed slopes at high altitudes.

North America has nine species of firs. Four are native to Canada and of these, three are found only in the west. It is sometimes very difficult to tell them apart, especially when they are young. When their cones have disintegrated, mature fir trees can pose problems of identification; and where distribution ranges overlap, some species produce intermediary offspring through hybridization—this is true of both the alpine and balsam firs.

The specific name, *lasiocarpa*, derives from the Greek *lasios* (woolly) and *karpos* (fruit), a reference to the cone-scales, which are covered with fine hairs. In 1839 the botanist W.J. Hooker first described it as a species of pine. It was not until 1876 that Thomas Nuttall, curator of the Harvard Botanical Gardens, assigned it to the genus *Abies*.

As many of its common names indicate, the alpine fir is a mountain species that is generally found growing at higher altitudes than other firs. It starts at elevations of 600 metres, continuing up to the timberline, where it occurs as a scrubby, low-spreading shrub. At this altitude it is found in association with the whitebark pine and the western white pine. The alpine fir has a very slender form even when growing in the open, and is the most widespread of the North American firs.

The branches of the alpine fir, like those of other subalpine species, are short and sturdy with tips curved downwards from the weight of the snow and ice supported during the winter months. It is also known as the caribou fir, attracting as it does many of the deer family, who nibble at its bark and, indeed, that of other fir trees.

The Indians used the wood of the alpine fir to make shingles. They chewed its resin (and that of other firs) to clean their teeth and plug holes in their canoes. Its fragrant needles were used to purify the air, and to make baby powder, perfumes and a green ointment.

The wood of the alpine fir is similar to that of white spruce, Engelmann spruce and other firs and is sold mixed with these species.

The alpine fir has a magnificent slender spire when found in its natural habitat, but, because it is adapted to high altitudes, it grows poorly in other areas.

C 211c

Amabilis Fir

Balsam fir, Cascades fir, lovely
fir, Pacific silver fir, red fir,
white fir

Sapin gracieux, sapin argenté,
sapin amabilis, sapin rouge

Abies amabilis (Dougl. ex Loud.) Dougl. ex Forbes

Pine family (Pinaceae)

Distribution
Coast Forest Region and coastal zone of the Subalpine Forest Region.

Distinctive features
Leaves. Flat needles, stalkless, arranged in three rows, those above pointing outwards, from 2-4 cm long, shiny dark green above with two white bands below; difficult to roll between the thumb and forefinger. **Cones.** Cylindrical, erect, purple, from 7-15 cm long, maturing in autumn of first season; shed cone-scales completely, leaving central axis. **Bark.** Smooth, grey blotched with white, raised aromatic resin blisters when young, becoming scaly later. **Size.** Height 20-40 m, diameter 60-100 cm.

The amabilis fir is an attractive tree in its natural habitat, with a nicely formed crown. Its shiny, dense foliage has a silvery cast; in open areas the branches droop down to the ground. It is easy to see why the Scottish botanist David Douglas (1798-1834) named this fir, *amabilis*, from the Latin *amare* (to love, or lovable, pleasing). The two white bands on the underside of the needles give the foliage its silvery appearance, accounting for the use of such descriptive terms as white, and silver, in the common names. The white bands are caused by rows of small natural openings called stomata, which allow gaseous exchanges between the leaf and its environment. The common name red fir is a misnomer inspired by its resemblance to the California red fir (*Abies magnifica* A. Murr.), a species native to the American southwest. Like the other firs, its bark is covered in blisters filled with a resin called Canadian balsam, or fir gum. This resin was the inspiration for the name balsam fir, which is shared by a number of fir species of the Canadian and American west.

The amabilis fir occurs mainly on the western slopes of the coastal Cascade Mountain chain at altitudes from 350 to 2000 metres. At high elevations, it shares the habitat of the Alpine Fir. The largest specimens are found in the Olympic Mountains of Washington State. They can reach 70 metres in height and live for over 300 years.

Like most firs, the wood of the amabilis fir is light, soft and not very decay-resistant. It is used mainly for manufacturing pulp or objects not requiring durability. It makes an attractive ornamental in its natural habitat.

C 211d

Grand Fir

Lowland balsam fir, lowland white fir, giant fir, lowland fir, western white fir

Sapin grandissime, sapin de Vancouver, sapin géant

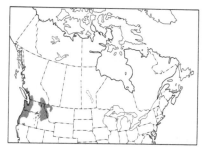

Abies grandis (Dougl. ex D. Don) Lindl.

Pine family (Pinaceae)

Distribution

Low elevations in the Coast and Columbia Forest Regions.

Distinctive features

Leaves. Flat needles, stalkless, 2-ranked arrangement in the same plane, from 2.5-5.0 cm long, shiny dark green above with two white bands below; difficult to roll between the thumb and forefinger. **Cones.** Cylindrical, erect, yellowish green, from 5-10 cm long, maturing in the autumn of the first season; shed cone-scales completely, leaving a central axis. **Bark.** Smooth, greyish, marked with raised aromatic resin blisters when young, becoming scaly later. **Size.** Height 30-70 m, diameter 50-100 cm.

The grand fir is admirably suited to its English and French names and its scientific designation; it is the largest fir in Canada and one of the largest of the genus. It is generally confined to the lower valleys of British Columbia at elevations ranging from sea level to 30 m; hence the common name lowland fir.

Like other firs, the grand fir tolerates shade and can regenerate under the cover of other trees. One of the fastest growing of the conifers, its annual growth can exceed 1 metre, some trees reaching a height of 16 metres in 20 years.

The grand fir can be recognized from afar by the top of its compact, conical crown. Close to, it can be identified by its long needles arranged in two ranks on its spread twigs. The balsam fir is the only other Canadian species to display this configuration of needles. The grand fir can be confused with a species from the American west whose needles are arranged in the same plane: known as the Colorado, or white fir (*Abies concolor* (Gord. & Glend.) Lindl.), and often planted as an ornamental, it has bluish-green needles with white bands on both surfaces. The grand fir, however, has shiny dark green needles on top with only the underside marked by white bands.

The grand fir has a very limited range in Canada and is consequently not important commercially. Its wood, light and of low resistance, is used in pulp-making and general construction.

The Indians did not distinguish between the grand fir and the amabilis fir. They made canoes from the wood of these trees, sometimes splitting it into planks. They extracted a pink dye from the bark, and by drying and crushing the needles they produced a powdery substance used as baby powder.

Introduced into England in 1830 by its discoverer, David Douglas, the grand fir is being planted increasingly in Europe. A beautiful tree in its natural range, it does not seem to thrive in the east.

C 211e

Eastern Hemlock

Canada hemlock, hemlock gum
tree, hemlock-spruce, hemlock,
tree-juniper (Maritimes),
weeping-spruce, white hemlock

Pruche du Canada, haricot
(Acadian), pérusse or prusse
pruche de l'Est, pruche, tsuga
du Canada, violon (Acadian)

Tsuga canadensis (L.) Carr.

Pine family (Pinaceae)

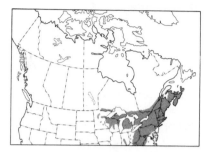

Distribution
Great Lakes-St Lawrence Forest Region, Acadian Forest Region and
to a lesser extent the Deciduous Forest Region.

Distinctive features
Leaves. Flat needles, stalked, arranged in two rows, 1-2 cm long;
shiny dark green above with two wide, bluish white bands beneath;
difficult to roll between thumb and forefinger. **Cones.** Very small, less
than 2 cm long, with short stalk; maturing in the autumn of the first
season but not falling until the next spring. **Size.** Height 20-25 m,
diameter 60-100 cm.

This tree's name, *Tsuga*, is borrowed from the Japanese. The genus
Tsuga is indigenous only to North America, and eastern Asia including Japan. This hemlock should not be confused with the famous
plant of the same name that killed Socrates—a herbaceous plant of the
genus *Conium*.

The eastern hemlock and two western species are the only native
conifers to have a spire and foliage that droop, giving them a graceful
profile; hence the name weeping spruce for the eastern hemlock. Its
spire usually bends eastward and can be used as a compass. Its
needles, flat and arrayed on the same plane (like the barbs of a
feather), differ from those of the fir in that their stalk is attached to a
small "peg" lying against the twigs. Its cones, unlike those of the fir,
fall whole, and the twigs, once they have lost their needles, are
stubble-like, as are those of the spruce.

The reddish, scaly bark was formerly a major source of tannic acid,
used in the tanning of hides and leather. The inner bark, red and
astringent, was used as a dye.

As self-pruning does not occur in the eastern hemlock, this species is
characterized by numerous, remarkably hard knots that can quickly
dull the blade of an axe. Those who like campfires or fires in the fire-
place should be warned—hemlocks, more than any other native conifer except the arborvitae, tend to flare up when burning and project
embers and burning wood a distance of several metres.

The eastern hemlock prefers cool, shady, rocky locations and requires considerable moisture. It is sometimes found in pure stands but
is usually mixed with pines and deciduous species.

Its light, hard wood is difficult to work with as it splits fairly easily.
It is mainly used in its rough state for the manufacture of beams, railroad ties, culverts and bridge planks. This wood is very much in de-

mand in the eastern United States, where spruce is becoming scarce as a result of insect infestations, forest fires and intensive logging. The eastern hemlock makes a very attractive compact hedge, but is quite slow-growing.

C 211f

Western Hemlock
British Columbia hemlock, Pacific hemlock, West Coast hemlock

Pruche occidentale, pruche de l'Ouest, tsuga de Californie, tsuga de l'Ouest

Tsuga heterophylla (Raf.) Sarg.

Pine family (Pinaceae)

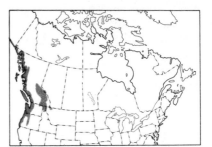

Rare in Alberta

Distribution
Coast and Columbia Forest Regions and rain belts of inland valleys.

Distinctive features
Leaves. Flat needles, stalked, arranged in two ranks, vary from 1-2.5 cm long on the same twig; shiny dark green above, two broad bluish-white bands below; difficult to roll between the thumb and forefinger. **Cones.** Oval when closed, hanging, 1.5-2.5 cm long; stalkless; opening, mature in the autumn of the first season, falling in winter. **Size.** Height 30-50 m, diameter 90-120 cm.

The specific name *heterophylla*, from the Greek *heteros* (different) and *phullon* (leaf), refers to the variation in needle length on the same twig. The generic name *Tsuga* is the Japanese word for hemlock.

Western hemlock reaches maximum size in moist, cool climates and deep soils, and under these conditions sometimes becomes a dominating species in the forest. It often grows together with the giants of our western forests: giant arborvitae, Douglas fir and Sitka spruce. It also forms pure stands with very thick foliage that the sun's rays can barely penetrate. Although able to reproduce under its own cover, it prevents other species from doing so (thus a forest of western hemlock remains unchanged unless it succumbs to the logger's saw or a forest fire). For this reason foresters and woodcutters, who frequently come across western hemlock when scouting out good specimens, consider it a harmful tree, inhibiting as it does the regeneration and growth of other, highly prized, species. Long ignored by lumbermen, who mistook it for the commercially unimportant eastern hemlock, it was not until the early part of this century that the quality of its wood began to become known. It rivals the Douglas fir in its durability and is often used as a substitute, e.g., in gymnasium flooring. It is British Columbia's greatest source of pulpwood.

In the 1930s the application of new chemical processes for separating cellulose from wood created a demand for western hemlock. Cellulose is the most important element in the structure of trees and the main component of pulp, from which paper is made. It can be treated chemically to produce cellophane or synthetic textile fibres such as viscose rayon, plastics, lacquers, safety glass and photographic film.

Canada imports most of the tannin it uses. Western hemlock and Douglas fir are high in this substance, with a content of up to 18 per cent in their bark. The tannin recovered in sawmills and pulp mills from these two species alone could adequately supply the tanning industry. Tannin is associated with tanning, but serves other purposes too. Commercial tannin, especially that extracted from western hemlock, is used as a stabilizing agent in dyes and pesticides and to check viscosity during oil-well drilling operations.

Western hemlock is easy to work. The Indians used it for woodcarving, making it into spoons, spears, hooks and sticks. The tannin from the bark was used in tanning and preparing dyes.

The western hemlock is an important species for British Columbia. It is often planted in western and northern Europe for its high-quality wood.

C 211g

Mountain Hemlock

Alpine hemlock, black hemlock, hemlock-spruce

Pruche subalpine, pruche de Mertens, pruche de Patton, tsuga de Mertens, tsuga des montagnes

Tsuga mertensiana (Bong.) Carr.

Pine family (Pinaceae)

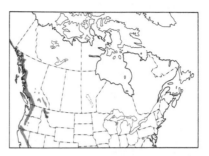

Distribution
Wetter areas of the Subalpine, Coast and Columbia Forest Regions.

Distinctive features
Leaves. Needles, semicircular in cross-section, stalked and extending all around twigs, 1-2 cm long, dark greyish green on both surfaces; easy to roll between thumb and forefinger. **Cones.** Hanging, cylindrical when closed, 2.5-7.5 cm long; stalkless; opening, mature in autumn of first season but not falling until the following spring or early summer. **Size.** Height generally 8-15 m, diameter 25-50 cm.

Mountain hemlock can easily be mistaken for spruce and many naturalists have done so. In fact, one of its common names is hemlock-spruce because of its close resemblance to spruce in shape, cone structure and arrangement of needles on the twigs. Until the mid 20th century some botanists considered the species a product of hemlock-spruce hybridization. However, genetic analyses have now confirmed its true nature.

The generic name, *Tsuga*, is the Japanese name for hemlock, and the specific name, *mertensiana*, is the latinization of Mertens—Karl Heinrich Mertens (1796-1830) was the German naturalist who discovered the species in Sitka, Alaska.

Mountain hemlock and its subalpine congeners range from low-spreading shrubs to towering trees, depending on altitude and exposure. These species characterize arborescent mountain flora (mountain Tsuga) on the fringes of forest vegetation. The very dense foliage of the mountain hemlock in forest conditions led woodcutters to name it black hemlock.

Mountain hemlock is cut only when western hemlock, the other western species, is found growing on the same site. The wood of these two species is similar in quality, and they are marketed together and used for the same purposes.

C 211h

Douglas Fir

British Columbia fir, bigcone-
spruce, Douglas pine, Douglas
spruce, Douglas tree, fir (many
North American Indians),
Oregon spruce, Oregon pine,
red-fir, yellow-fir

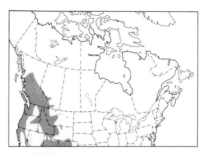

Douglas taxifolié, douglas,
douglas vert, douglas bleu,
fausse pruche, pin de Douglas,
pin de l'Oregon, sapin de
Douglas, sapin de l'Oregon

Pseudotsuga menziesii (Mirbel) Franco
    syn. *Pseudotsuga douglasii* Carr.
    syn. *Pseudotsuga taxifolia* (Lamb.) Britton

Pine family (Pinaceae)   var. *glauca*

var. *menziesii*

Distribution
Coast Forest Region, central British Columbia, and the Rocky Mountains west of Alberta.

Distinctive features
Leaves. Flat needles, pointed, flexible, with short stalk, 2-3 cm long, arranged in two ranks, shiny yellowish-green above, paler below; difficult to roll between the thumb and forefinger. **Twigs.** Smooth; covered in fine hairs, many droop; bright-red, pointed buds. **Cones.** Hanging, oval at maturity, 5-10 cm long; short, very visible 3-pronged needles (bracts) extending between the cone-scales; falling whole every year once seeds have fallen. **Bark.** Smooth, blotched with resin blisters in young trees, becoming deeply furrowed at maturity. **Size.** Height 50-80 m, diameter 90-200 cm.

The Douglas fir is the largest Canadian tree and is surpassed in size in North America only by the redwood (*Sequoia sempervirens* (Lamb. ex D. Don) Endl.). Its bark, over 30 cm thick, protects it well from fire, and its deep, wide-spreading roots anchor it firmly, sheltering it from the wind. The Douglas fir's lifespan exceeds 1000 years. It is a pioneer species that, because it cannot reproduce under its own cover, will be replaced over the centuries by other species such as western hemlock, giant arborvitae and grand fir, all of which are more tolerant of shade.

Two forms of Douglas fir are generally recognized. The typical coastal variety (var. *menziesii*) can easily reach 60 metres in height and 2 metres in diameter, has glossy green-yellowish leaves, and cones with straight 3-pronged bracts. It grows on Vancouver Island and adjacent lands on the continent. The variety found in the Interior (var. *glauca* (Beissn.) Franco) rarely reaches a height of 40 metres and has strongly reflexed 3-pronged bracts. In some areas the two varieties integrate.

It is clear from the diversity of both the common and the scientific names that the Douglas fir creates confusion among laymen and experts alike. On his voyage up the Pacific coast in 1778, Captain Cook was impressed by the majestic stature of the Douglas fir. He was the first to observe it and associate it with the firs. The soft, flat needles and the resin blisters on the bark of young specimens resemble the true firs of Europe (*Abies*). The position of the cones, however, is very different; the cones of the true European firs are erect on the branches, whereas those of the Douglas fir hang. The epithet spruce is a misnomer arising from the slight resemblance between the cones and pointed leaves of the Douglas fir and those of the spruce.

At the end of the eighteenth century, following the compilation of a herbarium by the Irish scientist Archibald Menzies (who accompanied Captain George Vancouver on his historic expedition along the Pacific coast), the Douglas fir was reclassified a pine by the English botanist Aylmer Bourke Lambert. It was given the name *Pinus taxifolia* Lamb. (pine with yew-like leaves). The needles of true pines, however, are grouped in clusters, whereas those of the Douglas fir occur singly on a twig.

In 1825 the Scottish botanist David Douglas rediscovered the "taxifolia pine" at the mouth of the Columbia River in Oregon; hence the names Oregon pine and Oregon spruce. In the nineteenth century the Douglas fir was variously classified as a pine (*Pinus*), a fir (*Abies*) and a hemlock (*Tsuga*). With the discovery in the Himalayas of trees resembling the Oregon pine, the French curator Elie Abel Carrière in 1867 proposed the Douglas fir's present generic name *Pseudotsuga*, meaning false hemlock. He named the Canadian tree *Pseudotsuga douglasii* in honour of David Douglas, later changing it to *Pseudotsuga taxifolia* (false hemlock with yew-like leaves). In 1950 the name was changed again—to the present-day *Pseudotsuga menziesii*, after Archibald Menzies.

One of the most economically important species, the Douglas fir produces some of the world's best timber. It is easy to work, light, solid, durable, good for painting or varnishing, does not warp and dries quickly. Its colour varies from dark yellow to reddish-brown (yellow fir and red fir). Because it is so large, the lumber can be cut to almost any length or thickness, making it ideal for masts and spars and the structural work involved in building ships and barges. Thousands of kilometres of railway track have been laid with treated Douglas fir ties. It is also used to make plywood and Kraft pulp. Its bark is used for a variety of products, including fertilizer. Since logging operations are located near the ocean, Douglas fir is shipped by sea to points around the world.

Towards the end of the nineteenth century, stocks of eastern white pine were becoming depleted, and lumberjacks, along with many commercial companies, were forced to move west and settle. This was the start of the golden age of the forestry industry in the Northwest, where the first sawmill had been set up as early as 1828 by John McLaughlin, a friend of David Douglas and an agent for the Hudson's Bay Company.

Both the Indians and the early settlers sought the bark of the Douglas fir as fuel, for its quality of heat and its smokelessness. The Indians used its strong, durable wood to build huts, make tools, harpoon handles and spears, and for structural supports. They also carved utensils and fishhooks from it and used the antiseptic resin (like fir "gum") to treat burns and wounds, repair canoes and as chewing gum. Infusions were made from the needles, to treat colds and other ailments.

C 211i

Western Yew
Pacific yew, bow plant

If occidental, if de l'Ouest

Taxus brevifolia Nutt.

Yew family (Taxaceae)

Distribution
Coast and Columbia Forest Regions.

Rare in Alberta

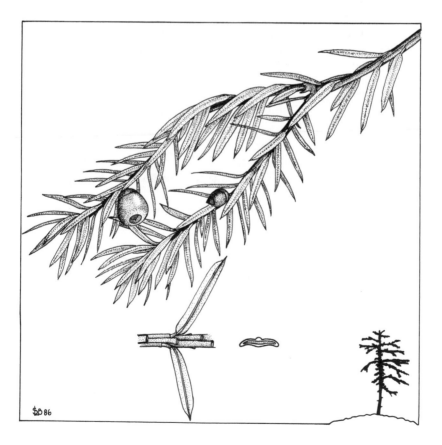

Distinctive features

Toxic plant. **Leaves.** Flat needles; long, ending in long, sharp point, dull yellowish-green above, 1.3-2.5 cm long, with twisted stalk; appearing two-ranked; soft to the touch; difficult to roll between the thumb and forefinger. **Twigs.** Slender and drooping, green underside. **Fruit.** Female tree: seed visible, dark blue, partly surrounded by a fleshy structure (aril), which is bright red at maturity. Male tree: has minute pollen cones. **Bark.** Scaly, reddish and thin. **Size.** Shrub or small tree. Height 5-15 m, diameter 15-30 cm.

A small, unkempt tree, often twisted and leaning, the western yew is found in moist soils near lakes, rivers and streams. Living in the understorey of the large conifers, it grows very slowly and tolerates shade extremely well. It is called the western yew to distinguish it from the Canada yew (*Taxus canadensis* Marsh.; a low-spreading eastern shrub not found west of southeastern Manitoba).

The generic name *Taxus* is the Latin name for the yew and means bow, referring to the use made of the wood of the English yew (*Taxus baccata* L.) by archers. The specific name, *brevifolia* (short-leaved), distinguishes it from the English yew, which has longer needles.

Still used in the manufacturing of bows, the wood of the western yew was prized by the Indians for its durability and strength (bow plant). The wood, though hard, is easy to carve and polishes well. It was used to make not only bows, but clubs, wood-splitting wedges and oars. This nonresinous wood was also carved into spoons, knives, arrowheads, fishhooks, combs and shovels. A red paint was produced by mixing the woodchips with fish oil. Indian youths tested their strength by trying to bend yew trees.

Some tribes ate the fruit of the western yew, but do not try this. *Warning:* although the aril may be considered edible, the seeds—and all parts of this tree—are extremely poisonous to man. Decaying leaves are particularly toxic to cattle and domestic animals.

Many varieties of the Japanese yew (*Taxus cuspidata* Sieb. & Zucc.) are hardy in Canada and are planted as ornamentals. Their bright red fruit, so attractive and tempting to children, can be fatal. Keep this in mind if you have an ornamental yew tree.

C 211j

White Spruce

Canadian spruce, cat spruce,
northern spruce (Labrador),
pasture spruce, single spruce,
skunk spruce

Épinette blanche, épicéa
glauque, épinette grise, épinette
du Canada, prusse blanche,
sapinette blanche

Picea glauca (Moench) Voss

Pine family (Pinaceae)

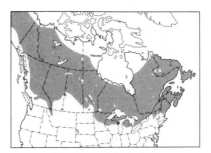

Distribution
Boreal Forest Region, Great Lakes-St Lawrence Forest Region, Acadian Forest Region, and to a lesser extent in the Deciduous Forest Region, mainly in plantations.

Distinctive features
Leaves. 4-sided needles, 1.8-2.2 cm long, dull bluish green with silvery bloom; easy to roll between thumb and forefinger. **Twigs.** Hairless. **Cones.** Hanging, 5-7 cm long; cylindrical when open, falling whole every year; cone-scales smooth-edged. **Size.** Height 24-40 m, diameter 50-100 cm.

The generic name *Picea* means pitch, or resin, and the specific name *glauca* refers to the glaucous colour of the needles. The absence of hairs on the twigs distinguishes white spruce from red spruce and black spruce, whose twigs are covered with hairs. The cones of the white spruce are supple, not breaking when squeezed with the fingers, and easily regaining their shape. When crushed, the needles sometimes give off an unpleasant odour reminiscent of the liquid sprayed by skunks; hence the names cat spruce and skunk spruce.

The white spruce with its conical crown, along with the balsam fir and the black spruce, is characteristic of the boreal forest. Widespread and abundant, it is one of the country's most important species for the pulp, paper and lumber industries.

Frequently used in plantations for reforestation, the white spruce is found today in deciduous forests. It is often used as a Christmas tree, a use for which it is ill-suited as it quickly drops its needles when indoors.

The Indians used the long roots of the white spruce, the black spruce and the jack pine to make a rope called *watap*, which they used to stitch the bark of the paper birch when making canoes. In the Mackenzie Basin and the Cordillera region, where paper birch was rare, bark for this purpose was taken from the white spruce instead. The seams were waterproofed with spruce, pine or fir gum. A tea made with the foliage of white spruce was used for its medicinal and antiseptic qualities.

All species of spruce are grouped together commercially and marketed as white spruce. Its resonance and its capacity to transmit vibrations better than any other material make it the ideal wood for manufacturing piano soundboards, organ pipes, guitars and violins.

Its wood contains little resin and is odourless and bland. When dried, it is the ideal wood for making food containers. Its bark contains tannic acid, used in tanning and in the manufacture of candles and varnish. Its seeds are an important food source for birds.

In Eastern Canada the white spruce is vulnerable to the spruce budworm (one of the most harmful defoliating insects in North America). However, it is less severely damaged than the balsam fir, the preferred host of the spruce budworm.

In western Canada the white spruce combines with the Sitka spruce and the Engelmann spruce to form hybrids that are very difficult to identify with any certainty.

C 211k

Engelmann Spruce
Mountain spruce, Rocky Mountain spruce, western white spruce

Épinette d'Engelmann, épinette des montagnes, épicéa d'Engelmann

Picea engelmannii Parry ex Engelm.

Pine family (Pinaceae)

Distribution

Southern part of the Subalpine Forest Region except in zones close to the Pacific coast.

Distinctive features

Leaves. 4-sided needles, arranged all around the twigs, 1.8-2.2 cm long; dull, silvery bluish green; easy to roll between the thumb and forefinger. **Twigs.** Covered with fine hairs when young. **Cones.** Hanging, 5-7 cm in length; fall whole annually; cone-scales jagged-edged. **Size.** Height 30-40 m, diameter 50-100 cm.

Experts disagree on the identity of the Engelmann spruce, which is so similar to the white spruce that some authors consider it to be a variety of it. Certainly difficult to tell apart, the only valid criterion for distinguishing the two species appears to be the cone-scale margin. To complicate matters, the Engelmann spruce hybridizes with the Sitka spruce in southern British Columbia.

The scientific name is in honour of George Englemann (1809-1884), an American botanist of German descent who was an expert on conifers. Other names reflect the fact that it is often found in the mountains.

Its wood, closely resembling that of eastern spruce, is used for the same purposes as white spruce.

C 211l

Black Spruce

Double spruce, bog spruce,
swamp spruce, water spruce

Épinette noire, épicéa marial,
épinette bâtarde, épinette des
marais, épinette des tourbières,
épinette de savane, épinette à
bière, sapinette noire

Picea mariana (P. Mill.) B.S.P.

Pine family (Pinaceae)

Distribution
Boreal, Great Lakes-St Lawrence and Acadian Forest Regions, and to
a lesser extent the Deciduous Forest Region.

Distinctive features
Leaves. 4-sided needles, arranged all around twig, 0.5-1.5 cm long,
dull bluish green; easy to roll between thumb and forefinger. **Twigs.**
Covered with rust-coloured hairs. **Cones.** Hanging, 2-3 cm long,
spherical when open, persisting on tree for 20-30 years; stiff, brittle
cone-scales, usually jagged-edged. **Size.** Height 5-18 m, diameter
15-30 cm.

The black spruce is a species characteristic of the Boreal Forest
Region. With the white spruce and the eastern larch, it marks the tree
line in the north.

The drooping branches and compact, narrow crown, give the
mature tree a distinctive appearance. To distinguish the black spruce
from the white spruce look for the rust-coloured hairs that cover the
twigs and for cones that, when dry, can be crushed by squeezing with
the fingers. It is often very difficult to distinguish this species from the
red spruce; for this reason some consider the two to be varieties of the
same species.

In 1731 the English botanist Philip Miller named it *Picea mariana*:
Maryland spruce. The black spruce, however, does not grow in Maryland. Its generic name *Picea* comes from the Latin *pix* (pitch).

The black spruce grows in a variety of soils, but thrives in a moist,
acidic environment. It is often found in sphagnum bogs. For this reason some of its English and French common names refer to wet places
(e.g., water spruce and *épinette des marais*). In the north, it grows in
well-drained valleys and on rocky slopes. Some stands develop following forest fires. Its cones, like those of the jack pine, can withstand
great heat, which causes them to open and drop their seeds. In addition to reproducing from seed, it can reproduce by layering: its lower
live branches, on becoming covered with mosses or leaf litter, can
grow into new trees.

The black spruce was formerly used to make spruce beer (in its day
a good source of vitamins and minerals), made by boiling the new
shoots with water and a little molasses, maple syrup or honey, and
adding yeast. In less than a week the beer was ready to be consumed.
Hardened blobs of the resin make excellent chewing gum.

The black spruce is one of the most widespread and abundant species in North America. It is used mainly in the pulp and paper industry; thus, along with other spruces and the balsam fir, it plays a vital role in the country's economy. The wood is little used in construction because of its small dimensions. It is used for the siding of houses and for making boxes and crates. It makes a poor Christmas tree, as its needles drop when they dry out. Its lower branches tend to die on the trunk over the years, making it a very poor choice as an ornamental.

Like other spruces, the black spruce is attacked by various insects such as the budworm and the weevil but (unlike the white spruce) is not seriously damaged by them. Its main enemy is a tiny parasitic plant, the dwarf mistletoe (*Arceuthobium pusillum* Peck). The latter deforms the tree, causing the formation of "witches' brooms", which eventually may cause its death.

C 211m

Red Spruce

Eastern spruce, Maritime
spruce, spruce he-balsam, yellow
spruce

Épinette rouge, épicéa rouge,
prusqueur rouge

Picea rubens Sarg.

Pine family (Pinaceae)

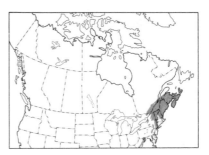

Distribution
Acadian Forest Region, parts of Great Lakes-St Lawrence Forest Region.

Distinctive features
Leaves. 4-sided needles, arranged all around twig, 1-2 cm long, bright yellowish green, often curved; easy to roll between thumb and forefinger. **Twigs.** Covered with brown hairs. **Cones.** Hanging, 3-5 cm long, ovoid when open, falling whole every year; stiff cone-scales with jagged to smooth edges. **Size.** Height 20-30 m, diameter 30-100 cm.

Some of the features of the red spruce (e.g., its height, and the length of its needles and cones) are sufficiently intermediate between those of the black spruce and the white spruce, to be considered by some to be a hybrid of these two species.

Its specific name *rubens* (red) refers to the light reddish brown colour of its bark, the common name yellow spruce refers to the yellowish green colour of its foliage.

It is often difficult to identify spruce with certainty, red spruce and black spruce being particularly hard to differentiate—they are similar in appearance, and their habitats overlap. They produce various forms of intermediary hybrids.

C 211n

Sitka Spruce
Coast spruce, tideland spruce,
tidewater spruce

Épinette de Sitka

Picea sitchensis (Bong.) Carr.

Pine family (Pinaceae)

Distribution
Coast Forest Region

Distinctive features
Leaves. 4-sided needles, somewhat flat, very pointed, arranged all around the branch, 1.5-2.5 cm long, yellowish green above the whitish below; difficult to roll between the thumb and forefinger. **Twigs.** Hairless. **Cones.** Hanging, 5-10 cm long, cylindrical when open, falling whole every year, cone-scales wavy to jagged edges. **Size.** Height 45-60 m, diameter 90-180 cm.

The Sitka spruce played a very important role during the last two world wars, its wood being used in almost all American, French and British airplanes. For aircraft construction, the quality of the wood of the Sitka spruce is unsurpassed. It is remarkably strong, yet light; an essential combination for the wooden parts of an airplane. Its resistance-weight ratio is among the highest. In Canada, the best specimens for aircraft construction are found in the Queen Charlotte Islands.

The Sitka spruce is characteristic of the Coast Forest Region, which stretches from Alaska to northern California. In Alaska, it is found mainly with western hemlock and in British Columbia principally with Douglas fir and giant arborvitae. Its common names aptly reflect its habitat. The Sitka spruce is confined to a narrow belt along the coast scarcely 80 kilometres wide, and to the adjacent islands. It is Alaska's main commercial species and was first observed at Sitka in southeast Alaska; hence its scientific name.

Of great industrial value, Sitka spruce wood is very important in British Columbia for the production of timber and pulp. It is the largest of all the spruces native to Canada, ranking among the giants along with the Douglas fir and the giant arborvitae, and giant specimens sometimes reach 90 metres in height and 3.5 metres in diameter. It is used in shipbuilding and the manufacture of masts and spars of all sizes. It is used to make plywood and is commonly used for such items as ladder rungs etc.

Spruce wood is renowned for its use in the construction of high-quality resonance chambers, the Sitka spruce producing some of the best wood for this purpose. It yields very large cuts of lumber from which flawless, straight-grained pieces of uniform density are obtained. These qualities are much sought after in the manufacture of musical instruments.

The Indians of the coast used its wood as fuel, or split it to form large planks. They used the roots as they did the roots of other spruces: to make rope, hats and tightly woven baskets used to carry water.

C 211o

Blue Spruce
Colorado blue spruce

Épinette bleue, épicéa piquant, épinette bleue du Colorado, épinette glauque, épinette du Colorado, épinette piquante

Picea pungens Engelm.

Pine family (Pinaceae)

Distribution

Species native to the United States' Rockies, frequently planted as an ornamental in Canada.

Distinctive features

Leaves. 4-sided needles, 0.5-3.1 cm long, distinctly bluish colour, silvery; very prickly, incurved; easy to roll between thumb and forefinger. **Cones.** Hanging, 5-10 cm long, cone-scales wedge-shaped and jagged-edged. **Size.** Height 20-30 m, diameter 30-100 cm.

This species is mainly used as an ornamental because of its silvery blue twigs. This characteristic is particularly striking in cultivars such as the blue spruce, "Glauca". The most common cultivars are "Koster" and "Moerheimii". The species name *pungens* (sharp-pointed) pertains to the long, prickly needles. The species has little commercial value, since its wood is knotty. Trees growing in the forest often fall victim to fires and insect pests.

C 211p

Norway Spruce
Common spruce.

Épinette de Norvège, épicéa
commun, pesse, sapin de
Norvège, sapin rouge

Picea abies (L.) Karst.
    syn. *Picea excelsa* Link

Pine family (Pinaceae)

Distribution
Species native to Europe, frequently used in eastern Canada as an ornamental and in forestation.

Distinctive features
Leaves. 4-sided needles, 1.2-2.5 cm long, yellowish green; easy to roll between thumb and forefinger. **Twigs.** Distinctly droopy. **Cones.** Hanging, 10-16 cm long; cone-scales wedge-shaped. **Size.** Height 20-30 m, diameter 30-100 cm.

The drooping branches of the mature Norway spruce give it a pleasing shape. Its specific name, *abies*, means fir, indeed, the early botanical authors mistook this tree for such, classifying it in the genus *Abies*. Its needles, more flattened than 4-sided, resemble those of the fir, but its hanging cones and its prickly foliage are more spruce-like. It plays an important role in the forest industry in Europe.

It is used in eastern Canada as a reforestation tree—it grows faster than our native species, and forms a good windbreak. Both natural and horticultural varieties are used as ornamentals. Because of its rapid growth, its dense, conical crown and its branches persisting to the ground, it is ideal for Christmas tree plantations. New shoots of Norway spruce are used in the making of spruce beer.

Deciduous Trees

Leaves Opposite, Compound

D 432

Blue Elder

Blueberry elder, blue elderberry

Sureau bleu

Sambucus cerulea Raf.
    syn. *Sambucus glauca* Nutt.

Honeysuckle family
(Caprifoliaceae)

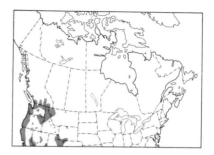

Distribution

Southern mainland British Columbia and eastern coast of Vancouver Island.

Distinctive features

Leaves. 12-20 cm long; 5-11 leaflets (5-15 cm long); grooved leaf-stalk; rank-smelling when crushed. **Flowers.** Cream-coloured, many in dense, nearly flat-topped clusters. **Fruit.** Bluish-black, round berries with 3 small stones, covered by thin whitish film; sweet, ripe at end of summer or autumn; edible when ripe, toxic when green. **Size.** Small tree or shrub. Height 6-8 m, diameter 10-20 cm.

The generic name *Sambucus* is derived from the Greek *sambuke* (an ancient stringed instrument probably fashioned from the wood of the European elderberry: *Sambucus nigra* L.), and *cerulea,* from the Latin *coeruleus* (bluish in colour) and *glauca* (blue-green), which also refers to the colour of the fruit.

The blue elder is the only elder in Canada reaching the size of a small tree. The American elder (*Sambucus canadensis* L.), a shrub elder with edible blue fruit, is found in eastern Canada and can be distinguished from the blue elder by the lack of a whitish bloom on its fruit. Another shrub elder, the red-berried elder (*Sambucus racemosa* L.) and its numerous varieties, are also found in Canada. Its fruit (red or blue, depending on the variety) is very bitter and considered poisonous. It differs from the blue elder and the elderberry in the arrangement of its flowers and fruit, which are in dome-shaped clusters—those of the two other species are almost flat-topped. A European species resembling the elderberry—the European elderberry—can be found growing wild. Like the blue elder and the elderberry, its black, delicious fruit, rich in vitamin C, is commonly used in pies, jellies, jams and wine. *Warning:* the red and green fruit, and the various parts of the elder contain toxic substances that may cause vomiting and diarrhea, particularly in children. Since heat destroys these toxic substances, the fruit must always be cooked. Cases of poisoning have been reported in children who used the hollow stems as straws or peashooters.

The blue elder and the American elder both played an important role in the home medicine of the pioneers. An infusion of or extract made from the flowers, bark and roots was used to cure the grippe and fever, or was used as a sudorific and laxative. An ointment, prepared by mixing the tree bark with lard, was used for treating skin irritations, ulcers and burns.

The Indians ate the fruit raw, made it into dried cakes for winter or stored it under the snow. From the hollowed stems, they made drinking straws, whistles, peashooters and pipe stems.

D 522a

White Ash

American ash, Canadian white ash, ground ash (Maritimes)

Frêne blanc, frêne d'Amérique, frêne blanc d'Amérique, franc frêne

Fraxinus americana L.

Olive family (Oleaceae)

Rare in P.E.I.

Distribution
Deciduous Forest Region, Great Lakes-St Lawrence Forest Region and Acadian Forest Region, except in their most northerly parts.

Distinctive features
Leaves. 20-35 cm long; 5-9 leaflets (6-14 cm long), hairless, much paler beneath than above; leaflets on stalks of 5-15 mm in length. **Twigs.** Hairless, with a thin waxy layer that peels off twigs of more than one year old. **Fruit.** Samara; wing does not surround the seed; stays on tree all winter. **Bark.** Firm ridges intersect to form diamond pattern. **Size.** Height 15-20 m, diameter 50-100 cm.

The ashes native to Canada are basically eastern species. However, a few specimens of Oregon ash (*Fraxinus latifolia* Benth.) were found in 1984 at Long Beach and Port Alberni on Vancouver Island. Oregon ash resembles white ash but has a wider leaf, as its specific name indicates. It was considered a species extinct in Canada. The only other reports of its presence date back to 1887 and 1893, when specimens were gathered by John Macoun. Still to be determined is whether these trees are indigenous or have escaped from cultivation.

The generic name *Fraxinus* was given to the European ash (*Fraxinus excelsior* L.) by the Romans. This name is derived from the Greek *phraxis* (hedges), referring to its frequent use as a hedge. The term white in the common name refers to the silvery green colour of the undersurface of the leaf, twigs and bark.

The white ash is tolerant of forest shade, and grows best in a rich but well-drained soil. Its hard, elastic wood is one of the most precious in North America; it is used to make the best hockey sticks, baseball bats and tennis rackets. This wood is also used to make tool handles, ploughing implements, boats, barrels, casks, ladders and furniture veneer. Formerly it was used in the construction of airplanes and auto bodies. As a fuel it is comparable in quality to oak and hickory.

With its large, compound leaves with autumn colours ranging from yellow to purplish-red, and its diamond-patterned bark, the white ash is a handsome ornamental. The Indians drew a bitter-tasting syrup from it and extracted a yellow dye from its bark. According to Michaud, an eighteenth-century botanist, the leaves of the white ash can be used to soothe the itching caused by mosquito bites and bee stings.

D 522b

Red Ash
Rim ash, river ash, soft ash

Frêne rouge, frêne, frêne de
Pennsylvanie, frêne pubescent,
frêne de rivage, frêne de savane

Fraxinus pennsylvanica Marsh.

Olive family (Oleaceae)

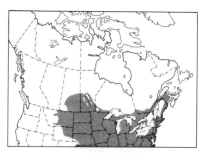

Rare in Nova Scotia

Distribution
Deciduous, Great Lakes St-Lawrence and Acadian forest regions and
southern fringe of the Boreal Forest Region (prairies of Manitoba and
Saskatchewan).

Distinctive features
Habitat. Wet soils. **Leaves.** 25-30 cm long; 7-9 leaflets (8-14 cm long),
hairy above, slightly paler beneath; leaflets on stalks 5 mm long or
less. **Twigs.** Hairy; no waxy layer present. **Fruit.** Samara; wing extends from the middle of the seed; stays on the tree almost all winter.
Bark. Firm ridges (less prominent than on white ash) intersect to form
diamond pattern. **Size.** Height 10-15 m, diameter 30-50 cm.

The generic name *Fraxinus* comes from the Greek *phraxis* (hedge),
and the common name red ash derives from the reddish cast of the
bark on the trunk and the reddish brown colour of the twigs. The specific name, *pennsylvanica*, refers to where it was harvested in colonial
times.

The red ash grows mainly in open, moist locations, and has little
tolerance of shade. For this reason it is found almost exclusively on
the edge of streams and swamps and rarely occurs in pure stands. In
general appearance resembling the white ash, it can be distinguished
from it by the pubescence of its leaves and twigs and by its frequently
reddish bark with its less pronounced diamond pattern. Some authors
distinguish several varieties of red ash, the most well known being the
green ash (var. *subintegerrima* (Vahl) Fern.) on the western plains and
the northern red ash (var. *austini* Fern.) in eastern Canada. Green ash
basically differs from red ash in its hairless twigs and its toothed
leaflets. Northern red ash can be recognized by its prominently-
toothed leaflets. All ashes with hairy twigs are red ash, but ashes with
hairless twigs may or may not be red ash.

The wood, although of poorer quality than white ash, is used for
the same purpose and is marketed under its name—as is the wood of
all ashes except black ash. A red dye is extracted from its bark. Potash
is obtained from its ashes. The fruit of ash trees is an important food
source for birds and small rodents. It remains on the tree all summer
and in the case of blue ash, for much of the winter. Moose, deer and
beavers feed on the leaves and young twigs of ash trees.

The red ash and its varieties are sometimes hard to identify. This is
not the case for ashes in general; indeed, the ashes, the blue elder and
the Manitoba maple are the only native trees to have leaves that are
compound and opposite.

According to an old belief, ash trees draw lightning.

D 532

Horsechestnut
Large chestnut tree

Marronnier d'Inde, faux-marron, marronnier commun

Aesculus hippocastanum L.

Horsechestnut family (Hippocastanaceae)

Distribution
A native of Eastern Europe (from the Caucasus to the Balkans), it is often planted as an ornamental. Often propagates by seed in southern Ontario and southwestern Quebec.

Distinctive features
Leaves. 10-25 cm long; usually 5-7 sessile (stalkless) leaflets (12-18 cm long); palmate (arranged like the fingers of a hand), rarely 5 leaflets. **Buds.** Large, dark reddish brown, shiny, very sticky in spring. **Fruit.** Spiny capsules containing 1-3 large, glossy brown seeds. **Size.** Height 12-20 m, diameter 30-150 cm.

In spring the horsechestnut offers an unforgettable sight. Its buds burst and release the leaves in the space of only a few days. Its specific name comes from the Greek *hippos* (horse) and *kastanon* (chestnut).

Sometimes used as fodder for horses, the nuts were also used by the Turks in a decoction made for treating horses with bad colds. Nut lovers should nevertheless beware: these nuts are inedible and should never be confused with the cultivated chestnut (*Castanea sativa* P. Mill.), a native of Eurasia. The generic name *Aesculus* comes from the Greek *aesea*, probably meaning food. The generic name was given by the Romans to an oak with edible acorns and was applied by Linnaeus to the horsechestnut.

The horsechestnut is often planted as an ornamental and shade tree in parks and along avenues. Its white flowers, tinged with red and yellow, grow in dense, erect clusters; these give the tree the appearance of a huge, multibranched candelabra. It is a shade tree with an immense, dome-shaped crown, and it requires considerable space.

A tree native to the United States, Ohio buckeye (*Aesculus glabra* Willd.) is probably also indigenous to southern Ontario. In fact, a population of large trees was confirmed on Walpole Island in 1982 (S.J. Darbyshire and K.M. Oldhman 1985). This tree, the state tree of Ohio, is also known as "fetid buckeye". It releases an unpleasant odour when the twigs, leaves, flowers and bark are crushed. Despite the fact that the seeds are sometimes eaten by squirrels, they are poisonous, as are those of all members of the genus *Aesculus*. The name buckeye probably refers to the seed which looks like the eye of a deer.

Horsechestnut, a compound leaf generally with 7 leaflets, can usually be distinguished from Ohio buckeye, which generally has 5 leaflets.

D 542a

Blue Ash

Frêne bleu, frêne anguleux,
frêne quadrangulaire

Fraxinus quadrangulata Michx.

Olive family (Oleaceae)

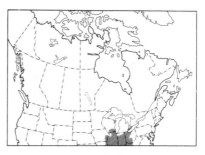

Rare in Ontario

Distribution
Deciduous Forest Region, Lake Erie area only.

Distinctive features
Twigs. Conspicuously 4-sided; corky ridges. **Leaves.** 20-30 cm long; 5-11 leaflets (8-14 cm long) on short stalks. **Fruit.** Samara, with the wing completely surrounding the seed. **Size.** Height 10-20 m, diameter 15-25 cm.

This species is confined to areas bordering sandy beaches, wooded bottomlands and shallow soils on limestone. In Ontario it is found at Pointe Pelee, on Pelee Island and in the valley of the Thames River. The populations located furthest upstream and downstream along the Thames River have been decimated. Clearing of land, pasturing, mining of rock quarries and viticulture all pose a potential danger to the species.

Its wood is marketed as white ash. It is, however, of no commercial value because of its scarcity.

As its specific name, *quadrangulata*, suggests, the twigs of the blue ash are 4-sided, owing to the presence of corky ridges or wings, making it easy to distinguish from all other ash species. Its sap becomes blue when exposed to the air (hence its common name), and its bark, when ground and steeped in water, yields a blue dye.

D 542b

Black Ash
Basket ash, brown ash
(Maritimes), hoop ash, swamp
ash, water ash

Frêne noir, frêne à feuilles de
sureau, frêne de grève, frêne
gras

Fraxinus nigra Marsh.

Olive family (Oleaceae)

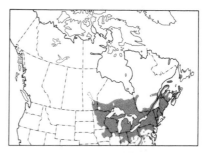

Rare in Newfoundland

Distribution
Deciduous, Great Lakes-St Lawrence and Acadian forest regions and southeastern portion of the Boreal Forest Region.

Distinctive features
Twigs. Round, grey, hairless; terminal bud separated from laterals. **Buds.** Almost black. **Leaves.** 25-40 cm long; leaflets (7-13 cm long) are sessile (stalkless), tufts of hair at the joints where they are attached to main stalk. **Fruit.** Samara, with the wing completely surrounding the seed. **Bark.** Soft, scaly, easily rubbed off by hand. **Size.** Height 10-20 m, diameter 30-50 cm.

The black ash is confined to moist, open places, cool, swampy soils, and the edges of ponds and of streams that flood regularly. It is the only ash found in Newfoundland. It sometimes forms pure stands but is usually found in association with white elm, red maple, speckled alder, willows, balsam fir and eastern arborvitae. In winter, it can easily be recognized by its soft bark and its blue-black buds (from which it derives its specific name). Its bark does not have the diamond pattern (formed by intersecting ridges) characteristic of white ash and red ash; it differs distinctly from other species of ash in its almost square-ended fruit and its almost black, pointed buds.

Its wood, much softer and heavier than white ash, is used in some interior finishing and in cabinet work. If immersed in water and then pounded, the wood separates readily into thin sheets; the Indians and the early settlers used these to make woven baskets, barrel hoops (hence the names basket ash and hoop ash), chair seats and other, similar articles. The ash from this tree is rich in potash.

D 542c

European Ash

Grand Frêne, frêne commun,
frêne élevé (Europe)

Fraxinus excelsior L.

Olive family (Oleaceae)

Distribution
Species native to Europe, often used as an ornamental, sometimes spreading along roads and near towns, and becoming established in Newfoundland and Nova Scotia.

Distinctive features
Twigs. Round, greenish grey. **Leaves.** 25-35 cm long; 9-13 sessile leaflets (6-14 cm long); no tufts of hair at joints where leaflets are attached to the main stalk. **Fruit.** Samara; wing completely surrounds the seed. **Bark.** Firm and ridged. **Size.** In its native range it may reach a height of 40 m.

The specific name *excelsior* (higher) probably arose from comparison with the flowering ash (*Fraxinus ornus* L.), which is smaller in size.

The European ash resembles the black ash in its leaf, fruit and twigs, but differs from it in its bark, which is firm, cracked and not scaly.

The European ash has been used by man since ancient times. Its bark was used as a writing surface long before the invention of paper. Its wood, when steam-pressed, can take various forms, and this characteristic was turned to advantage by the war industry. According to Old Norse mythology, the human race emerged from a hollow tree— the European ash.

D 572

Manitoba Maple
Ash-leaved maple, box-elder

Érable négundo, érable à
Giguère, érable à feuille de
frêne, érable du Manitoba, frêne
à fruits d'érable, plaine à
Giguère, plane négundo

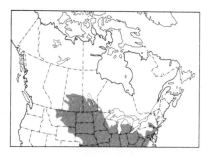

Acer negundo L.

Maple family (Aceraceae)

Distribution
Native to the Prairie provinces, naturalized in places in the Deciduous Forest Region and the Great Lakes-St Lawrence Forest Region, planted across Canada.

Distinctive features
Twigs. Often covered with a waxy, whitish bloom. **Leaves.** 15-25 cm long; 3-9 leaflets (5-12 cm long) with the terminal leaflet often lobed. **Fruit.** Samara, or 2-winged keys, persisting on the tree almost all winter, with only a narrow angle separating the wings, 3-4 cm long. **Size.** Height 20 m, diameter 30-60 cm.

The French name *érable à Giguère* (Giguere maple) was in use as early as the beginning of the nineteenth century. Its origin is uncertain. Some believe that Giguère was the name of the person who introduced the species into Quebec, others believe that the name is a deformation of *érable argilière* (clay-bed maple). The specific name *negundo* derives from the Sanskrit and Bengali *nurgundi*, which describes the chaste tree (*Vitex agnus-cactus* L.), a tree with compound leaves, native to India. The leaf of the Manitoba maple somewhat resembles that of the elder (*Sambucus*), and its wood is often used for making boxes, hence its common name, box elder. The Manitoba maple is the only one of our maples to have compound leaves. The resemblance of its trunk and leaves to those of the white ash have earned it the name ash-leaved maple. Understandably, it is often confused with the white ash. However, nature has endowed it with 2-winged keys, the fruit typical of maples. Unlike other indigenous maples, the Manitoba maple is a unisexual species, with male and female flowers on different trees.

The tree is called the Manitoba maple because it is native to the Prairies, where it is used as a windbreak and shade tree. It grows along streams and on lake shores. A hardy tree, highly drought-resistant, it has a scraggy appearance, with a rather crooked trunk. It was introduced into Europe (in France) in 1688 and is grown in eastern Canada. It is unremarkable except for its fast growth.

In the United States it was frequently planted along streets, but its abundant fruit and the susceptibility of its branches to breakage make it unsuitable for this use. The long clusters of 2-winged keys remain on the tree almost all winter, providing a food source for grosbeaks.

As with all maples, the sap of the Manitoba maple can be used to make sugar, but it is the least productive species for this purpose. Nevertheless, when the Prairies were first settled and sugar was scarce, even the Manitoba maple was tapped.

D 932
Blue Elder (*see* D 432)

Deciduous Trees
Leaves Opposite, Simple

E 522a

Eastern Flowering Dogwood

Arrowood, bitter red berry, common dogwood, cornel, dogtree, dogwood, florida dogwood, flower cornel, flowering dogwood, great-flowered dogwood, Virginia dogwood, white cornel

Cornouiller fleuri, bois de flèche, bois-bouton, cornouiller à grandes fleurs, cornouiller de Floride, cornouiller à fleurs

Cornus florida L.

Dogwood family (Cornaceae)

Distribution
Deciduous Forest Region.

Distinctive features
Leaves. 5-15 cm long; curved veining; lateral veins bend and follow the margin. **Flowers.** Encircled by 4 large white bracts notched at tip, resembling petals; flower bud shaped like dome or pagoda. **Fruit.** A group of 3-6 bright red drupes, 1-1.5 cm long, with bitter pulp. **Bark.** In roughly 4-sided segments, resembling alligator skin. **Size.** Small tree or shrub. Height 4-10 m, diameter 10-20 cm.

The generic name *Cornus* comes from the Latin *corneolus* (of horn) or *cornum* (dogwood). The wood of dogwood is in fact very hard, and the Romans used it to make spears and arrows; hence its common name: arrowood.

The specific name *florida* comes from the Latin *flos* (flower, or flowery), referring to the white bracts that have the appearance of a 4-petalled flower. The eastern flowering dogwood and the western flowering dogwood are the only tree species of the dogwood family in Canada to have this type of flower arrangement; hence their names. The bunchberry (*Cornus canadensis* L.), a small herbaceous plant, has a similar flower arrangement.

Dogwood may derive its name from a decoction made from its bark, and at one time used in England for the cleaning of dogs. Alternatively it may derive from the word daggerwood (or dagwood), referring to a dagger or a skewer on which to cook meat.

The eastern flowering dogwood has had a number of uses. Its wood, heavy, hard and fine-textured, was formerly used to make tool handles, rolling pins, shuttles for weaving, spindles, bobbins and golf clubs. The Indians used its roots to make a scarlet dye used for colouring the porcupine quills and eagle feathers with which they made headdresses. When dried and ground up, the bark is an excellent substitute for quinine in reducing a fever, and in the last century was used to treat malaria. A boiled drink made from its bark has astringent properties and can be used to treat mouth ailments. The twigs can be used as a toothbrush, said to make the teeth extremely white.

Because of its small size and its scarcity, the eastern flowering dogwood is of little commercial value. It is mostly appreciated for its qualities as an ornamental: its attractive, large "flowers", which appear before the leaves, its brilliant red fruit and its handsome red fall foliage. Unfortunately, it thrives only within its natural range. A wide variety of birds and small rodents feed on its fruit in autumn and early winter. As with all dogwoods, its fruit, a bitter red berry, is non-poisonous but almost inedible when raw. When seeded and mashed, it can be mixed with other fruit or made into a jam or jelly.

Two exotic dogwood trees are presently used as ornamentals: the Kous dogwood (*Cornus kousa* Hance), which resembles the eastern flowering dogwood but blossoms two or three weeks later, and the cornelian cherry (*Cornus mas* L.), grown for its early flowering, its profusion of yellow blossoms and its edible fruit.

E 522b

Western Flowering Dogwood

Flowering dogwood, mountain dogwood, Pacific dogwood, western dogwood

Cornouiller de Nuttall, cornouiller du Pacifique

Cornus nuttallii Audubon ex T. & G.

Dogwood family (Cornaceae)

Distribution

Southern part of the Coast Forest Region and almost all of Vancouver Island.

Distinctive features
Leaves. 8-15 cm long; arched venation, i.e., lateral veins that bend and follow the margin. **Flowers.** Surrounded by 4-6 (usually 5) large white, petal-like structures (bracts) flowering in spring and often in autumn; floral bud is domed or pagoda-shaped. **Fruits.** Dense clusters of 30-40 scarlet berry-like bodies, 1-1.2 cm long, bitter pulp. **Bark.** Thin, dark purple, not broken into block-like segments like the eastern flowering dogwood even when old. **Size.** Shrub or small tree. Height 4-12 m, diameter 30-50 cm.

Because the western flowering dogwood so closely resembles its eastern counterpart, David Douglas mistook it for such during his voyage of 1825. Sent by the Royal Horticultural Society on a special mission to the Pacific Coast to study the forest and collect seed specimens, he did not even report upon the seeds of this species. The western flowering dogwood differs from the eastern flowering dogwood in that it has larger "flowers" (5 floral bracts compared to the 4 of the other) and virtually smooth bark.

Thomas Nuttall, a British-American botanist and ornithologist, was the first to recognize this dogwood as a new species (later named in his honour by his friend John James Audubon). He observed these first trees in 1834 at Fort Vancouver, noticing that the fruit was a favourite food of the band-tailed pigeon. This is one of the reasons Audubon included this tree in his painting of the band-tailed pigeon in his famous collection of paintings "Birds of America".

The generic name *Cornus* refers to the tree's fine-grain, hard wood. The North American Indians used it for making bows, arrows, tool handles, combs, needles and, until recently, knitting needles.

As with the eastern flowering dogwood, the pioneers used the extract boiled down from its bark as a substitute for quinine, a cure specifically for malaria.

The western flowering dogwood lives in the shade of large trees and requires a minimum of light to flower. It is particularly brilliant in spring, with large "flowers" more than 12 cm in diameter, white or cream at first, tinted with pink thereafter. This tree (the floral symbol of B.C. from 1956) is dazzling in autumn, offering an uncommon sight for a Canadian species: against a red, orange and yellow background, sparkling with clusters of fruit, its large beautiful "flowers" bloom for a second time. The western flowering dogwood is a perfect ornamental species, much sought after for landscaping; but, like the eastern species, it has difficulties enduring the cold and grows poorly outside its range.

In British Columbia, the western flowering dogwood and the cascara are the only trees protected by law.

E 522c

Alternate-leaved Dogwood (*see* G 522g)

E 542a

Nannyberry
Blackhaw, sweet viburnum,
sheepberry, wild raisin

Viorne lentago, alisier,
bourdaine, viorne alisier, viorne
à manchettes

Viburnum lentago L.

Honeysuckle family (Caprifoliaceae)

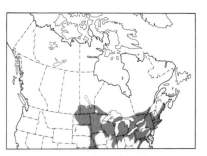

Rare in Saskatchewan and
New Brunswick

Distribution
Deciduous Forest Region, Great Lakes-St Lawrence Forest Region
and some areas in the southern portion of the Boreal Forest Region.

Distinctive features
Leaves. Blade 5-10 cm long; tiny dark dots scattered on undersurface;
leaf stalk usually grooved and winged and often rust-coloured.
Flowers. Large number grouped in round-topped clusters. **Fruit.**
Bluish black drupe, edible and sweet-tasting; oval stone, flat and
rough. **Size.** Shrub or small tree. Height 4-7 m, diameter 10-20 cm.

Viburnum is the Latin name for plants of this genus, and derives from
viere (to link) in reference to the suppleness of the twigs of some
members of the genus. The specific name *lentago* is an old generic
name meaning flexible; it was transferred to this species by Linnaeus.

The nannyberry is the largest Canadian viburnum. It grows on rich
soils along streams and at the edge of ponds and swamps, as well as in
maple-dominated stands and copses. Its finely-toothed leaves and its
sessile (stalkless) flower cluster distinguish it from the witherod
(*Viburnum cassinoides* L.), which has nearly entire leaves, and flower
clusters with long stalks.

The wood of the nannyberry is hard and heavy, but too small to be
of commercial value. When broken, it gives off an unpleasant, linger-
ing odour. The fruit is edible, sweet and fleshy. It is a major food
source for birds, which definitely contribute to the spreading of the
species. The nannyberry is used as an ornamental because of its attractive and sweet-smelling flowers, its fruit and its bright red twigs, and
also because it forms a handsome hedge. It readily sprouts from the
roots, making it undesirable on a small property.

E 542b
Cascara (*see* G 542f)

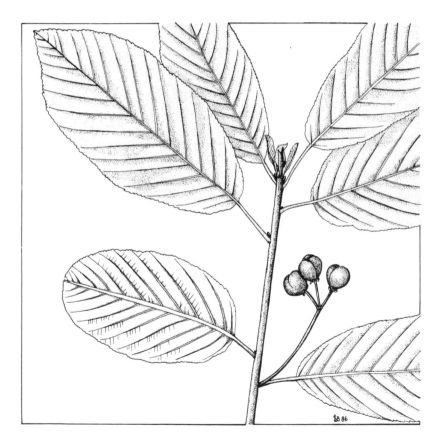

E 683a

Sugar Maple

Bird's-eye maple, curly maple, hard maple, head maple, rock-maple, sugartree, sweet maple

Érable à sucre, érable sucrier, érable dur, érable franc, érable du Canada, érable piqué, érable franche, érable moiré, érable ondé

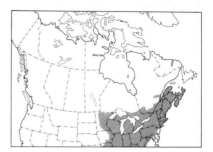

Acer saccharum Marsh.
     syn. *Acer saccharaphorum* K. Koch

Maple family (Aceraceae)

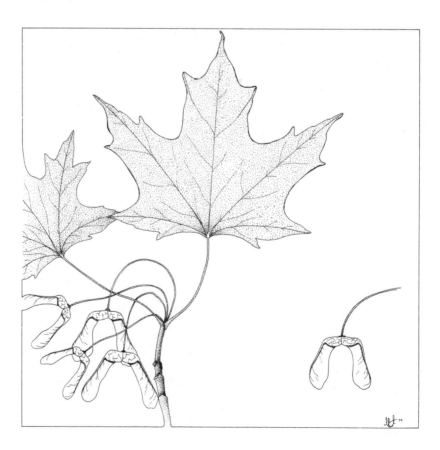

Distribution
Deciduous Forest Region, Great Lakes-St Lawrence Forest Region and Acadian Forest Region.

Distinctive features
Leaves. Blade 8-15 long, generally 5 lobes; undersurface of leaf hairless; sinus rounded. **Fruit.** Samara, 2-winged key, wings almost parallel or diverging slightly, forming a U shape, 1-2 cm long; falling in autumn. **Bark.** Dark grey, ridged and scaly on older trees. **Size.** Height 20-30 m, diameter 50-150 cm.

The generic name *Acer* is the Latin name for maple, and it comes from the Celtic *ac*, referring to the hardness of the wood. The sugar maple is highly shade-tolerant—more so than all our other maples. It is found in association with other deciduous species, with conifers, or in pure stands. In French, all stands dominated by maple are called *érablières*, and those dominated by the sugar maple are called *érablières sucrières*. In English such terms as sugar maple stand, sugar maple forest, sugar maple basswood forest, and beech sugar maple forest are used. Latin, French and English names all reflect two major features of the sugar maple: the hardness of its wood and its sweet sap.

Its wood, one of the most highly valued in Canada for furniture-making, is hard, strong, and durable, and takes an admirable finish. It is ideal for the flooring of bowling alleys, and is used in cabinetmaking and wood turning, and as a veneer. It is also used in the manufacture of ploughing implements, tool handles, panelling, sports articles, musical instruments and other objects requiring a hard, strong wood.

The close grain of the wood sometimes results in irregularities and a wavy or speckled appearance (hence the names curly maple and bird's-eye maple), which is highly valued, making the wood much sought after for the making of high-quality furniture. In the past the wood was used for making wagons, carts, carriages and even rails—the first trains did not travel on iron but on wooden rails, which were made from this wood.

Sugar maple makes excellent firewood, giving off considerable heat and forming very hot embers. The Indians taught the early settlers to use the potash-rich ashes as fertilizer. In the mid nineteenth century, potash became such a booming industry in Quebec that the province supplied 80 per cent of the American potash market. The ashes were also used for soap making. Today, potters use this ash to produce a beautiful glazed finish to their pieces.

Although there are some 160 species of maples throughout the world, the sugar maple is found only in North America. Our ancestors learned from the Indians the art of making maple sugar and syrup, an art they hastened to master. The sugar cabin with its rising clouds of steam and the tradition of "sugaring off", with its attendant festivities and folklore soon came into being. Sap can be tapped in autumn, but the ideal season is spring. A good flow of sap requires temperatures that remain below freezing point at night and rise to about 5 °C during the day. It generally takes 40 litres of sap to produce 1 litre of syrup.

Around 1880, with the invention of the chimney-equipped evaporator, maple sugar products began to be marketed. Today, the grower no longer transports the sap by hand; as in other sections of agriculture, production has been modernized. The sap pails have been replaced by plastic tubing, which carries the sap directly to the processing site. To increase production and make the sap flow more evenly, a vacuum system is used to draw the sap. The traditional wood fires for heating the evaporators have given way to oil or gas which in turn will be replaced by percolation and thermocompression, allowing for evaporation without a flame.

Maple forests are in danger. For the last ten years biologists and maple-sugar producers have noted signs of "maple decline" in sugarbushes in Quebec. The number of premature deaths of maple and its companion species (ashes, beech, birches) is increasing every year. This phenomenon seems to be caused by a combination of natural stresses such as drought, severe defoliation, and extremely cold winters, aggravated by atmospheric pollution and the resulting acidic precipitation.

E 683b

Black Maple
Black sugar maple

Érable noir.

Acer nigrum Michx. fil.

Maple family (Aceraceae)

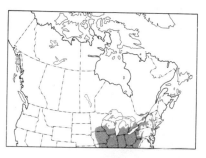

Rare in Quebec

Distribution
Deciduous Forest Region, Great Lakes-St Lawrence Region as far as Montreal.

Distinctive features
Leaves. Blade 10-15 cm long; generally 3 shallow lobes; ends of lobes drooping, wilted; undersurface densely hairy. **Fruit.** Samara, 2-winged key joined at base, wings similar to that of the sugar maple; 1-2.5 cm long, falling in autumn. **Bark.** Blackish grey, generally more ridged than on the sugar maple. **Size.** Height 20-30 m, diameter 50-150 cm.

The specific name *nigrum* means black, or dark, and refers to the colour of the foliage (dark green) and the bark (blackish grey); the generic name *Acer* means hard.

The black maple is similar in appearance to the sugar maple. Where their ranges overlap, they hybridize, giving rise to trees with intermediate characteristics. Some botanists do not consider the black maple a species but, rather, a variety of the sugar maple. Its wood, marketed as "hard maple", is used for the same purposes as the wood of the sugar maple. The sap, like that of the sugar maple, is collected for making syrup.

E 683c

Bigleaf Maple

British Columbia maple,
broadleaf maple, common
maple, Oregon maple

Érable grandifolié, érable à
grande feuilles, érable de
l'Oregon

Acer macrophyllum Pursh

Maple family (Aceraceae)

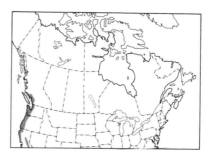

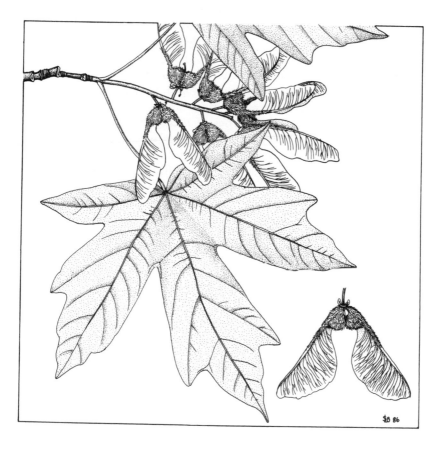

Distribution
Coast Forest Region, confined to southwestern British Columbia. Introduced north of Vancouver Island.

Distinctive features
Leaves. Very large, 20-30 cm long, 5-7 deep lobes; sinus is rounded.
Fruit. Samara, 2-winged key, in hanging clusters, wings almost parallel or diverging slightly, forming a narrow V, 3-4 cm long; seeds covered with dense bristly hair; falling in autumn. **Bark.** Dark grey, deeply furrowed and scaly on older trees. **Size.** Height 15-30 m, diameter 60-100 cm.

The leaves of the bigleaf maple cannot be confused with those of any other native maple, and their size (sometimes reaching 50 cm) has earned it its scientific and common names. It is one of the rare Pacific coast hardwoods with a measure of commercial importance, and the only western maple to grow to the size of an average tree. In southwestern Oregon, it is one of the principal forest species; hence the name Oregon maple. Its light, uniformly textured wood is used by the furniture industry for making kitchen cabinets and for other uses where hard wood is required. Irregularities in its dense wood produce a lovely speckled or rippled grain, much sought after as a veneer.

The Indians carved various types of utensils, fish hooks, combs, and particularly oars, from the wood. They used the inner bark to make a woven rope. They even boiled the sprouting seeds and ate them. The wood makes excellent fuel, producing a hot, smokeless flame.

The bigleaf maple is a beautiful ornamental, planted for its shade and foliage, which turns lovely shades of orange in autumn. Like the sugar maple, it can be tapped and produces good quality syrup. However, it cannot endure cold winters.

E 683d

Norway Maple

Érable de Norvège, érable plane,
érable platanoïde, plane

Acer platanoides L.

Maple family (Aceraceae)

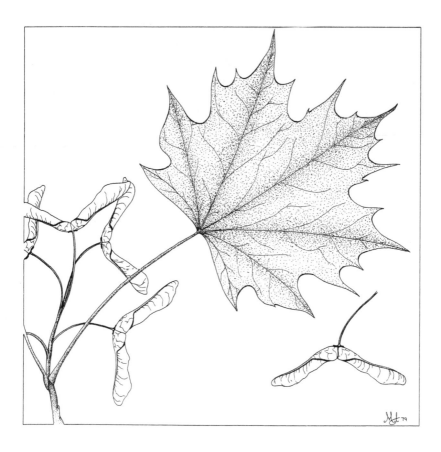

Distribution
Native to Europe; frequently planted as an ornamental in North America.

Distinctive features
Leaves. Blade 8-15 cm long; a milky juice appears when leaf stalk or buds are cut. **Fruit.** Samara, 2-winged key, wings spread widely to almost 180°, 3-5 cm long; falling in autumn. **Bark.** Slightly ridged; not scaly. **Size.** Height 15-20 m, diameter 30-60 cm.

The generic name *Acer* (hard) is the Latin name for maple. The specific name *platanoides* comes from the Greek *platanos* (plane tree), and *idea* (appearance), indicating that the leaves of this species resemble those of the plane tree (*Platanus*). The tree is called the Norway maple because it was first introduced into England from Norway.

The Norway maple embellishes our streets, parks and gardens. It is a great favourite with landscapers because of its fine symmetrical crown, which is dense and round, and its dark green foliage that turns pale yellow in autumn. It keeps its foliage two weeks longer than our native maples. It grows quickly, tolerating dust, smoke and air pollution better than do native species, and is more resistant than they to insects and fungus diseases. "Crimson king", one of the many popular cultivars, beautifies our gardens and streets throughout the season, with its magnificent red foliage.

E 693a

Red Maple

Curled maple, scarlet maple, soft maple, swamp maple, water maple

Érable rouge, érable tendre, plaine, plaine rouge, plane rouge

Acer rubrum L.

Maple family (Aceraceae)

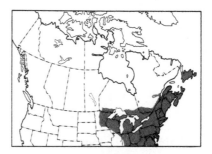

Distribution
Deciduous, Great Lakes-St Lawrence and Acadian forest regions and fringe of Boreal Forest Region.

Distinctive freatures
Leaves. Blade 5-15 cm long; 3-5 lobes with sharp, shallow notches.
Fruit. Samara, 2-winged key, wings diverging slightly, 1.5-2.5 cm long; falling early summer. **Twigs.** Shining red, with small red buds, no unpleasant odour when broken. **Size.** Height 20-25 m, diameter 40-130 cm.

Its reddish twigs, buds, flowers, fruit and leafstalks, and its scarlet autumn foliage, have earned this tree its specific name, *rubrum*, and its common name, red maple. Its generic name is *Acer* (hard). It usually flourishes in cool, moist places, spring-fed or swampy (hence the names water and swamp maple), but it is sometimes found on dry or even rocky soils. As with the silver maple, its flowers appear well before the leaves. The red maple is one of the most common trees of eastern North America. It grows from the eastern fringe of the Boreal Forest Region to the swamps of southern Florida.

Although its sap is only half as sweet as that of the sugar maple, it is possible to make sugar from it. Its light brown wood is heavy but has neither the resistance nor the strength of sugar maple wood. Nevertheless, like sugar maple, it is used as pulpwood and in the manufacture of boxes and crates. It is often planted as an ornamental or shade tree. Horticultural varieties have been developed that produce an attractive red autumn foliage.

The colonists of Pennsylvania boiled its bark to obtain a dark red ink or dye. Today, red, brown or black dyes can be obtained from it by using different mordants such as alum, cream of tartar, salt, vinegar or chrome (potassium dichromate).

E 693b

Silver Maple
White maple, river maple

Érable argenté, érable blanc,
érable à fruits cotonneux, plaine
de France, plaine blanche, plane
blanche

Acer saccharinum L.

Maple family (Aceraceae)

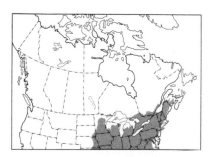

Distribution
Deciduous Forest Region, southeastern part of Great Lakes-St Lawrence Region (Ontario and Quebec), and Acadian Forest Region (southwestern New Brunswick); introduced elsewhere in Canada.

Distinctive features
Leaves. Blade 8-15 cm long; 5 lobes with deep notches shaped like Gothic arches. **Twigs.** Give off an unpleasant odour when broken. **Fruit.** Samara, 2-winged key, wings widely diverging, 3-7 cm long; falling early in spring. **Size.** Height 20-30 m, diameter 50-100 cm.

The origin of its specific name *saccharinum* is unclear, and some consider it to be the result of a misspelling of *saccharum*; others believe, perhaps correctly, that it means sweet, for although its sap is only half as sweet as that of the sugar maple, it yields a delicious pale syrup. It would be difficult to produce this syrup on a large scale, the silver maple being significantly less common than the red or the sugar maple. The terms white, and silver, in the common names, both English and French, refer to the whitish undersurface of its leaves. The name river maple refers to the moist, swampy habitat that it prefers. In autumn its leaves turn a pale brownish yellow.

The silver maple blossoms at the same time as the red maple, and they are the first of the maples to blossom in spring. Its fruit is the largest of all our native maples. Sometimes one of the 2-winged seeds in the key aborts, favouring the growth of the other.

Although commonly planted as an ornamental for its hardiness and rapid growth, it has fragile branches that can be broken by even a minor storm or the weight of ice; its roots often interfere with sewer pipes and drainage tiles around houses. Its wood is often used for the same purposes as that of the sugar maple.

E 693c

Striped Maple

Moose-wood, moose maple,
whistle-wood, goose-foot maple,
moosewood

Érable de Pennsylvanie, bois
barré, bois noir, bois d'orignal,
érable strié, érable jaspé
(Europe), érable barré

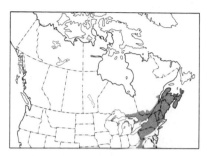

Acer pensylvanicum L.

Maple family (Aceraceae)

Distribution
Great Lakes-St Lawrence Forest Region and Acadian Forest Region.

Distinctive features
Small understorey tree. **Bark.** Vertical, greenish white stripes that darken with age. **Leaves.** 3 lobes, very large, 10-18 cm wide. **Fruit.** Samara, 2-winged key, wings widely diverging, 1.5-2.5 cm long; in hanging clusters; falling in autumn. **Size.** Small tree or shrub. Height 4-10 m, diameter 7-20 cm.

This tree owes its name to its striped bark. After the leaves are fully grown, long, drooping clusters of yellow flowers appear. They are succeeded by 2-winged keys distinguished by their indented pericarps (seed envelopes). The generic name is *Acer* (hard); *pensylvanicum* means of Pennsylvania.

Its large, thin, drooping leaf somewhat resembles a goose foot; hence its common name, goose-foot maple.

Often found in association with mountain maple, it prefers cool, shady locations, and like the mountain maple it can reproduce vegetatively by layering.

The settlers saw deer and moose nibbling the young shoots, especially in winter, and gave the tree the name moosewood. The word moose itself derives from the Algonquian *mousou*, meaning twig-eater. Beavers and hares eat the bark. The fruit, like that of all maples, is part of the diet of a number of birds and rodents. The wood is not used commercially, but is sometimes used as firewood.

The striped maple is planted as an ornamental. Its handsome leaves, large and droopy, turn an attractive pale yellow in autumn, and these, along with its striped bark, are probably the reason for its introduction into Europe.

E 693d

Mountain Maple

Dwarf maple, low-moose maple, whitewood (N.B.), whiterod, white maple

Érable à épis, bâtarde, érable bâtard, fouéreux, plaine, plaine bleue, plâne bâtard

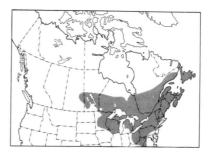

Acer spicatum Lam.

Maple family (Aceraceae)

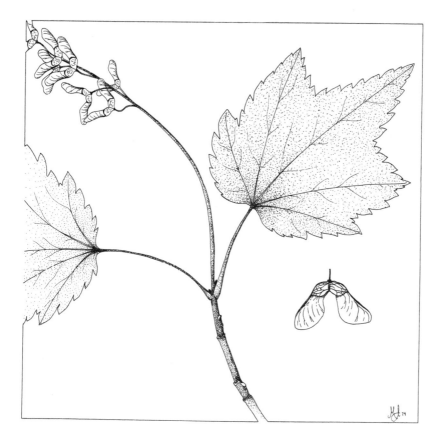

Distribution
Deciduous, Great Lakes-St Lawrence and Acadian forest regions and southwestern part of Boreal Forest Region.

Distinctive features
Leaves. Blade 8-12 cm long, 3-5 lobes (usually 3). **Fruit.** Samara, 2-winged key, wings slightly diverging, 1-2 cm long; in erect clusters; falling in autumn. **Twigs.** Covered with very short hairs. **Size.** Shrub or small tree. Height 3-5 m, diameter 7-20 cm.

The French name *érable à épis* is related to the Latin name *spicatum*, which comes from *spica* (point, or spike), *épi* referring to the way in which the flowers appear in upright clusters once the leaves are fully grown. The generic name *Acer* means hard. In autumn, the fruit is often a scarlet red, and on its keys, as on those of the striped maple, the seed envelope (pericarp) is indented on one side. The mountain maple, with its short, crooked trunk and the tendency of its lower branches to take root in the leaf litter, has a shrubby appearance and sometimes forms an impenetrable thicket. It is much sought after by deer and moose. The inhabitants of Quebec's Ile-aux-coudres call it *bois fouéreux* (mushy wood). The mountain maple is the smallest and most northerly of our maples. It is found in shady, cool and wet locations, and in rocky mountainous forests, as its name implies.

The Indians, in order to soothe eye irritation caused by campfire smoke, boiled the inside of young maple twigs, adding a pinch of alum; this solution they used as an eye-drop.

The mountain maple has no commercial value but plays a major role in preventing erosion on banks and steep slopes. It is sometimes used as an ornamental tree or shrub, for its colour, its fruit and its handsome autumn foliage.

E 693e

Douglas Maple

Dwarf maple, Rocky Mountain
maple, western mountain maple

Érable nain

Acer glabrum Torr.
var. *douglasii* (Hook.) Dippel

Maple family (Aceraceae)

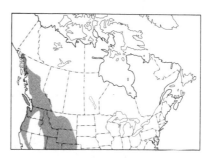

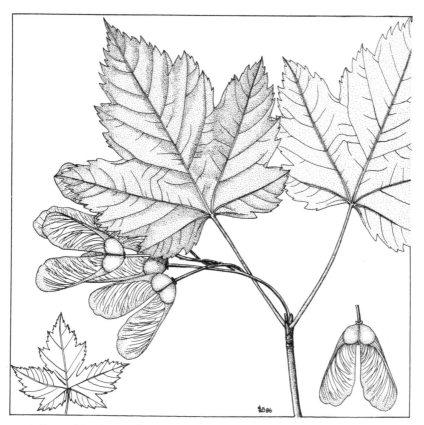

variation of leaf margin

Distribution
South of latitude 56 degrees North. From the east coast of Vancouver Island to the Rocky Mountains.

Distinctive features
Leaves. Blade 6-10 cm long, 3-5 lobes sometimes separated into 3 leaflets; hairless. **Fruit.** Samara, 2-winged key, wings parallel or slightly diverging, 1.5-2.5 cm long, forming a narrow V; falling in autumn. **Size.** A shrub or small, multiple-stemmed tree. Height 1-10 m, diameter 17-25 cm.

The specific name *glabrum* (smooth, or without hairs) refers to the leaves—hairless on both surfaces. They resemble the leaves of the mountain maple; hence the usage in the common names. The Douglas maple is widespread and two varieties of the same species are believed to exist: that found in Canada, which grows in the northern part of its range (var. *douglasii*), and the specific variety (var. *glabrum*) (not found in Canada), which extends southward in the Rocky Mountains.

Unlike the vine maple, this species does not tolerate shade and generally grows in open areas. Usually a shrub, it grows to tree size only along the coast and on the neighbouring islands, and in southern British Columbia. The Douglas maple is atypical of Canadian maples in being usually a dioecious species, i.e., with male and female flowers on different trees.

Like the vine maple, the seeds of the Douglas maple are eaten by small rodents and birds. Deer feed on the leaves and twigs.

The autumn colours of the Douglas maple's foliage are not as brilliant as those of the vine maple. Planted as an ornamental, it forms lovely groves. The North American Indians used its wood for the same purposes as that of the vine maple. It makes a good fuel.

E 693f

Vine Maple

Érable circiné, érable à feuilles rondes

Acer circinatum Pursh

Maple family (Aceraceae)

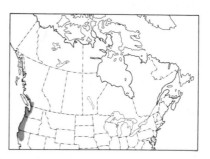

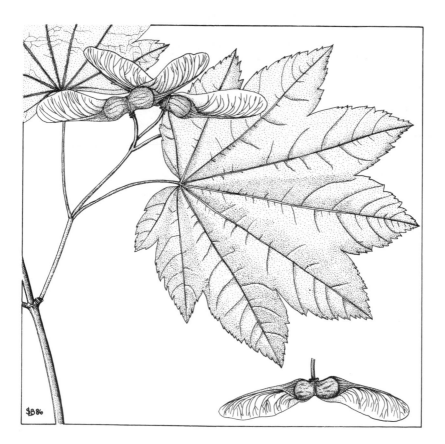

Distribution
Limited to southern Coast Forest Region, rare on Vancouver Island.

Distinctive features
Leaves. Blade 6-12 cm long, almost round, 7-11 lobes (rarely, 5).
Fruit. Samara, 2-winged key; fruit wings spread widely, to almost
180°, 2.5-4 cm long; falling in autumn. **Twigs.** Hairless, lacking terminal buds. **Size.** Shrub or small tree. Height 5-9 m, diameter 7-15 cm.

Mostly a contorted shrub, the vine maple grows in the shade of large
trees. Its branches, arching under the weight of snow, sometimes
cover up to 10 metres of ground, giving it the appearance of a vine
(hence its name). The coureurs de bois called it Devil's wood because
they stumbled over its low-spreading branches hidden under the forest
carpet as they walked half blind, loaded down with canoe and packs.
Rarely a single-stemmed tree, it usually grows as a bush in clearings
and prefers moist, deep soils.

Its specific name *circinatum* (to coil) refers to the branches, which
tend to coil around other trees, like a vine. The generic name *Acer*
(hard) is very appropriate to the vine maple. The first settlers used its
very strong, durable wood to make cart shafts, tool handles and
yokes. The wood is almost impossible to burn when green, and it
served as a cauldron hook over the fire. The Indians used this strong,
flexible wood, and that of the Douglas maple, to make fishing net
frames, snowshoes and sometimes bows, arrows and baby baskets.
Hidden under the cover of other trees, it remains unnoticed until
autumn, when it proudly displays its splendid scarlet and orange
leaves along with its bright red twigs and fruit. For these reasons it is
grown as an ornamental.

E 723

Northern Catalpa

Cigartree, catawbatree, hardy
catalpa, Indian bean tree,
western catalpa

Catalpa remarquable, catalpa à
feuilles cordées, catalpa du
Nord

Catalpa speciosa (Warder ex Barney) Engelm.

Bignonia family (Bignoniaceae)

Distribution
Native to the United States, planted widely in Canada as an ornamental.

Distinctive features
Leaves. Blade 10-30 cm long; either opposite or verticillate (more than
2 leaves at same level on stem). **Fruit.** A long capsule, 20-50 cm long
and 1.5 cm wide, resembling a cigar, hanging from tree almost all
winter; seeds flat with rounded, wide-fringed wings at each end.
Flowers. White, marked with purplish brown and yellow, very large,
roughly 6 cm in diameter, in erect terminal clusters. **Size.** Height 10-
15 m, diameter 20-40 cm.

The catalpa unfurls its large, tropical-looking leaves in late spring;
only after they have fully developed, in June or July, do the large, attractive flowers open out, to be pollenized by insects. At first frost,
the leaves blacken and fall. The fruit remains on the tree throughout
the winter, giving it a distinctive appearance and earning it the name
cigartree and Indian bean. The generic name *Catalpa* is the name
given it by the Indians of Carolina. The specific name, *speciosa*,
derives from the Latin *species* (form, or appearance), and *osers* (full
of), referring to the striking flowers. The name catawbatree harks
back to the days when the large caterpillar of the moth *Ceratomia
catalpae*, commonly known as the catawba worm, was in great demand as fish bait.

The northern catalpa is a fast-growing tree with a light wood slow to
rot when in contact with the soil; because of these two qualities it is
frequently grown in the United States in dense plantations to produce
wood for fence posts.

There is another catalpa, the southern catalpa (*Catalpa
bignonioides* Walt.), but it is much less hardy in our regions. It may be
distinguished from the northern catalpa by its smaller size and its
smaller flowers, more numerous per cluster, as well as by the unpleasant odour that its leaves give off when crushed.

Deciduous Trees
Leaves Alternate, Compound

F 422

Ailanthus
Tree-of-Heaven, Chinese sumac,
stinking-ash

Ailante glanduleux, ailante,
faux-vernis du Japon, frêne
puant

Ailanthus altissima (P. Mill.) Swingle
    syn. *Ailanthus glandulosa* Desf.

Quassia family (Simaroubaceae)

Distribution
Native to northern China. Naturalized in southern Ontario.

Distinctive features
Leaves. Very large, sometimes up to 100 cm, divided into 11-25 (maximum 41) glossy leaflets; unpleasant odour when crushed; leaflets have small glands and large teeth at base. **Flowers.** Small and greenish; male and female generally on separate trees; unpleasant odour. **Fruit.** Reddish bodies, 5 cm long, arranged in dense clusters at end of branch; seed in middle. **Size.** Height 15-30 m, diameter 30-100 cm.

A native of northern China, the ailanthus was introduced into England by Jesuit missionaries in 1751 and into North America in 1874. Widely planted as an ornamental, it now grows wild. The ailanthus is not always recommended for planting; the leaves and male flowers have an unpleasant odour, the pollen causes allergic reactions such as hay fever, and its strong roots may damage wells and drainage systems. The ailanthus sends out shoots and produces new stems from rootsuckers. Once established, it is very difficult to eliminate. It grows in poor soils and tolerates city air and pollution very well.

The generic name appears to be the translation of a Chinese phrase meaning "a tree that can reach to heaven," though the tree seldom reaches 30 metres. It could also be derived from *ailanto* or *aylanto*, the Chinese name for the tree-of-heaven. The specific name *altissima*, comes from the Latin *altus* (high). The small glands on the teeth of the leaflets release an unpleasant odour when rubbed; hence the origin of the names *glandulosa*, and stinking ash. Although the ailanthus has compound leaves and seeds, it is unrelated to the ash family. Like the ash, it has compound leaves, but these are arranged alternately on the twig whereas those of the ash are opposite. It is sometimes called the Chinese sumac because its large leaves and silhouette are similar to those of a sumac—the varnished tree (*Rhus verniciflua* Stokes), an Asian species used to make a toxic black varnish.

F 432a/F 442a

Staghorn Sumac
Sumac, sumac vinegar tree, velvet sumac

Sumac vinaigrier, sumac amarante, vinaigrier sumac

Rhus typhina L.

Cashew family (Anacardiaceae)

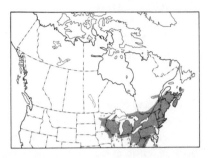

Distribution
Deciduous and Great Lakes-St Lawrence forest regions and in the Acadian Forest Region.

Distinctive features
Leaves. 25-50 cm long, 11-31 leaflets (8-13 cm long) covered with hairs beneath. **Fruit.** Erect, cone-shaped mass of bright red, woolly drupes, remaining on tree all winter. **Size.** Shrub or small tree. Height 6-10 m, diameter 5-15 cm.

The generic name comes from the Greek and the Latin *rhous* or *rhoys*, which formerly designated the sumacs of Sicily and means "to flow", in reference to the twigs of the species of this genus. These twigs when broken emit a milky sap that turns black on exposure to air. The specific name, *thyphina*, suggests a resemblance to the velvety texture of the compact, cylindrical spear of the cat-tail (*Typha*).

A small tree, often crooked with a flat crown, the staghorn sumac colonizes open, rocky, dry areas, at forest edges, in thickets, on slopes, in abandoned fields and along streams. Its fruits, covered with acid-tasting hairs, explain the common name, vinegar tree. Its twigs, also covered with hairs, resemble the velvet that covers the antlers of deer in summer, hence the name staghorn sumac. This species may be confused with another, closely related, one; the smooth sumac (*Rhus glabra* L.), which can be distinguished from the staghorn sumac by the lack of hairs on its branches, twigs and leaves (indicated in its Latin and English names). Furthermore, it is a shrub with a restricted range in Canada (rare in Quebec).

There are, in the same family, three highly poisonous species: poison-ivy (*Rhus radicans* L.), poison sumac (*Rhus vernix* L.) and poison-oak (*Rhus diversilobum* T. & G.). The staghorn sumac can be distinguished by the presence of hairs on its twigs and leaves. The fruit, bark and leaves of this tree are rich in tannic acid, which the Indians used to tan hides. They also used the sap to remove warts, mixed the leaves with others to make a smoking blend, prepared a beverage similar to lemonade with the fruit, and gargled with a liquid derived from the leaves and fruit.

One can nibble the fruit of this tree, or make it into jelly or a thirst-quenching beverage, which, however, it is wise to drink in moderation and avoid boiling for too long, because of its high tannic acid content. A black ink can be obtained by boiling the leaves and fruit. When it flowers, around mid June, the staghorn sumac yields a great quantity of pollen and nectar, resulting in increased honey production. Fruits stay on the tree throughout winter. The fruit and twigs, are a food source for various members of the deer family, rodents and birds such as pheasants and grouse.

The graceful leaves hang fernlike from the branches. In autumn the foliage assumes colours from red-orange to purple. The staghorn sumac is often planted as an ornamental as its highly visible fruit gives it a striking appearance. The cultivar "Laciniata", with deeply jagged leaves, is particularly popular. However, this tree tends to spread very quickly and is thus unsuitable for a small property.

The wood has no commercial value but is sometimes used as rough construction wood or employed in turning.

212

F 432b/F 442b

American Mountain-ash
American rowantree, catberry,
dogberry, mountain-ash,
pigberry, roundwood, rowan
berry, rowan tree, servicetree

Sorbier d'Amérique, cormier,
maska, maskouabina

Sorbus americana Marsh.
    syn. *Pyrus americana* (Marsh.) DC.

Rose family (Rosaceae)

Distribution
Southern portion of Boreal Forest Region (from Manitoba border eastward), Great Lakes-St Lawrence Forest Region.

Distinctive features
Leaves. 12-30 cm long; 11-17 thin, sharp-pointed leaflets (5-10 cm long), length 3 to 5 times the width. **Flowers.** White, arranged in flat or round-topped clusters. **Fruit.** Pome; round, bright orangey red, edible, acidic; 4-6 mm in diameter. **Twigs.** Glabrous (hairless); buds are shiny, black and gummy. **Size.** Shrub or small tree. Height 4-10 m, diameter 10-20 cm.

The American mountain-ash baffled European settlers, who mistook it for an ash, as its name indicates. Like the ash (*Fraxinus*) it has leaves composed of numerous leaflets. There the similarity ends. The leaves of the American mountain-ash are arranged alternately on the twig, while those of the ash are opposite. It can be recognized by its narrow, round-topped crown, its clusters of white flowers and its hanging bunches of glossy orange fruit.

The generic name *Sorbus* means to absorb, or stop. The specific name *americana* (of America), distinguishes this species from the European mountain-ash (*Sorbus aucuparia* L.). The synonymous name *Pyrus* comes from the Latin *pirus* (pear tree).

This tree is found in moist soils on the edge of lakes and swamps and on rocky hillsides, but is more abundant in fir forests.

In Canada, only American mountain-ash and showy mountain-ash reach tree height. Two shrubby species of mountain-ash are found in British Columbia and Alberta. The first is the Sitka mountain-ash (*Sorbus sitchensis* Roemer), first discovered in Sitka, Alaska. The second is the cascade mountain-ash (*Sorbus scopulina* Greene), a species found at high altitudes. As its specific name *scopulina* (like a small broom), indicates, it is only a stunted shrub at such altitudes.

The Algonquins prepared a mild pick-me-up by boiling in a little wine the young twigs of American mountain-ash with new twigs of white spruce, leaves of wintergreen (*Gaultheria procumbens* L.), and flowers of Canada elderberry (*Sambucus canadensis* L.). Some Indians gathered the fruits, dried them and ground them into meal. When gathered after the first frosts, they have a bittersweet taste and can be made into juice, jelly, jam or marmalade. They can be eaten raw, but in moderation owing to their high tannin content. They can also be used for making wine or for flavouring liqueurs. They are used in folk medicine. Rich in vitamin C and iron even when dried, they are mildly laxative, diuretic, astringent and digestive. They are the ideal accompaniment to foods hard to digest. They are much appreciated by various species of birds, especially grouse, Cedar waxwings, thrushes and grosbeaks, as well as by black bears, who feel no compunction about climbing into the tree or pulling its branches down. The wood of the American mountain-ash is of no commercial value.

It is sometimes planted as an ornamental.

F 432c/F 442c

Showy Mountain-ash
American mountain-ash, northern-ash dogberry, northern-ash, showy northern-ash

Sorbier plaisant, sorbier décoratif, sorbier des montagnes, sorbier monticole

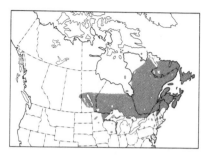

Sorbus decora (Sarg.) C.K. Schneid.
syn. *Pyrus decora* (Sarg.) (Hyl.)

Rose family (Rosaceae)

Distribution
Boreal Forest Region (from central Manitoba to Newfoundland),
Deciduous, Great Lakes-St Lawrence and Acadian forest regions.

Distinctive features
Leaves. 10-25 cm long; 13-17 firm, abruptly short-pointed leaflets (5-8
cm long); length 2-3 times the width. **Flowers.** Like those of American
mountain-ash but larger and appearing 10-12 days later. **Fruit.** Pome,
resembling that of American mountain-ash, but larger, 8-12 mm in
diameter. **Size.** Shrub or small tree. Height 10 m, diameter 10-30 cm.

The generic name is the Latin name for mountain-ash. *Decora*
(elegant, or ornamental) refers to the showy flowers and brilliant red
fruit that make this tree a favourite of landscape designers.

So much does this species resemble the American mountain-ash that
at one time it was classified as a variety of it. Today it is considered a
separate species. In particular, it can be distinguished by its larger
flowers and fruits, and by its leaflets, which have edges almost parallel
to each other. These characteristics, however, are not in themselves a
reliable identification.

The fruits are a major winter food source for various species of
birds. It is said that when native species are grown along with the
European mountain-ash, birds eat the fruits of the native species first.
The increase in the population of cedar waxwings in urban areas in
winter is probably due to the great popularity of mountain-ash (both
native and introduced) as an ornamental.

The European mountain-ash (*Sorbus aucuparia* L.) is an introduced
species. It is often planted in gardens, but sometimes escapes from
cultivation and grows in the wild state, probably as a result of birds
spreading its seeds. It can be distinguished by its young twigs, which
are much hairier than those of our native species, and by its winter
buds, which are not gummy, but covered with a whitish down.

The specific name *aucuparia* comes from the Latin *aucupari* (I catch
birds). In Europe, bird catchers use the fruit of the mountain-ash as a
lure with which to trap their prey. The name rowan-tree is derived
from an old Scandinavian word meaning red, in reference to the brilliant colour of the fruits. Rowans are much appreciated as a spice in
Scandinavian countries, where, fresh or dried, they add flavour to
sauces and game, especially fowl.

F 432d/F 442d

Butternut

Lemon walnut, oilnut, white walnut

Noyer cendré, arbre à noix longues, noyer à beurre, noyer gris, noix longues, noyer tendre

Juglans cinerea L.

Walnut family (Juglandaceae)

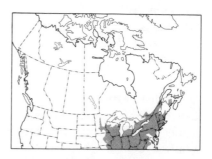

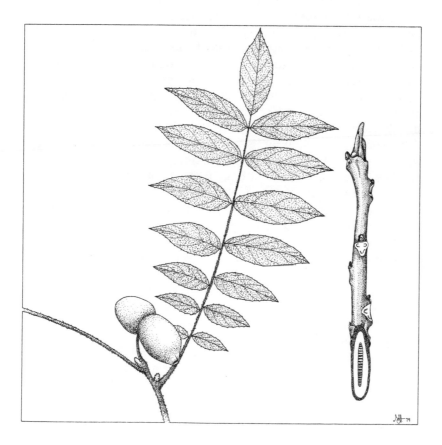

Distribution
Deciduous Forest Region, southeastern part of Great Lakes-St Lawrence Forest Region and western section of Acadian Forest Region.

Distinctive features
Leaves. 30-60 cm long; 11-17 leaflets (8-12 cm long) with the terminal leaflet usually present and about the same size as the larger leaflets. **Fruit.** Lemon-shaped, 4-6 cm long; nut with sweet-tasting kernel, enclosed in a very sticky, hairy shell; stains the fingers. **Twigs.** Pith is dark brown, chambered; leaf scars have downy line across top. **Bark.** Light grey, separated by crevices into flat-topped, intersecting ridges. **Size.** Height 12-20 m, diameter 30-60 cm.

The generic name is the contraction of two Latin words, *Jovis* and *glans*, meaning Jupiter's acorn. The specific name comes from the Latin *cineris* (dust, or ash), referring to the light grey colour of the bark. The butternut is found in maple-dominated stands, often in very hilly areas or along streams; it is never found in a pure stand. It prefers a fertile, moist, well-drained soil, but it grows also on dry, rocky soils, particularly those of limestone origin. It has a short trunk divided into large, ascending branches. The crown is broad, open and slightly rounded or flat on top.

In winter, the butternut is easily distinguished from the black walnut by its sticky twigs and its upper margin of leaf scars with hairy pad (the black walnut has nonsticky twigs and heart-shaped leaf scars without hairy pad).

The wood is soft (hence the tree's common name in French, *noyer tendre*), weak and much lighter than the wood of the black walnut; it is light brown, darkening quickly when exposed to air. Of no commercial value, it is sometimes used for interior finishing and the making of furniture, boxes and toys.

A yellow or orange dye can be extracted from the husks and root bark. During the United States Civil War, foot soldiers wore durable, homemade uniforms dyed with an extract of the husks and outside bark of the butternut, with no mordant to fix the colour. The leaves yield a brown or bronze dye requiring alum as a mordant. The outside bark, dried, is used to make a tea to cure toothache and dysentery.

Both humans and rodents are fond of butternuts. Squirrels play a major role in the natural dissemination of the nuts; they hide them in holes in the ground, and those that they forget may subsequently germinate. The nuts contain a kernel that is hard to extract but mild, sweet and delicious when fully ripe. In the Montreal area there was once a commerce in these nuts. They can be prepared in the same manner as the nuts of the English walnut (*Juglans regia* L.). They can be eaten plain, salted or hickory-smoked, or used as an ingredient in pies or candies. When marinated, the young nuts are an excellent condiment to accompany meat.

The Indians boiled butternuts, extracting an oil that they used as butter (hence the name oilnut); the kernels were then dried and ground, and added to cornmeal mush to give it richness.

The butternut and the black walnut can be tapped like the sugar maple. Their sweet-tasting sap yields an excellent syrup.

F 432e/F 442e

Black Walnut
American black walnut,
American walnut, eastern black
walnut

Noyer noir, noyer noir d'Amérique

Juglans nigra L.

Walnut family (Juglandaceae)

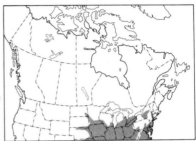

Distribution
Deciduous Forest Region; planted in some parts of Quebec.

Distinctive features
Leaves. 20-60 cm long; 15-23 leaflets (5-9 cm long); terminal leaflet usually absent, if present, much smaller than the others. **Fruit.** Almost round, 4-6 cm in diameter; aromatic nut with sweet kernel enclosed in a nonviscous shell; stains the fingers. **Bark.** Dark brown, almost black, with deep, round, intersecting ridges. **Twigs.** Pith is cream-coloured, chambered; heart-shaped leaf scar. **Size.** Height 20-27 m, diameter 60-120 cm.

The black walnut has magnificent, lustrous, rich chocolate brown wood. Probably the most precious and sought-after deciduous species in North America. The ancient Greeks called the walnut the royal tree, and the Romans dedicated it to Jupiter, the most powerful of the gods.

The generic name is the contraction of two Latin words, *Jovis* and *glans*, meaning Jupiter's acorn. The specific name refers to the dark colour of the bark.

In cross-section the twigs of this species (like those of other walnuts) show a chambered pith, light brown or cream-coloured in the black walnut and dark brown in the butternut. This characteristic helps to distinguish them from their close cousins the hickories, which have solid pith. When growing in the forest the black walnut has a rounded form and long trunk with dark, ridged bark. It prefers deep, rich, well-drained, silty soils. It does not grow in pure stands but is found in association with other deciduous trees.

The wood of the black walnut is one of the most sought after because of its numerous qualities: it is hard, heavy, strong, and resistant to shock and decay; it is usually straight-grained.

It is easy to work with: it can be glued, takes a good polish, stains well, does not shrink and does not warp over the course of time. It is the ideal wood for manufacturing rifle butts and stocks, boats and high-quality furniture. It is also much in demand for making the veneer used in cabinetmaking. This wood is so precious and scarce that an unfelled tree can fetch $5 000 at an auction.

The nuts are edible and they, too, are much sought after, because of their flavour. But beware! they can leave permanent stains on clothing. They can be prepared in the same manner as butternuts. Unfortunately, the kernel is hard to extract, but efforts are being made to develop new varieties with thinner husks. Even the husks were once in great demand, since they not only yielded a blackish dye and tannin but were also made into high-quality coal for use in the filters of gas masks during the First World War. During the 1930s they were ground into a type of meal that was used as an insecticide. The Indians ground the husks to make a poison to kill fish. This practice is now illegal.

In Canada the supply of black walnut is almost exhausted. However, there are reforestation programs in southern Ontario and Quebec.

When planted as an ornamental or shade tree, it requires considerable space to reach its full size. It is hard to transplant, having a long taproot. Its roots secrete a substance called juglone, which inhibits the growth of some cultivated plants (tomatoes, alfalfa) and prevents numerous other trees and its own seedlings from sprouting around it.

F 432f/F 442f

Bitternut Hickory
Swamp hickory

Caryer cordiforme, arbe à noix amères, carya amer, caryer amer

Carya cordiformis (Wang.) K. Koch

Walnut family (Juglandaceae)

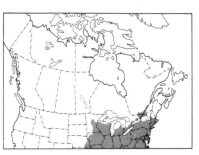

Distribution

Deciduous Forest Region and southern portion of Great Lakes-St Lawrence Forest Region.

Distinctive features
Leaves. 15-30 cm long; 7-11 leaflets (usually 9) 10-15 cm long. **Twigs.**
Slender and smooth or slightly hairy; buds sulphur yellow; pith solid
(not chambered). **Fruit.** Round, 2-3 cm long; nuts with very bitter
kernels, encased in very thin, smooth shell; yellowish green; opening
into 4 valves at maturity. **Bark.** Light grey or brown in the adult, with
shallow crevices, not peeling off in scales or strips. **Size.** Height
15-20 m, diameter 30-50 cm.

The generic name comes from the Greek *karuon*, the old name for the
walnut, the fruit of which somewhat resembles those of the hickories.
While the two genuses have numerous similarities, the hickory may be
distinguished by the pith in its twigs, the shell on its fruit, which comes
away from the nut in four valves at maturity, and the white to reddish
brown colour of its wood. The walnut has chambered pith in its twigs,
the shell on its fruit does not open at maturity, and its wood goes from
light brown to dark brown. The specific name *cordiformis* derives
from the Latin *cor, cordis* (heart) and *forma* (form), referring to the
shape of the fruit.

Of the five Canadian species of hickory, the bitternut hickory is the
easiest to identify, being the only one to have sulphur-yellow buds.
This feature also serves to identify it in winter. Different from the
"true hickories" with its distinctive buds, its fruit with 4-winged husks
and its leaves with a greater number of leaflets, it belongs to the
"pecan hickory" group. The pecan, the delicious and well-known ingredient of pecan pies, comes from a hickory of the eastern United
States, the sweet pecan (*Carya illinoensis* (Wang.) K. Koch). In terms
of its taste the fruit of the bitternut hickory is definitely not related to
the pecan. It is so bitter (hence the names bitternut and *arbre à noix
amères*) that even squirrels pass it over or eat it only as a last resort.

The bitternut hickory is the most common hickory, followed by the
shagbark hickory. It is found in low, moist locations and in rich soils
on higher ground, in places well protected from the wind. It is fairly
shade tolerant and is found in association with other hardwood
species such as the sugar maple and the American beech.

Its wood is heavy, hard and strong, but is not as resistant to shock
as that of other Canadian hickories. It burns intensely, leaving few
cinders; it is recommended for smoking meat, to which it gives a distinctive flavour. In the past it was used for making wooden wheels.
Now it is used in the making of tool handles, sporting goods, panelling
and fine furniture. Early settlers extracted oil from the nut and used it
in lamps; it seems that this oil was also useful in bringing relief from

rheumatism. Although it is the most common and abundant hickory in Canada, reserves are insufficient to meet the demand, thus industries using it obtain their supplies almost entirely from the United States.

F 432g/F 442g

Mockernut Hickory
Bigbud hickory, bullnut
hickory, white hickory,
whiteheart hickory

Caryer tomenteux, carya
tomenteux, caryer cotonneux,
noyer à noix douces, noyer
blanc, noyer dur

Carya tomentosa (Poir.) Nutt.
   syn. *Carya alba* (P. Mill.) K. Koch

Walnut family (Juglandaceae)

Distribution
Deciduous Forest Region: only at the eastern end of Lake St Clair and the eastern and western ends of Lake Erie.

Distinctive features
Leaves. 15-30 cm long; 7-9 leaflets (10-20 cm long) occasionally only 5, undersurface of leaflets covered with fine hairs; leaflets very fragrant when crushed. **Twigs.** Sturdy and pubescent (covered with hairs); terminal bud reddish brown, very broad (about 2 cm long) and pubescent; pith solid (not chambered). **Fruit.** Round, 4-5 cm long; nut with sweet, edible kernel, encased in very thick shell; splitting to middle at maturity. **Bark.** Dark grey with shallow furrows, not peeling off in scales or strips. **Size.** Height 25-30 m, diameter 50-100 cm.

The generic name *Carya* is an ancient Greek name for the walnut, and the specific name *tomentosa* (down-covered) refers to the pubescence of the twigs and buds and the undersurface of the leaflets.

The great variety that exists within each species complicates the task of identifying hickories. Furthermore, there are a number of hybrids that are hard to classify, making identification even more difficult. However, the mockernut, pignut and big shellbark hickories are relatively rare species in Canada and are found only in southern Ontario. In order to identify the different species of hickories accurately, all data must be taken into account.

Unlike the bitternut hickory, the mockernut hickory is not shade-tolerant and prefers rich, well-drained slopes. While not abundant in Canada, it is very common in the southern United States.

The name mockernut probably refers to the fact that such a large nut contains such a small kernel—but how delicious this kernel is! The wood of the mockernut hickory is considered superior to that of other hickories, but since it is scarce in Canada is not used commercially. The Indians extracted a black dye from it by boiling the bark in a vinegar solution. A beige dye is extracted from its leaves and twigs, using cream of tartar as a mordant. A yellow dye is made from its bark, using alum as a mordant.

228

F 522a

Honey-locust
Sweet-locust, thorny-locust,
tree-thorned acacia, honeylocust

Févier épineux, carouge à miel,
févier à trois épines, févier
d'Amérique

Gleditsia triacanthos L.

Pea family (Leguminosae)   Rare in Ontario

$B 84

Distribution

Deciduous Forest Region, along the shores of Lake Erie; is planted as an ornamental and has escaped from cultivation.

Distinctive features

Leaves. 15-30 cm long, singly or doubly compound leaf; an even number of leaflets (18 or more), 2.5-5 cm long. **Twigs.** Armed with formidable thorns, either simple or branched; no terminal bud. **Fruit.** Long pods, 30 cm or longer; thin, flat and generally aromatic, twisted like a corkscrew and very numerous on tree. **Trunk.** At maturity, bristling with a mass of thorns measuring up to 30 cm. **Size.** Height 15-25 m, diameter 60-100 cm.

The generic name was given in honour of Johann Gottlieb Gleditsch, a director of the Berlin Botanical Garden during the eighteenth century. The specific name comes from the Greek *treis* (three) and *akantha*, (thorn), in reference to the three thorns usually found on each bud. There is a variety on the market (var. *inermis* Pursh) that has few or no thorns and bears fruit that is shorter and reddish in colour.

The honey-locust is also called the thorny-locust; it owes this name to the clusters of long, sharp thorns on its twigs. These hard and very dangerous thorns, formerly used as nails or pins, serve to protect the tree. The pods contain a sweetish substance with a taste suggesting a mixture of castor oil and honey; hence the name honey-locust.

This species, probably introduced into Canada a very long time ago, grows naturally only in southern Ontario. It is cultivated throughout southern Ontario, and is found as far north as Renfrew County and as far east as Carleton County and western Quebec. Its hard, heavy, wood, easy to polish, is sometimes used in cabinetmaking and carpentry. The tree may be used as a protective hedge or in gardens as an ornamental. It was introduced into Europe during the sixteenth century to embellish parks and gardens.

Various wild and domestic animals eat its foliage. Its striking flowers and sweet-tasting pods attract large numbers of bees. Its fruit can be used to make beer. The roots of the honey-locust, unlike most Leguminosae, do not have nodules caused by the presence of nitrogen-fixing bacteria.

230

F 522b

Kentucky Coffee Tree
Coffeebean, coffeenut,
coffeetree

Chicot févier, café du Kentucky,
caféier du Kentucky, chicot
dioïque, chicot du Canada, gros
févier, gymnocladier dioïque

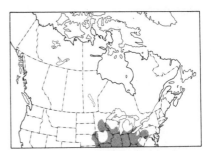

Gymnocladus dioicus (L.) K. Koch

Rare in Ontario

Pea family (Leguminosae)

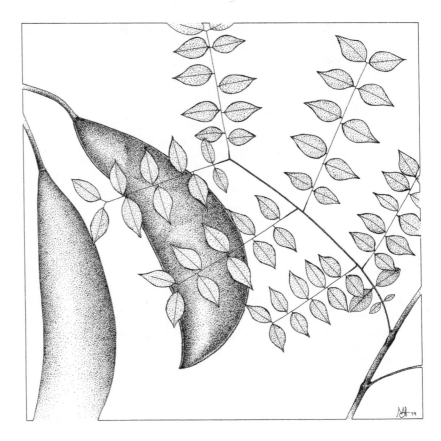

Distribution
Deciduous Forest Region, extreme southwest of Ontario. Planted as an ornamental elsewhere in Canada.

Distinctive features
Leaves. Usually composed of an even number of leaflets (40 or more); very large leaves, doubly compound (bipinnate), up to 1 m long and 0.6 m wide, leaflets seldom opposite each other, 4-6 cm long. **Twigs.** Very stout, with only a few on each branch. **Fruit.** Reddish pods, flat and tough, 8-25 cm long, remaining on the tree through the winter. **Size.** Height 15-23 m, diameter 40-60 cm.

The generic name comes from the Greek *gymnos* (naked) and *klodos* (twig, or branch), referring to the denuded appearance of the tree for half the year (it leafs out much later in spring than do the other species in its group). The specific name comes from the Greek *di* (two) and *oikor* (house), in reference to plants that have male and female flowers on different trees.

The tree is formed of a few large branches and very stout, stocky twigs; their stumplike appearance give it its French name, *chicot* [stump] *du Canada*.

In the past its black seeds were used as a bitter-tasting coffee substitute, hence the name Kentucky coffee tree. The Indians roasted the seeds and ate them like nuts, hence the name coffeenut. The seeds can be roasted and ground for use as a coffee substitute, but it is essential to roast the seeds, since they and the pulp inside the pod are toxic when raw.

The Kentucky coffee tree does not appear to be a food source for wildlife. Indeed, it is said that cattle became sick after drinking water contaminated by its leaves or fruit.

It has not been possible to find the populations represented by the samplings taken in 1950 and earlier. Because of its rarity, this tree has no commercial value. It is cultivated as an ornamental for its unusual foliage.

F 522c

Black Locust
Common locust, false acacia, white locust, yellow locust

Robinier faux-acacia, acacia blanc, acacia commun, faux-acacia, robinier

Robinia pseudoacacia L.

Pea family (Leguminosae)

Distribution
Species native to the United States, now planted as an ornamental, sometimes escaping from cultivation.

Distinctive features
Leaves. 20-35 cm long, uneven number of leaflets (from 7-19), 2-5 cm
long. **Twigs.** Zigzag; armed with pair of short thorns at each bud.
Flowers. White, fragrant, hanging in clusters, resembling pea flowers.
Fruit. Flat, smooth pods, dark brown to black at maturity, 7-10 cm
long, poisonous, remaining on tree through the winter. **Size.** Height
9-15 m, diameter 30-60 cm.

The generic name *Robinia* was given to this tree by Linnaeus in
honour of Jean Robin and his son Vespasien Robin, herbalists to the
kings of France in the sixteenth and seventeenth centuries. They were
the first to cultivate the black locust in the gardens of the Louvre and
to popularize its use in France. The specific name *pseudoacacia* comes
from *pseudo* (false) and *acacia*, from the Greek *acakia*, designating
the acacia. The black locust is wrongly classified as an acacia. True
acacias, although of the same family (Leguminosae), are mainly
found in the tropical and subtropical regions of the world.

The first settlers in New England confused this tree with the Carob
(*Ceratonia siliqua* L.) or biblical locust, which St. John the Baptist
described in the Gospel of St Mark, and whose fruit (carobs) he ate to
survive in the wilderness. The fruit of the black locust is not edible.
Black refers to the colour of the fruit.

The black locust, with its irregular, open crown and crooked
branches, is a very invasive, fast-growing tree that can adapt to a
variety of soils. It has a highly-developed creeping root system and
often multiplies by shoots or suckers springing up from the roots, up
to 5 m from the parent plant. Because of these characteristics, it is
often planted to prevent soil erosion. The roots are so strong that they
are used to support dikes.

The black locust was introduced into Europe in the early seventeenth century to embellish gardens and stabilize soils. There are
several cultivars on the market, with and without thorns. Today it is
naturalized throughout Europe.

In Canada there are other species of locust planted as ornamental
trees. One of these is the clammy locust, (*Robinia viscosa* Vent. ex
Vaug.), which can be distinguished from the black locust by its
odourless pink flowers, and its twigs, leaf-stalks and pods—viscous
and sticky to the touch.

When small, the black locust may be confused with the prickly-ash
(*Zanthoxylum americanum* P. Mill.) (which in Canada is a shrub)
because of the presence of short thorns in both species and the similar
shape of their leaves. However, the prickly-ash can be distinguished

by its shrubby appearance, the tiny translucent dots on its leaves (aromatic when crushed), the presence of thorns on its leaf-stalk, and its round fruit.

The greenish-yellow wood of the black locust is very hard, heavy and durable. It is very slow to decompose in the soil, and is therefore much valued for making railroad ties, posts, stakes and piles. Carpenters like this wood, for its volume varies only slightly despite climatic changes. It can be used as firewood, but with caution: it flares up and projects sparks, like the wood of the hemlock and the arborvitae.

The inside bark, leaves and seeds of the black locust are poisonous: cattle have been poisoned as a result of eating its leaves or bark; children have become seriously ill from chewing its bark. But rabbits, hares, pheasants and mourning doves eat its seed with no apparent ill effect. The Indians used to make arrows from its poisonous wood. As with most Leguminosae, the black locust has root nodules. These root nodules are caused by the presence of nitrogen-fixing bacteria, which serve to enrich the soil.

F 522d

Hoptree

Common hoptree, stinking-ash, tree-leaved hoptree, wafer-ash

Ptéléa trifolié, bois puant, orme de Samarie, orme de Samarie à trois folioles

Ptelea trifoliata L.
  syn. *Ptelea angustifolia* Benth.

Citrus family (Rutaceae)

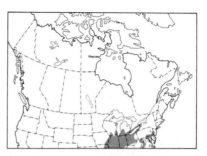

Rare in Ontario

Distribution
Deciduous Forest Region, used as an ornamental, sometimes escaping from cultivation.

Distinctive features
The leaves, flowers, bark and twigs emit highly unpleasant odour when crushed. **Leaves.** Scattered with tiny translucent dots visible by holding leaf to the sun; 3 leaflets, 5-10 cm long. **Fruit.** Samara surrounded by a circular wing, remaining on tree almost all winter. **Size.** Large shrub or small tree. Height 4-5 m, diameter 8-12 cm.

This tree does not belong to the elm but to the citrus family. The resemblance of its fruits to those of the elm gave rise to the French name *orme de Samarie* (Samaria elm). Its generic name *Ptelea* is the common Greek name for elm, and it was transferred by Linnaeus to this genus. Its specific name comes from the Latin *tres* (three) and *folium* (leaf), in reference to the leaf's three leaflets.

A common name for the hoptree is stinking-ash, and for good reason, almost all its parts giving off an unpleasant odour. Even its flowers emit an odour of rotting flesh—in order to attract carrion insects as pollinators. Formerly the fruit was used as a substitute for hops in the making of beer, hence the name hoptree. The wafer-shaped fruit justifies the first part of the name wafer-ash; the ash bears no resemblance to the hoptree, however, except in having compound leaves.

This small tree, capable of living in the understorey of a forest, is slow-growing and short-lived. Its wood—hard, heavy, close-grained and brownish yellow in colour—is too small for commercial use. The hoptree is sometimes used as an ornamental or a hedge plant. Many populations of this species are protected in parks and nature reserves, but a number of others are threatened by waterfront development.

F 522e

Poison Sumac

Poison-dogwood, poison-
elderberry, poison-elder, poison-
oak, swamp sumac

Sumac lustré, arbre du vernis,
bois-chandelle, sumac à vernis,
sumac vénéneux

Rhus vernix L.
    syn. *Toxicodendron vernix* (L.) Kuntze

Cashew family (Anacardiaceae)

Rare in Quebec

Distribution

Southern parts of the Deciduous Forest Region and a few places in the Great Lakes St-Lawrence Forest Region.

Distinctive features

Poisonous plant: **All parts are extremely toxic. Leaves.** 15-30 cm long; 7-13 shiny leaflets 3-6 cm long. **Fruit.** Glossy white drupes, in clusters remaining on tree throughout winter; nonterminal, situated at axil of leaf. **Size.** Shrub or small tree. Height 4-6 m, diameter 6-8 cm.

Of all trees, it is important to be able to recognize the poison sumac. It is a small tree that grows in swampy woodlands and bogs and near peaty lakes (swamp sumac). Its small rounded crown is formed by moderately stout branches bearing large alternate leaves composed of leaflets which have no teeth and are dark green and glossy, hence the French name *Sumac lustré* (glossy sumac). These leaves resemble the compound leaves of a thorny shrub of the same family as the hoptree: the prickly-ash (*Zanthoxylum americanum* P. Mill.). It, however, has thorny leaves and twigs, whereas those of poison sumac are smooth. Two other poisonous species of this family are found in Canada: poison-ivy (*Rhus radicans* L.), found all across the continent, and poison-oak (*Rhus diversilobum* Torr. & Gray), found on the Pacific coast. These three species contain a milky or colourless oil to which many people are allergic. Only the poison sumac reaches tree size; the other two are creepers or small shrubs.

The generic name *Rhus* probably derives from the Greek or Latin *rhous* or *rhoys* (to flow), which formerly designated the sumacs of Sicily; but some botanists believe the name is of Celtic origin and means red. The specific name, *vernix* (varnish) originates from an error of Linnaeus, who believed that this species was the source of Chinese lacquer, which actually comes from a similar Asian species, the lacquer tree (*Rhus verniciflua* Stokes). Some consider that the poisonous plants do not belong to the genus *Rhus* but rather to the genus *Toxicodendron*, from the Greek *toxikon* (poison) and *dendron* (tree). The specific name of poison ivy, *radicans* (rooting), refers to the roots propagating by sending up suckers, and the specific name of the poison oak, *diversilobum*, refers to the irregularly lobed leaf.

The greenish fruit grows in clusters from the axils of the leaves and becomes globular and white or ivory-coloured. The poison sumac retains its fruit during the autumn and winter, greatly facilitating identification during this period. In autumn its showy fruits stand out against their dark background, giving it a characteristic appearance. People unfamiliar with the harmful effects of the poison sumac have gathered sprays of it to use as decoration, paying dearly for their folly.

Prolonged contact with any part of the plant causes painful skin eruptions. The itching is caused by an oil, present in all parts of the plant throughout the year, which does not evaporate and can contaminate clothes. Pets and other animals can also transmit the poison. No part of the plant should be burned, since the smoke carries the toxic substance through the air. The severest cases of poisoning have been caused by contaminated smoke coming into contact with the skin or eyes or with the mucous membranes of the mouth, nose and throat: anyone affected should wash thoroughly as soon as possible, with warm water and soap. Never use oily or fatty substances, since they tend to dissolve and spread the toxin. This toxin, also present in the fruit, does not appear to affect the birds that eat it.

This tree has no commercial value. Its sap was formerly used to make an indelible ink and a shiny black varnish (hence the French name *arbre du vernis*, varnish tree). This practice was abandoned when the final product proved toxic.

F 542a

Shagbark Hickory

Scalybark hickory, shellbark
hickory, upland hickory

Caryer ovale, arbre à noix
piquées, caryer à fruits doux,
caryer à noix douce, caryer
blanc, noyer blanc, noyer
écailleux, noyer tendre

Carya ovata (P. Mill.) K. Koch
syn. *Carya carolinae-septentrionalis* (Ashe) Engl. & Graebn.

Walnut family (Juglandaceae)

Distribution
Deciduous Forest Region and southern portion of Great Lakes-St Lawrence Forest Region.

Distinctive features
Leaves. 20-30 cm long; 5 leaflets (occasionally 7) 8-18 cm long, toothed, fringed with numerous hairs visible under magnifying glass. **Twigs.** Stout, shiny, hairless; terminal bud greenish brown, very large (1-2 cm long) and hairy. **Fruit.** Round, 2-4 cm long; nut with sweet, edible kernel encased in thick, reddish brown shell; splitting to the base at maturity. **Bark.** Peeling off in curly strips or plates on mature trees; dark grey. **Size.** Height 19-25 m, diameter 30-60 cm.

The shagbark hickory and the big shellbark hickory are the only trees in our flora to have a trunk with bark that peels off in long strips, giving them a shaggy appearance; hence the name shagbark hickory. It can be distinguished from the big shellbark hickory by its leaves with 5 leaflets and by the almost total absence of hairs on the undersurface of the leaf. The leaf of the big shellbark hickory generally has 7 leaflets and a dense coating of hairs; a rare species in Canada, it is confined to a few sites in southern Ontario. The shagbark hickory has a larger natural range in southern Ontario and the St Lawrence Valley.

The generic name *Carya* is an old Greek name for the walnut, and the specific name *ovata* comes from the Latin *ovum* (egg), referring to the shape of the fruit. The nuts of this species were a major food source for a number of tribes of Indians: when ground up and boiled in water, these nuts yield a ''milk''—an oily substance resembling cream and used as an ingredient in corn bread and cornmeal mush. The early settlers were quick to make use of the hickory nut and its milk. The name hickory may be a deformation of the Indian name *Pocohicora*, or *Pauchohiceora*.

The wood of the shagbark hickory is one of the best. It is hard, strong, resilient and extremely heavy. It is used in the manufacture of wheel spokes, tool handles, ploughing implements, machine parts, and sporting goods such as skis, fishing rods, bows and lacrosse sticks. Canada produces some 98 per cent of the world supply of lacrosse sticks. Only hickory wood has both the strength and the elasticity required for this product.

The shagbark (like other hickories) gives off considerable heat when burning, similar to the white oak. Its wood is used for producing high-quality charcoal and for smoking meat. In common with the walnut, it can be tapped like the sugar maple to collect its sweet-tasting sap.

A yellow dye is extracted from its inside bark. In the eighteenth century this dye was patented, but was never much in demand because more intense yellows were available. The shagbark hickory and its improved varieties produce an edible nut that can be eaten on its own or used in any recipe calling for nuts or pecans.

F 542b

Big Shellbark Hickory

Bigleaf, big shagbark hickory, bottom shellbark, kingnut hickory, shagbark hickory

Caryer lacinié, caryer à écorce laciniée

Carya laciniosa (Michx. fil.) Loud.

Walnut family (Juglandaceae)

Rare in Ontario

Distribution

Scattered throughout the Deciduous Forest Region.

Distinctive features
Leaves. 25-50 cm long; 7-9 leaflets (usually 7) (12-20 cm long); hairy beneath; toothed margins hairless. **Twigs.** Similar to shagbark hickory but light orange in colour. **Fruit.** Similar to shagbark hickory but larger, 5-6 cm in diameter. **Bark.** Dark grey, peeling off in plates or strips, similar to shagbark hickory. **Size.** Height 20-30 m, diameter 60-100 cm.

While similar to the shagbark hickory, this fast-growing hickory differs in that its leaves have 7 leaflets (in rare cases 5 or 9). Unlike other hickories, its twigs are orange-coloured.

The specific name *laciniosa* comes from the Latin *lacinia* (cut in shreds), in reference to the characteristic bark of this species. Its wood has the same technical qualities as that of other hickories and is used for the same purposes. Its nuts, encased in thick husks, are edible and can be used in place of pecans in pies. The largest of all the hickory nuts, they have earned this species the name kingnut. (The meaning of the word nut is vague, encompassing a variety of fruits, from the true nuts (Juglandaceae) to the exotic nuts: Brazil nut, coconut, kola nut, nutmeg.)

The edible nuts of our hickories are much sought after by mammals such as black bears, foxes, hares, muskrats, squirrels and chipmunks. Ducks and quail eat the nuts occasionally. As with walnuts, the hickory's green husk was once ground up and used to poison fish.

F 542c

Pignut Hickory
Black hickory, broom hickory,
smoothbark hickory

Caryer glabre, carya glabre,
caryer à cochon, caryer des
pourceaux, noyer à cochon,
noyer à noix de cochon

Carya glabra (P. Mill.) Sweet
    syn. *Carya leiodermis* Sarg.

Walnut family (Juglandaceae)

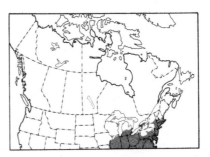

Rare in Ontario

Distribution
Deciduous Forest Region, especially on the peninsula south of Lake Ontario.

Distinctive features
Leaves. 15-30 cm long; 5-7 leaflets; hairless. **Twigs.** Slender, smooth and shiny, without hairs. **Fruit.** Pear-shaped, 1.5-3 cm long; nut with a usually bitter kernel; encased in thin shell; often not splitting to base at maturity. **Bark.** Thin, with shallow crevices; does not peel off in long plates or strips. **Size.** Height 15-20 m, diameter 30-100 cm.

The pignut hickory is quite variable and resembles an American species, the red hickory (*Carya ovalis* (Wang.) Sarg.), not found in Canada. In order to identify the pignut hickory, all characteristics must be considered. Its pale bark is much less jagged than that of the shagbark and big shellbark hickories; the narrow, crisscross ridges are rounded. Like the mockernut and big shellbark hickories, it is a rare species in Canada—all three species are much more widely distributed in the United States, and are common south of the Appalachians.

The pignut hickory's specific name, *glabra* (smooth, or hairless) refers to the total or nearly total absence of hairs on its leaves and twigs. *Leiodermis* comes from the Greek *leios* (smooth) and *derma* (skin). The fruit of the pignut hickory is bitter and contains little edible matter; nut lovers leave it to the pigs, preferring the fruit of the big shellbark and shagbark hickories. Its wood was formerly used for making brooms (broom hickory). It is not harvested in Canada because of its scarcity, but it has the same properties and is used for the same purposes as the wood of other hickories.

Deciduous Trees

Leaves Alternate, Simple

G 422

Silky Willow
Satin willow, satiny willow

Saule satiné

Salix pellita Anderss. ex Schneid.

Willow family (Salicaceae)

Distribution
From Nova Scotia to Saskatchewan. Not found on Prince Edward Island.

variation of leaf margin

249

Distinctive features

Leaves. 4-13 cm long, 0.5-2.5 cm wide, stipules absent or tiny and deciduous; dark green and hairless above, and velvety, often silky, densely covered with glossy white hairs below; curled edge. **Flowers.** Catkins (groups of male or female flowers) appear before or simultaneously with leaves. **Twigs.** Range from yellowish to reddish brown, smooth and often covered with thin wax film, strong. **Size.** Shrub or small tree. Height 5 m.

The specific name *pellita* (film) refers to the twigs, covered with a thin waxy film. The other names refer to the leaf's velvety underside. The silky willow, a species found mainly in northeastern Canada, is sometimes found in the form *psila* (smooth). It is characterized by leaves with dull blue-green, hairless underside.

The silky willow's counterpart west of Saskatchewan, the drummond willow (*Salix drummondiana* Barr. ex Hook.), does not reach tree size. Some taxonomists consider it a variety of the silky willow, but most works refer to it as a distinct species. It was named in honour of Thomas Drummond (1780-1853), a Scottish botanist.

In eastern Canada, the silky willow can be mistaken for a willow introduced from abroad and now growing wild; the osier (*Salix viminalis* L.). Native to Europe and Asia, it is grown as an ornamental and as a source of wicker for wickerwork. Its twigs are considered the best in both quality and quantity for the making of furniture and baskets. Its specific name, *viminalis* (able to make links), refers to this unique feature. The osier is a small tree or shrub reaching 8 metres or more in height with long, very flexible greenish-yellow twigs. It differs from the silky willow mainly in its very erect twigs and the absence of a thin whitish film upon them.

The Russian olive (*Elaeagnus angustifolia* L.), a species of the Oleaster family (Elaeagnaceae), is a native of western Asia and southern Europe, and is often grown here in parks and gardens. It can easily be mistaken for the willow due to the similarity of their leaves. The Russian olive has alternate, spear-shaped, toothless leaves, dark green above and silvery below. However, it can be recognized by the presence of shiny scales on the underside of its leaves, on its twigs and on its fruit, which resemble small olives.

G 432a

American Chestnut
Chestnut, sweet chestnut

Châtaignier d'Amérique,
châtaignier, châtaignier denté

Castanea dentata (Marsh.) Borkh.

Beech family (Fagaceae)

Rare in Ontario

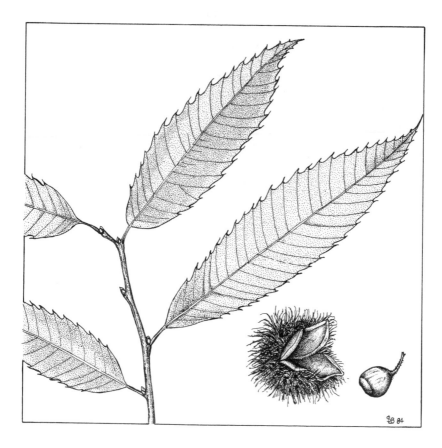

Distribution
Deciduous Forest Region.

Distinctive features
Leaves. 15-21 cm long, 5-7 cm wide; lateral veins parallel, prominent, extending through the teeth to form short bristles. **Fruit.** Nut (chestnut) is dull brown, smooth, in groups of 1-3 in spiny bur; kernel edible and sweet-tasting, matures in autumn of first year. **Size.** Formerly a large tree, now rarely exceeds 10 m in height and 15 cm in diameter.

At the turn of the century, the American chestnut was commercially important in North America because of its wood, used in construction, and for its nuts. In less than one generation entire stands were decimated by a serious disease, introduced around 1900 and known as chestnut blight, which causes uncontrolled cell growth in the bark. Unlike white pine blister rust, which attacks the eastern white pine via an intermediate host (*Ribes*), chestnut blight spreads from tree to tree by spores carried in the wind. In 1937 a study showed that 99 per cent of the chestnut trees in the United States had been killed. The chestnut has survived to the present day through suckers, which sometimes bear seed before being killed in turn.

The generic name comes from the Greek *kastanou* or *kastanea* (chestnut); the specific name, *dentata* (toothed), refers to the toothed margin of the leaves.

According to folklore, a jelly made by boiling the leaves eases burns and sweaty feet; a tea made from the bark of the American chestnut soothes inflamed tonsils when gargled, and when mixed with a little honey is said to cure whooping cough.

G 432b

Chinquapin, or Chinkapin Oak

Rock oak, yellow chestnut oak,
yellow oak

Chêne jaune, chêne chincapin,
chêne de Mühlenberg, chêne à
chinquapin

Quercus muehlenbergii Engelm.

Beech family (Fagaceae)

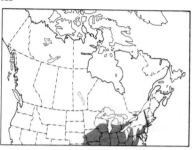

Distribution
Deciduous Forest Region and northeast of Lake Ontario.

Distinctive features
Leaves. 10-15 cm long, 3-8 cm wide; parallel lateral veins (8-13) extending to teeth on each side of the blade. **Twigs.** Hairless; end bud similar to laterals. **Fruit.** Egg-shaped acorn with edible kernel; 1.2-2.5 cm long in deep, thin cup covered with hairy scales; matures in autumn of first year. **Bark.** Pale grey; scaly. **Size.** Height 12-15 m, diameter 30-60 cm.

The generic name *Quercus* is the name given by the Romans; the specific name *muehlenbergii* was given in honour of Henry Ernst Mühlenberg (1753-1815), a Pennsylvania botanist first to identify this species.

This medium-sized oak, scarce within its range, can be distinguished from the American chestnut by its acorn and by the absence of short bristles at the ends of the teeth on its leaves. It can be confused with another oak, the dwarf chinquapin oak (*Quercus prinoides* Willd.), but the latter is a small shrub, and its leaves generally have six teeth on each side. A number of books state that the chestnut oak (*Quercus prinus* L.) is to be found in the southern tip of Ontario. Specimens upon which these statements were based were painstakingly examined by an expert, who concluded that this species is not part of the Canadian flora. All the specimens had been erroneously identified and in fact were specimens of chinquapin oak.

The crown of the chinquapin is made up of many branches and is narrow and rounded on top. Its bright yellowish-green foliage has earned it the name yellow oak. Because of the resemblance of its leaves to those of the American chestnut, it is also called the yellow chestnut oak (indeed, *chinquapin* is an Indian word meaning chestnut). The chinquapin belongs to the category of chestnut oaks, along with the swamp white oak and the chestnut oak. This group is characterized by leaves that are generally toothed, notched or shallowly lobed, rather than deeply lobed as are most oaks.

The acorns of the chinquapin are milder than those of other oaks. Its wood, of no great commercial value, is sold under the name white oak, and is used in construction, made into railroad ties or burned as firewood. The Chinquapin is sometimes planted as an ornamental or a shade tree.

G 442a

Black Cherry
Cabinet cherry, rhum cherry, timber cherry, wild black cherry, wine cherry

Cerisier tardif, cerises d'automne, cerisier d'automne, cerisier noir

Prunus serotina Ehrh.

Rose family (Rosaceae)

Distribution
Deciduous Forest Region, southern portions of the Great Lakes-St Lawrence Forest Region and the Acadian Forest Region.

Distinctive features
Leaves. 6-12 cm long, widest at middle of blade; thick and leathery, with fine, incurved teeth; top surface dark green, waxy; undersurface paler, with hairs ranging from white to red on either side of midrib. **Twigs.** Reddish brown, with a single bud at the end of the twig; give off strong odour when broken. **Fruit.** Drupe; cherries, almost black, arranged in elongated clusters, edible, slightly bitter, juicy. **Bark.** Smooth on young trees, with conspicuous horizontal whitish markings (lenticels), becoming rough and coming off in curved strips. **Size.** Height 20-30 m, diameter 30-100 cm.

The generic name is the Latin name for the plum tree and derives from the Greek *prunos* (plum, or cherry). The specific name *serotina* comes from the Latin *serus* (late), in reference to the late appearance of the flowers and fruit, which sometimes remain on the tree until mid October.

The black cherry is the only sizable cherry tree native to Canada, reaching a height of 30 metres in some areas. All other native cherries are either small trees or shrubs. The black cherry grows in a variety of soils and is found in maple-dominated stands, rocky woodlands or wooded areas along rivers.

Its wood—hard, close-grained and regular—polishes well. It is used in cabinet work and panelling, and in the making of musical instruments and tool handles. In quality it equals the wood of the black walnut, and its rich, reddish-brown colour is reminiscent of mahogany; because of these characteristics it was used for much of the colonial-style furniture produced at the beginning of Canada's development. The black cherry was one of the first trees to be introduced into English gardens (in 1629). Formerly its wood was the most sought-after for the framing of engravings and etchings. The tree was so extensively exploited that today it is scarce throughout its range.

The leaves give off prussic acid, which becomes a deadly poison when acted upon by the enzymes contained in the stomach. Cattle have been poisoned by eating the wilted leaves, and children have become poisoned and have even died after chewing the twigs. In folk medicine, the leaves and inner bark were once used as a tonic or sedative, or as a treatment for bronchial disorders—a practice to be condemned because of the toxicity of these parts. The flesh of the fruit may be eaten raw or made into jelly, syrup, wine or juice, or baked in a pie. The black cherry was once a valuable tree to humans and its fruit continues to be a major food source for birds and various mammals. The pits, while toxic for man, are much appreciated by chipmunks and deer mice, which have no qualms about storing them away.

G 442b

Pin Cherry

Bird cherry, cherrytree, fire
cherry, hay cherry, pigeon
cherry, red cherry, wild cherry,
wild red cherry

Cerisier de Pennsylvanie, arbre
à petites merises, cerisier d'été,
merise, merisier, petit merisier

Prunus pensylvanica L. fil.

Rose family (Rosaceae)

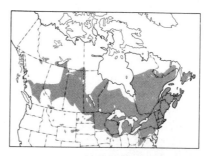

Rare in N.W.T.

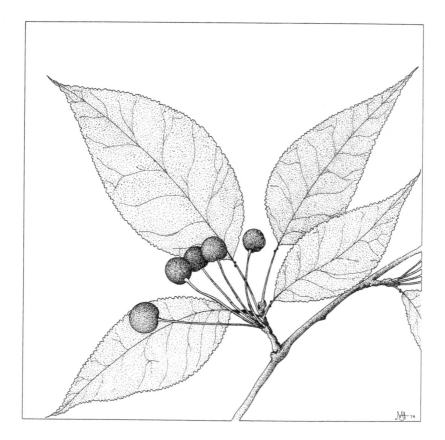

Distribution
In almost all forest regions in Canada, from Newfoundland to central British Columbia.

Distinctive features
Leaves. 4-12 cm long, the widest part in the lowest third of the blade; thin, fragile, hairless; shiny on both surfaces. **Twigs.** Several buds clustered at the end of the twig, shiny red, bitter tasting, with a pronounced odour when broken. **Fruit.** Drupe; bright-red wild cherry, on long stalk, in short clusters of 2-6; edible but very acidic. **Bark.** Smooth, reddish brown, varnished-looking, with conspicuous orange, powdery, horizontal markings (lenticels). **Size.** Small tree or shrub. Height 5-15 m, diameter 10-30 cm.

The straight-trunked pin cherry is considered by some the most attractive native cherry. The generic name *Prunus* comes from the Greek *prunos* (plum tree, or cherry tree). Its specific name *pensylvanica* commemorates an old spelling of the former colony. Some of the common names reflect important characteristics of the species. Birds feed heavily on the fruit and are the main agents for seed dispersal; hence the name bird cherry. The name pin cherry reflects the arrangement of the clusters of fruit on long stems resembling pins in a pincushion. It is sometimes called the fire cherry because of its ability to spring up in burned-over areas. It is also known as hay cherry, because its fruit ripens during the hay season. The bright red colour of its fruit has earned it the name red cherry.

The pin cherry is one of the first trees to display its white flowers in spring, before or at the same time as its leaves appear. A pioneer species, it is intolerant of shade and quickly disappears when under the cover of other trees. Needing considerable sunlight in order to grow, it invades recently cut-over or burned-over areas, blueberry patches, pastures, abandoned fields and copses, and is often found along fences and on roadsides. The fruit is much too heavy to be spread by the wind like those of poplars, willows and birches, and therefore, like all cherries, it depends on animals (chiefly birds) for its propagation.

In spring, where the range of the pin cherry overlaps that of the Canada plum and the wild plum, it is liable to be confused with them, since the arrangement of the flowers in the three species is similar. But the other two species have thorny twigs and much larger flowers (1.5-3 cm in diameter). The fruit of the pin cherry, although more bitter than that of the black cherry, can be prepared in the same ways. As with all cherries (both native and introduced), the leaves, inner bark and pits contain a poison: prussic acid.

This small tree, too small to be of commercial value, is sometimes used to stabilize soil and contain erosion. It plays a highly important role as a "nurse tree" (following a forest fire), creating shade to enable more tolerant species to become established. It is sometimes planted as an ornamental, but tends to spread too quickly.

260

G 442c

Narrowleaf Cottonwood

Mountain cottonwood, willow
cottonwood, willow-leaved cottonwood, yellow cottonwood

Peuplier angustifolié, peuplier à
feuilles étroites, liard amer

Populus angustifolia James

Willow family (Salicaceae)

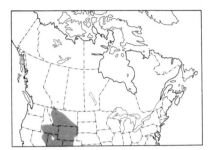

Rare in Saskatchewan

Distribution
Southwestern Saskatchewan and some valleys in southern Alberta.

Distinctive features
Leaves. 5-12 cm long, flattened leaf stalk; willow-like, underside frequently stained with brownish resin blotches. **Twigs.** Slender, bright white; smooth, pointed, slightly gummy, fragrant buds. **Bark.** Yellowish green and smooth; furrowed and greyish brown on older trees. **Size.** Height 10-15 m, diameter 20-30 cm.

The name narrowleaf cottonwood is the literal translation of the scientific name *Populus* (the common Latin name for poplars), probably meaning "people", and *angustifolia*, from the Latin *angustus* (narrow) and *folium* (leaf). The colour of its bark and leaves inspire its other common names. The narrowleaf cottonwood was discovered in 1805 by Lewis and Clark during their expedition to the Northwest. It is a common poplar in the Rocky Mountains of the United States (mountain cottonwood) but is rare in Canada.

At first glance the narrowleaf cottonwood can easily be mistaken for a willow. Like several species of willow, it has spear-shaped leaves and prefers moist locations along bodies of running water. However, its flowers are arranged in hanging catkins, whereas those of willows stand erect on the branches. The buds of poplars are covered with several scales—unlike willows, which have only one scale. Moreover, the resin-covered buds release a distinctive fragrance, particularly in the spring, indicating that they belong to the balsam poplar group and not to the willows. Like most of the willow species, the poplar species produce many hybrids, making identification difficult. The narrowleaf cottonwood and the balsam poplar hybridize easily, thus typical narrowleaf cottonwood specimens are rare. The narrowleaf cottonwood can also be crossed with the eastern cottonwood, producing the lanceleaf cottonwood (*Populus* x *acuminata* Rydb.)

Like all members of the Salicaceae family, the narrowleaf cottonwood contains salicin, an analgesic. Infection of the gums can be relieved by moistening the woolly fruit and applying it to the gums, and toothache can be treated with an extract obtained by boiling the fruit.

Small in size and rare in Canada, the narrowleaf cottonwood has no commercial value. Its highly developed root system helps to reduce the erosion of banks and slopes.

G 442d

Black Willow
Swamp willow

Saule noir

Salix nigra Marsh.

Willow family (Salicaceae)

Distribution
Deciduous Forest Region, southern portion of Great Lakes-St Lawrence Forest Region and Acadian Forest Region.

Distinctive features

Leaves. 5-15 cm long, 0.5-2 cm wide; stipules, always denticulate (minutely toothed), much in evidence on vigorous shoots; almost the same shade, dark green on both surfaces, only slightly paler beneath; often without a gland at the point where the stalk joins the blade.

Twigs. Fine and very brittle at the base, yellowish to reddish brown, hairy at first, becoming smooth soon afterward; buds sharply pointed.

Size. Large shrub or tree. Height 3-20 m, diameter 50-100 cm or more.

The largest willow native to Canada, the black willow owes both its English name and its species name (*nigra*, Latin for black) to the black bark on old specimens, which is deeply ridged and often rough, coming off in scales. It grows on dunes and banks, near streams in places subject to spring flooding, in swamps and in the forest. It is the willow most often occurring in tree form. The generic name *Salix* is an old Latin name for willow, derived from the Celtic *sal* (near) and *lis* (water), in reference to the habitat of willows in general. The trunk often tends to divide from the base into several branches or stems, giving this tree a very characteristic shape. Among the narrow-leaved willows, it is the only one with leaves that could be described as uniformly green on both surfaces, and the only one to retain conspicuous stipules on the vigorous shoots until autumn.

Twigs of the black willow tend to break off in storms, and then readily take root; this characteristic, together with the fact that the tree often grows along streams, promotes vegetative multiplication and natural spreading—the twigs that break off are carried downstream and take root wherever they wash ashore, and the miniscule seeds with their silky white hairs will germinate in a sunny, moist location. Unlike the heavy fruits of oaks, hickories and most conifers, these seeds contain very small nutritional reserves and so must germinate within 24 hours of falling. Produced in vast numbers, these seeds are light enough to float in the air and are spread by the wind. Even if regeneration by seed is ineffective, the black willow, like all other willows, is able to reproduce readily by sending up shoots or suckers from its roots or base. This characteristic is often exploited, and willow cuttings are planted on river banks in order to stabilize them and contain erosion.

While it is easy to distinguish willows from other species of trees, it is not as simple to recognize the different species of native willows. The characteristics needed in order to make an identification are not always all in evidence on the tree, since willows are dioecious plants—i.e., the male and female flowers are borne by different trees.

Also, the leaves of the suckers are often different from those of the mother plant. To add to these difficulties, willows hybridize, producing trees with intermediate characteristics.

The black willow, of no commercial value, is sometimes used locally as building timber and as fuel or is made into charcoal. During the American Revolution and the early days of settlement, its wood and that of other willows was used to make a very fine charcoal, in its turn used to manufacture cannon powder. The Indians long used extracts from this willow to soothe headaches.

G 442e

Peachleaf Willow

Peach-leaved willow, peach willow

Saule à feuilles de pêcher, saule amygdaloïde

Salix amygdaloides Anderss.

Willow family (Salicaceae)

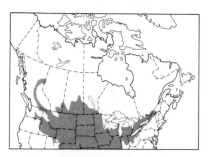

Distribution
Deciduous Forest Region, Great Lakes-St Lawrence Forest Region
and Grasslands.

Distinctive features
Leaves. 5-14 cm long, 1-3 cm wide; stipules small or absent in most
cases; smooth, yellowish green to dark green above and much paler
beneath; glands at point where blade is joined to stalk are either very
small or absent altogether. **Twigs.** Smooth, yellowish brown, flexible,
somewhat droopy; buds sharply pointed; yellow bud scales. **Size.**
Large shrub or tree. Height 10-20 m, diameter 30-40 cm.

This tree, whose leaves strongly resemble those of the peach tree,
prefers riverbanks, swamps, ponds and woodlands at low altitudes.
The specific name *amygdaloides* is from the Greek *amygdalos* (almond) and *oides* (appearing like), in reference to the almond shaped
leaf. The generic name is the Latin name for willow. Riverbanks owe
much to this tree, for its tenacious roots have saved many of them
from erosion. Peachleaf willow is a pioneer species, often found in the
company of eastern cottonwood and silver maple. With its trunk
dividing into branches not far from the base, it resembles the black
willow but differs from it in the following: its leaves are larger,
glaucous beneath, and not incurved; its stipule is often absent; and its
twigs are droopy and not brittle.

To soothe a headache one has only to chew a piece of bark from a
twig of this tree—the bark of all willows contains salicin, a substance
similar to aspirin. Like most willows, this tree has no commercial
value, although its wood is used for fence posts, firewood and sometimes charcoal. Tannin and a light-brown dye can be extracted from
its bark. Willows are important to wildlife, providing food and shelter
for various birds and mammals. Pollination is assured not only by the
wind but also by insects, as the flowers contain nectar. They open in
the early spring, providing bees with an important source of nectar.

G 442f

Shining Willow

Saule brillant, saule laurier, saule luisant

Salix lucida Mühl. ssp. *lucida*

Willow family (Salicaceae)

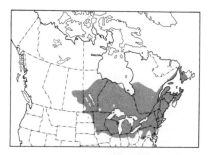

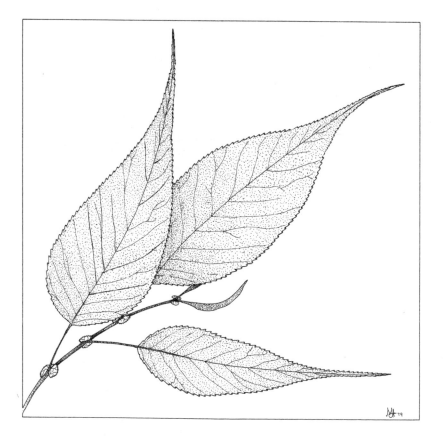

Distribution
Deciduous, Great Lakes-St Lawrence and Acadian forest regions, Grasslands and southern portion of Boreal Forest Region.

Distinctive features
Leaves. 4-15 cm long, 1.5-4.5 cm wide; semicircular stipule sometimes absent; smooth, shiny on both surfaces; dark green, slightly paler beneath; long drawn-out tip; young leaves often reddish, with rust-coloured hairs; glands at the point where the blade is joined to the stalk. **Twigs.** Very shiny, smooth, yellow to reddish brown; bud scale is light brown. **Size.** Shrub or small tree. Height 4-10 m, diameter 15-20 cm.

This small tree, one of our most attractive native willows, grows naturally in wetlands, on shores, in marshes and peat bogs and on sand banks along creeks. The delicate sheen on its twigs and the magnificent dark green, leather-like lustre of the leaves explains the qualification "shining" (*lucida* in Latin) in its names. Landscape designers are inclined to use it as an ornamental.

The leaf of the shining willow resembles that of the peachleaf willow, but is shinier and glossier beneath. The willows are the only alternate-leaved native trees with buds completely covered by a single scale and pressed against the twig. The sycamore and the cucumber-tree also have buds covered by a single scale, but they jut out from the twig. Although the buds of the shining willow are small and sometimes hard to see, they represent an unambiguous characteristic of the genus.

On willows, as on other tree species, there are often large, spherical cone-like blisters or pimple-like growths that deform the leaves or twigs. These galls are caused by small insects (flies, wasps or aphids) that live on plants as parasites. The female lays eggs on the leaf or twig, and the tissues of the plant react by developing a tumour from which the adult insect emerges later in the season. Each type of insect causes the formation of a characteristic gall at a particular point on a given plant. Fungi, too, can cause galls to form.

G 442g

Pacific Willow

Western shining willow, western
black willow, yellow willow

Saule du Pacifique, Saule à
étamines velues, saule brillant de
l'Ouest, saule laurier de l'Ouest

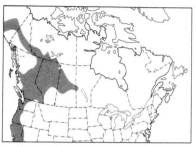

Salix lucida Mühl. ssp. *lasiandra* (Benth.) E. Murray
    syn. *Salix lasiandra* Benth.

Willow family (Salicaceae)

Distribution
From Alaska to western Manitoba.

Distinctive features
Leaves. 6-15 cm long, 1.5-3 cm wide; semicircular, clearly visible stipule; smooth, dark green and shiny above, whitish below; long, pointed tip; glands at junction of stalk and leaf-blade. **Twigs.** Shiny, smooth, ranging from yellow to reddish brown; pale brown bud-scales. **Size.** Shrub or small tree. Height 4-12 m, diameter 30-35 cm.

One of our largest native willows, the Pacific willow (along with the black cottonwood and red alder) is a tree typical of riverbanks, swamps and ponds. The French name, *saule à étamines velues* (willow with woolly stamens) is a literal translation of the scientific name, *Salix* (willow), and *lasiandra*, from the Greek *lasios* (woolly) and *andros* (male), referring to the (male) flowers with hairy stamens. It is sometimes called western shining willow, because its shiny leaves resemble those of the shining willow. Both trees have so many features in common that some botanists classify the Pacific willow as a variety or subspecies of the shining willow.

Where their ranges overlap, the Pacific willow is sometimes confused with the peachleaf willow. The Pacific willow can be recognized by the presence of glands at the junction of the leaf-stalk and the leaf-blade and by its clearly visible stipules. The peachleaf willow either does not have glands or, if they are indeed present, they are very small and the stipules are absent or very small.

The Indians used to light their fires by rubbing together two pieces of the light, soft wood of the Pacific willow. Its inner bark was used to make rope.

G 442h

Heart-leaved Willow
Erect willow

Saule à tête laineuse, saule rigide

Salix eriocephala Michx.
   syn. *Salix rigida* Mühl.

Willow family (Salicaceae)

Distribution
From the Atlantic provinces to western Saskatchewan.

Distinctive features
Leaves. 5-15 cm long, 1-4 cm wide; stipule generally large and in-deciduous; vary greatly, dark green above, whitish below, often with hair on either side of midrib. **Twigs.** Smooth or slightly hairy, ranging from yellow to reddish brown. **Size.** Multiple-stemmed shrub or small tree. Height 3-9 m, diameter 8-15 cm.

The heart-leaved willow is an excellent example of the complexity of the willows. Some botanists consider it to be a species whose forms vary greatly, others view it as a group of similar, difficult-to-identify species. A number of works use the name *Salix rigida* Mühl., but Argus (1980) stressed that the real name of this group is *Salix eriocephala* Michx.

The specific name *eriocephala* (woolly-headed) refers to the woolly flowers that appear before or simultaneously with the leaves; *rigida* (rigid) refers to the leaves, which become rigid in autumn. The base of the leaf is often heart-shaped, hence the name heart-leaved willow.

Bites from small insects cause the formation of silvery galls. An in-fusion of these was used to relieve urine retention.

G 442i

Shrubby Willow
Littletree willow

Saule arbustif

Salix arbusculoides Anderss.

Willow family (Salicaceae)

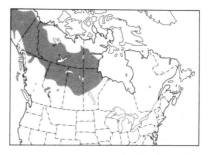

Rare in Ontario

Distribution
Mainly in the northern part of the Boreal Forest Region from Alaska to northwestern Ontario. At Mistassini Lake in Quebec.

Distinctive features
Leaves. 2-7 cm long, 0.5-1.5 cm wide; very small stipules that fall early; shiny, dark green, hairless above, whitish and silky below. **Twigs.** Slender, slightly hairy when young, yellowish brown. **Size.** Multiple-stemmed shrub or small tree. Height up to 6 m, diameter 10 cm.

The shrubby willow, characteristic of the Boreal Forest Region, is a species that varies greatly. It ranges from a small, low-spreading shrub only 30 centimetres high to a small tree over 5 metres in height. The tree's size is related to its habitat. It frequents riverbanks and peat bogs. Its specific name *arbusculoides*, means resembling the *Salix arbuscula* L. (a species of willow native to northern Europe).

It forms very closed, pure stands or is found in association with white spruce and birches.

G 442j

Slender Willow
Basket willow, meadow willow, stalked willow

Saule pétiolé, saule à long pétiole

Salix petiolaris Sm.
  syn. *Salix gracilis* Anderss.

Willow family (Salicaceae)

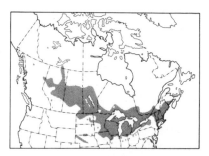

Rare in N.W.T.

Distribution
From eastern British Columbia to New Brunswick.

Distinctive features
Leaves. 2-12 cm long, 0.5-2 cm wide; long stipule falls early (generally absent); shiny, dark green above and dull blue-green below, both surfaces usually hairy, young leaves often reddish and silky. **Twigs.** Slender, silky when young, becoming almost hairless later on, ranging from yellowish to reddish brown. **Size.** Multiple-stemmed shrub or small tree. Height 2-7 m, diameter 5-10 cm.

The erect twigs on the slender willow usually form continuous willow-dominated forests along with other willows on lake shores, river and stream banks, and near ponds. This tree also frequents marshes and wet meadows. Its specific name, *petiolaris*, refers to the presence of a leaf-stalk; *gracilis* describes the slender, erect twigs—sometimes used to make baskets (basket willow). This species was first described by the Englishman Sir James Edward Smith (1759-1828) when studying specimens of willows introduced into England. In 1784 he purchased Linnaeus's Herbarium and became the founder of The Linnaean Society in England.

G 442k

Sandbar Willow

Basket willow, coyote willow, narrowleaf willow, pink-barked willow, rope plant, silver willow, slenderleaf willow

Saule des bancs de sable, saule à feuilles exiguës, saule de l'intérieur

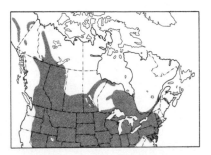

Salix exigua Nutt.
    syn. *Salix interior* Rowlee

Willow family (Salicaceae)

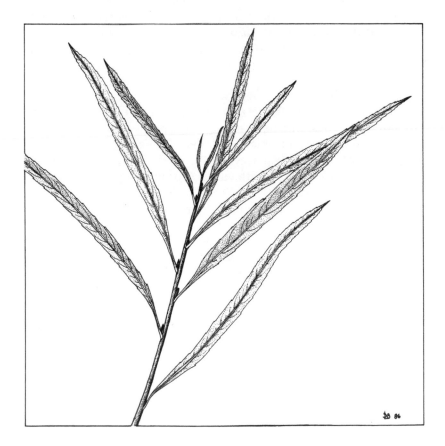

Distribution
From eastern British Columbia to New Brunswick.

Distinctive features
Leaves. 5-15 cm long, very narrow, 0.5-1.5 cm wide; tiny stipule (generally absent); from 5-15 mm in width, spaced teeth or toothless, leaf-stalk very small; yellow-green, hairless above, paler beneath, with or without hair. **Twigs.** Slender, erect, ranging from yellowish brown to dark reddish brown. **Size.** Shrub or small tree. Height 1-6 m, diameter 4-15 cm.

A species typical of flooded lands and alluvial plains, the sandbar willow, as its name indicates, colonizes recently-formed sandbars along rivers, streams and lakes. It tolerates very dry or very moist soils where it spreads vigorously via underground rootsuckers that rise to the surface. The sandbar willow is quick to form copses and stabilizes the soil, thereby preparing it for other species of willows, poplars and alders. The specific name *exigua* (meagre) refers to the very narrow leaves, and *interior* indicates that it is essentially a species found inland.

The sandbar willow has a very wide geographic range and is to be found over most of North America, from Alaska to Mexico. Several types of this species, with its changing characteristics, have developed according to the environmental conditions. These types vary in shape and in the hairiness of their leaves. Specialists consider the sandbar willow to be either a species with varying forms or a group of similar, difficult-to-identify species.

A similar species exists in southwestern British Columbia and on Vancouver Island, and plays the same role. Called the northwest willow (*Salix sessilifolia* Nutt.), it reaches 8 metres in height, and is characterized by leaves that are larger than its counterpart's (1-3.5 centimetres), velvety underneath and sessile or without a leaf stalk—hence its specific name. It was discovered at the mouth of the Willamette River and was named by the botanist and curator of the Harvard Botanical Gardens, Thomas Nuttal (1784-1859).

The Indians used the flexible twigs and bark of the sandbar willow (and those of other willows) to make rope, string and baskets. They wove the fibres of the bark to make clothing, bags and blankets. The wood was used to smoke meat, fish and animal skins and to make lightweight snowshoes and bows. They brushed their teeth with willow twigs and shredded the inner bark to make diapers and sanitary napkins.

G 4421

Weeping Willow
Babylon weeping willow

Saule pleureur, saule, saule de
Babylone, saule parasol

Salix babylonica L.

Willow family (Salicaceae)

Distribution
Native of northern China; introduced into North America from Europe around 1800. Planted as an ornamental, sometimes escaping from cultivation.

Distinctive features
Leaves. 5-12 cm long, 0.5-2 cm wide; lanceolate stipules; yellowish green and smooth above, whitish and smooth beneath; either no glands, or tiny glands at the point where the blade is joined to the stalk. **Twigs.** Very long, slender; drooping, sometimes to the ground; highly brittle at the base; yellowish brown. **Size.** Height 8-12 m, diameter 50-80 cm.

This exotic species has characteristic arching branches, long branchlets drooping down to the ground and deeply ridged bark. Because of its striking shape, it is one of the few willows that is readily identifiable year round. Its specific name, *babylonica*, stems from an error made by Carl Linnaeus (the originator of binomial nomenclature by genus and species), who mistook this tree for the biblical willows of Babylon. In fact, the latter were poplars (*Populus euphratica* Oliver). Perhaps he was referring to a Jewish legend concerning the Babylonian Captivity, according to which the exiled Jews hung their harps from this tree or wept under it in mourning. The generic name, *Salix*, derives from the Celtic *sal* (near) and *lis* (water), referring to the environment in which this tree is most often found.

The weeping willow, which has been planted in almost every park in the world, is found in Canada as a female tree only. Propagation must therefore be carried out vegetatively; by planting bud-bearing twigs. This willow, like most, bears male and female flowers on different trees. It is one of the first trees to leaf in the spring and one of the last to shed in the fall.

G 442m

White Willow
Common willow, French willow

Saule blanc, osier jaune, saule,
saule argenté

Salix alba L.

Willow family (Salicaceae)

Distribution

Native to Eurasia; thoroughly naturalized in Canada.

Distinctive features

Leaves. 4-12 cm long, 0.5-2 cm wide; stipules small or, in many cases, absent; green above, whitish beneath, both surfaces somewhat silky; tiny glands often present at the point where blade is joined to stalk. **Twigs.** Covered with long, silky hairs; break readily at the base; often drooping, olive-brown to yellowish brown; often bright yellow. **Size.** Height 15-25 m, diameter 60-120 cm.

This highly appreciated ornamental willow is not a native species but is very well adapted to Canada. The crown of ascending main branches and long, sometimes hanging, branchlets is supported by a trunk with dark grey bark that becomes ridged with age. It owes its specific name, *alba* (white) to the presence of white hairs on its leaves, which give it a silvery grey appearance. Its generic name, *Salix*, is the Latin name for willow. The most common willow in Europe, the white willow is often planted in this country because it is fast-growing. It readily hybridizes with the crack willow, resulting in trees with intermediate characteristics. The golden willow (*Salix alba* var. *vitellina* Wimmer), which has limber, yellow twigs and an absence of hairs on its leaves and twigs, is a variety of white willow. In Europe, the slender twigs of willows are used in wickerwork. In order to obtain a large quantity of wicker, the tree is often pollarded, so as to form tufts of twigs at the top of the trunk.

The wood is light, solid and even, and does not split; it is used in carving and in the manufacture of clogs. In England, it is the preferred wood for croquet balls and mallets.

G 442n

Crack Willow
Brittle willow, snap willow

Saule fragile, saule, saule cassant

Salix fragilis L.

Willow family (Salicaceae)

Distribution
Native to Asia Minor and Europe, often escaping from cultivation and now naturalized in northeastern North America.

Distinctive features
Leaves. 7-15 cm long, 1-3 cm wide; stipules small or absent; hairless on both surfaces; dark green above, glaucous beneath; often with glands at the point where blade is joined to stalk. **Twigs.** Smooth, shiny and brittle, reddish to greenish brown; breaking at the base. **Size.** Height 20-30 m, diameter 100-200 cm.

The crack willow was imported from Europe in colonial times. It owes both its common name and specific name *fragilis* (fragile) to the ease with which its twigs break off. Its broken twigs litter the ground after a storm, and with a little moisture they will take root. At one time the wood of this tree was made into charcoal in order to produce cannon powder. It also makes a fine parasol for those seeking refuge from the sun.

This tree is not exploited commercially but is sometimes used for firewood. It is the largest of all the willows. Naturalized in North America, the crack willow is found in parks and gardens, along streams and in swamps and wet woodlands. Streams help to spread it by carrying its twigs.

It should be noted that pure specimens of crack willow are rare in Canada: there are trees with characteristics between those of the crack willow and the white willow.

G 442o
Silky Willow (*see* G 422)

variation of leaf margin

G 462

Silky Willow (*see* G 422)

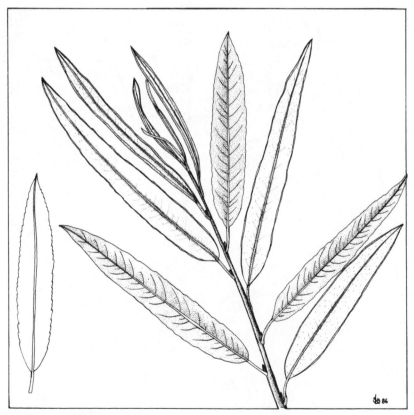

variation of leaf margin

G 522a

Bebb's Willow
Beak willow, long-beaked
willow

Saule de Bebb, chatons

Salix bebbiana Sarg.

Willow family (Salicaceae)

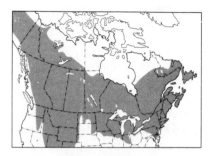

variation of leaf margin

Distribution
Throughout Canada except in the Coast Forest Region.

Distinctive features
Leaves. 2-8 cm long, 1-3 cm wide; stipules small and deciduous; dull green above, glaucous or whitish beneath; veins often rough and conspicuous. **Flowers.** Catkins (clusters of male or female flowers) appearing at same time as leaves. **Twigs.** Reddish brown; either pubescent and remaining so for several years, or hairless. **Size.** Shrub or small tree. Height 3-7 m, diameter 6-15 cm.

Bebb's willow, the most common of all willows, is probably the most variable in the shape and form of its leaf and the hairiness of its twig. This variability is found not only among the many varieties of this species within its geographical range, but even on an individual tree. Indeed, over the course of a season the margins of the leaves often vary in appearance from one leaf to another on a single twig: the first leaves may be untoothed, followed a little later by other leaves on the same twig that may well have small pointed or rounded teeth.

The specific name *bebbiana* was given in honour of Michael Schuck Bebb (1833-1895), an American expert on willows.

Because of its abundance, this willow is a major food source for birds and mammals. Moose, beavers, muskrats and hares eat the twigs and bark; ptarmigans, grouse and grosbeaks eat the leaves and buds. The wood is sometimes used for carving and wickerwork, and in earlier times it was made into charcoal to be used in cannon powder.

G 522b

Pussy Willow
Glaucous willow, Pussy feet

Saule discolore, chatons, minous, petits minous, petits-chats

Salix discolor Mühl.

Willow family (Salicaceae)

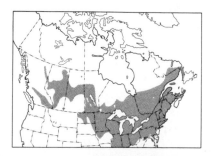

Rare in the N.W.T.

Distribution

In all forest regions except the Coast Forest Region.

Distinctive features

Leaves. 3-10 cm long, 1-3 cm wide; stipules small, prominent on vigorous shoots; vivid dark green above, glaucous beneath; hairless when mature. **Flowers.** Catkins (clusters of male or female flowers) appear long before the leaves. **Twigs.** Reddish brown, smooth and shiny or occasionally with thin waxy coating. **Size.** Shrub or small tree. Height 3-6 m, diameter 10-20 cm.

The appearance of the flowers or catkins of the pussy willow toward the end of April is a harbinger of spring. The female flowers are much in demand at that time of year for use in bouquets. This willow, like all other willows, is a dioecious plant: the male and female flowers are borne on different trees. Sometimes male flowers, which resemble the females, are mistakenly gathered for home decoration; this should be avoided as they drop their yellow stamens and pollen in the house.

The specific name *discolor* (having two colours) refers to the contrasting colours of the leaf, and a number of common names in both English and French refer to the silky flowers.

During the winter, catkins can be forced by putting the willow twigs in a warm place. The early flowering of this tree provides a major food source for bees and other insects, thus favouring pollination. Insects attracted by the pollen on the male flowers complete the tree's life cycle, once again demonstrating the close ties existing between the animal and plant kingdoms.

G 522c

Sitka Willow
Coulter willow, silky willow

Saule de Sitka

Salix sitchensis Sanson & Bong.

Willow family (Salicaceae)

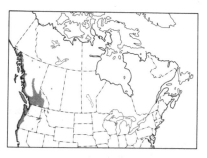

Rare in Alberta

Distribution
The Coast Forest Region and the Columbia Forest Region, sporadic inland up to the Rocky Mountains of Alberta.

Distinctive features
Leaves. 4-10 cm long, 2-4 cm wide; dark green above and covered with grey hairs creating a satiny effect below. **Flowers.** Catkins (groups of male or female flowers) appearing simultaneously with the flowers. **Twigs.** New shoots are velvety and silvery, losing their downiness almost entirely in the second season, reddish in colour; break easily at the base. **Size.** Multiple-stemmed shrub or small tree. Height 1-8 m, diameter 5-20 cm.

The Sitka willow can be recognized by its leaves, which are broader at the tip than at the base, and by its silky, satiny underside (silky willow). It can be mistaken for the Scouler Willow, whose leaves are similar but have an underside usually covered with rust-coloured hairs that do not create the same satiny effect. The name Sitka willow designates the southeastern part of Alaska, where this tree was first sighted and collected.

The Sitka willow prefers rich, moist soils along running water, where its reddish roots often float on the water's surface like seaweed.

The Indians made baskets and rope from the tree's flexible twigs. They made string from the peeled bark and concocted a tonic from the boiled bark. They used the wood for fuel.

G 522d

Scouler Willow
Fire willow, mountain willow

Saule de Scouler

Salix scouleriana Barr. ex Hook.

Willow family (Salicaceae)

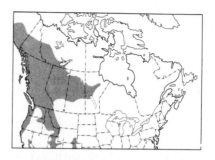

Distribution
From western Manitoba to British Columbia.

Distinctive features
Leaves. 5-10 cm long, 1.5-4 cm wide; stipules small; dark green above and usually hairless below; often covered with rust-coloured hair. **Flowers.** Catkins (groups of male or female flowers) appearing long before the leaves. **Twigs.** From dark brown to yellowish brown; covered with grey hair for several seasons; strong. **Size.** Shrub or small tree. Height 4-12 m, diameter 10-30 cm.

Unlike most other willows, the Scouler willow grows far from bodies of running water. Inside forests it associates with alders and maples, or birch, spruce and poplars. It is found in mountains up to altitudes of approximately 3000 metres, where it grows as a small shrub (mountain willow). Like the trembling aspen and some alders, the Scouler willow invades soils by disseminating seeds after fires, hence the name fire willow. The specific name *scouleriana* refers to John Scouler (1804-1871), a Scottish naturalist and physician who collected plants on the northwestern shores of North America.

The Indians used the wood to make utensils and knitting needles. The wicker twigs were used to sew the bark canoes and make hoops.

Like several other willows, the Scouler willow constitutes an important source of food for various species of deer, especially in winter.

G 522e

Hooker Willow

Beach willow, bigleaf willow,
coast willow, pussy willow,
shore willow

Saule de Hooker

Salix hookeriana Barr. ex Hook.

Willow family (Salicaceae)

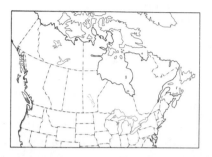

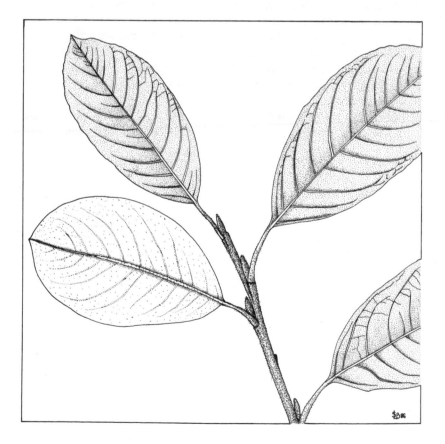

Distribution
Mainly in the southern part of the Coast Forest Region.

Distinctive features
Leaves. 4-15 cm long, 2.5-7.5 cm wide; very large for a willow; light green above and with or without hair, dull blue-green below and covered with hair at maturity; often with hair either side of the midrib. **Flowers.** Catkins (male or female groups of flowers) appear long before the leaves. **Twigs.** Dark brown, often densely covered with silvery grey hairs for several seasons; strong. **Size.** Multiple-stemmed shrub or small tree. Height 2-6 m, diameter 10-20 cm.

Very early in the spring the Hooker willow shows the large, velvety catkins (pussy willow) of its female flowers (in Victoria they appear around February). This tree is often found by the deep waters of ponds and lakes; hence the names beach willow, and shore willow. The Hooker willow can be recognized by its leaves, which are quite a bit larger (bigleaf willow) than the other willows and are hairy on the underside. It was named in honour of the renowned Scottish botanist Sir William Jackson Hooker (1785-1865). Joseph Barratt (1796-1882) first described this tree in a work by Hooker entitled *Flora Boreali Americana*.

The Indians twisted the fibres of the inner bark of willows to make long ropes; in the spring they wore the catkins as a leafy finery.

G 522f

Alaska Willow
Feltleaf willow

Saule de l'Alaska, saule feutré

Salix alaxensis (Anderss.) Cov.
syn. *Salix longistylis* Rydb.

Willow family (Salicaceae)

Rare in Alberta

Distribution
Mainly in the southern part of the Boreal Forest Region.

Distinctive features
Leaves. 4-10 cm long, 1.5-4 cm wide; presence of erect, clearly visible stipule; dull green above and almost hairless, felt-like texture below and densely covered with shiny white hair; edge often curled. **Flowers.** Catkins (groups of male and female flowers) appear long before the leaves. **Twigs.** Reddish brown, usually velvety, densely covered with white hair for more than one season; strong. **Size.** Gnarled shrub or small tree. Height 1-10 m, diameter 5-15 cm.

The Alaska willow can be recognized by its two-coloured leaves with their felt-like texture, and by its velvety twigs. It is found at all elevations, from sea level to past the timberline where it is no more than a small, recumbent, low-spreading shrub. It prefers the rocky soil along rivers and lakes and grows on high mountain slopes.

Although it is essentially a southern species, the range of the Alaska willow extends into Siberia. The specific name *alaxensis* (from Alaxa) is an old Russian connotation for Alaska; *longistylis* (long style) refers to the female flowers.

In certain outlying regions the Alaska willow and the shrubby willow are often the only source of wood for heating. The inner bark has enabled people to survive in emergency situations.

G 522g

Alternate-leaved Dogwood
Blue dogwood, green osier,
pagoda dogwood, pagoda tree

Cornouiller alternifolié,
cornouiller à feuilles alternes

Cornus alternifolia L. fil.

Dogwood family (Cornaceae)

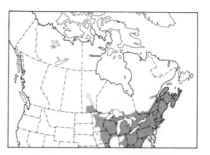

Rare in Newfoundland

Distribution
Deciduous Forest Region, Great Lakes-St Lawrence Forest Region
and Acadian Forest Region, extending northwards in eastern Canada
to the southern fringe of the Boreal Forest Region.

Distinctive features
Leaves. 4-13 cm long; often clustered at the ends of branchlets; lateral veins curve and follow margin. **Flowers.** Arranged in numerous clusters that are flattened on top. **Fruit.** Inedible drupe, dark blue or bluish black, on short stem. **Twigs.** Almost horizontal. **Size.** Small tree or shrub. Height 4-8 m, diameter 5-15 cm.

The generic name, *Cornus*, comes from the Latin *corneolus* (of horn), or from *cornum* (dogwood). The wood of trees in this genus is, indeed, very hard and firm, like the horns of cattle. The specific name, *alternifolia*, refers to the alternate leaf arrangement. Excepting a species native to eastern Asia, the alternate-leaved dogwood is the only species of the genus to have alternating leaves. Its branches, also arranged in an alternating pattern, are layered, giving it somewhat the appearance of an oriental temple (pagoda tree). The common name dogwood may derive from the fact that in England the bark of this tree was at one time used to make a rinse for ridding dogs of mange. The name could also be a distortion of the word daggerwood, or dagwood, referring to a dagger or a skewer on which to cook meat.

An understorey species, the alternate-leaved dogwood is found in maple-dominated stands, in copses, along streams, and near the bottom of steep slopes.

Its wood is hard and resistant but of no commercial value. With the addition of vinegar its roots yield a light-to-darker brown dye. Its fruit is a major food source for rodents and several species of birds, including the ruffed grouse. Its leaves and twigs are nibbled by the white-tailed deer. The alternate-leaved dogwood and its different varieties are used as ornamentals because of their distinctive appearance, their profusion of white or cream-coloured flowers and their scarlet autumn foliage.

Several shrubby dogwoods are found in Canada, including the red osier (*Cornus stolonifera* Michx.), which grows all across the country. The term red refers to the reddish colour of its bark and wood. The specific name signifies that it multiplies by layering, meaning that the aerial stems or stolons take root in leaf litter. It is a highly variable species that prefers moist places. Usually a shrub with a multiple trunk, oval leaves opposite, white flowers in flat clusters, and white or bluish fruit, it makes a fine ornamental. Another dogwood, the roundleaf dogwood (*Cornus rugosa* Lam.) is widely distributed in Canada, from southern Manitoba to the Maritimes. It is a shrub or small tree with light blue fruit and almost circular leaves (silky white underneath and rough on top) arranged opposite on the twigs, which are green with purple marks.

G 522h

Arbutus
Madrona, madroño, madrone,
Pacific madrona

Arbousier Madroño, arbousier
de Menzies, arbousier d'Amérique, madrona, madroño

Arbutus menziesii Pursh

Heath family (Ericaceae)

Distribution
Southwest British Columbia along the coast and on Vancouver Island.

Distinctive features
The only broad-leaved evergreen native to Canada. **Leaves.** 7-15 cm
long; leathery texture, shiny green above, lasting for more than one
season. **Flowers.** In the shape of small cups, creamy white, in clusters
at end of branches. **Fruit.** 1 cm berry, orangey red, floury, edible, but
very sour. **Bark.** Thin, yellowish-green and red blotches; cracking into
small flakes; peeling off in uneven papery strips during summer and
autumn. **Size.** Height 10-30 m, diameter 30-90 cm.

The arbutus cannot be confused with any other Canadian tree, particularly during winter. As a broad-leaved evergreen with deciduous
bark, it is unique. Like a number of conifers, its leaves have a two-
year cycle. They turn red or orange towards the middle of the second
summer and fall to make way for new leaves, which rapidly unfold.
The bark is shed throughout summer and autumn. It comes off in
scales, peels off in vertical strips, rolls up and then breaks off. The
newly exposed yellowish-green inner bark quickly turns red. This
tree's charm lies in the different shades of its deciduous bark. It is a
beautiful ornamental, but requires maintenance almost six months of
the year in order to clear the ground of its leaves, bark and fruit.
Its family name comes from "heath" (*Erica*), a small shrub in
France, not found among American flora. This lack is more than
compensated for by the widespread presence of species such as the
blueberry, cranberry, and rhododendron. Many species of Ericaceae
compose the mass of vegetation of peat bogs and tundras.
The generic name *Arbutus*, is the Latin name for the strawberry tree
(*Arbutus unedo* L.), a southern European species. The Canadian
species was dedicated to the Scottish naturalist A. Menzies, who
described it in 1792. He participated as both scientist and physician in
the expedition headed by Captain Vancouver.
Approximately twenty species of this tree are native to Mediterranean regions and Central America. Three species are found in North
America, one of which, the arbutus, is native to Canada; it is the most
northern of the group and reaches the limit of its range in southern
coastal British Columbia. Of all species of Ericaceae, the arbutus is
the most stately.
Madroño (the Spanish name for the strawberry tree) was the name
given the arbutus by a Spanish monk, resembling as it does species in
his country. The name applies to North American species.

The small, sweet-smelling, honey-bearing flowers of the arbutus resemble those of the blueberry (*Vaccinium*), and appear in spring. At the end of summer, the tree is heavy with fruit. Band-tailed pigeons and thrushes, among others, feast on it, thereby promoting its dissemination. As described by its specific name *unedo* (I eat only one) in reference to the fruit of the strawberry tree, the bitter fruit of the arbutus is edible if your taste buds can tolerate it. The Indians ate the fruit plain or cooked. Overindulgence causes cramps, moreover, the fruit seems to possess narcotic properties.

The wood of the arbutus is hard and heavy but has a tendency to crack when being dried. It has no commercial value in Canada. Rich in tannin, its bark was used for tanning leather. Boiled, it was used by the Indians to dye oars and fishhooks.

G 522i

Pawpaw
False banana, pawpaw custard
apple, tall (or common) pawpaw

Asiminier trilobé, corossol,
faux-bananier

Asimina triloba (L.) Dunal

Custard-apple family
(Annonaceae)

Rare in Ontario

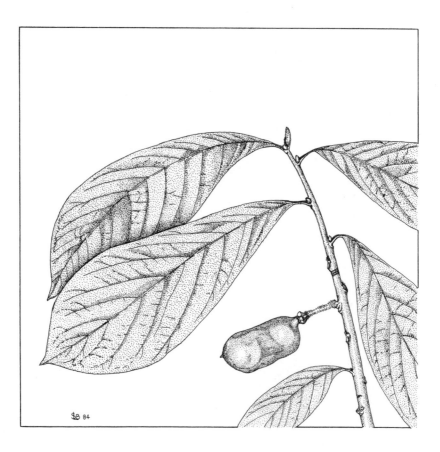

Distribution
Southern portion of the Deciduous Forest Region.

Distinctive features
Leaves. Thin, drooping foliage; leaves up to 30 cm long. **Flowers.**
Reddish purple, very showy, 3 sepals and 6 petals (3 small, 3 large).
Fruit. Berry, yellowish when ripe; pear-shaped. **Size.** Shrub or small
tree. Height 3-6 m, diameter 10-20 cm.

Rarely exceeding the size of a small tree, the pawpaw belongs to a
family of which most members are a tropical or subtropical species.
The genus *Asimina* is found only in North America. The generic name
derives from *assimin*, the Indian name for pawpaw, and the specific
name *triloba* (three-lobed) refers to the parts of the flower, which are
grouped in threes or multiples of three.

The pawpaw has no commercial value other than as an ornamental.
It is found in the northernmost part of its family's range. The number
of pawpaws in Canada has considerably decreased as a result of defor-
estation. Today, only birds and small mammals consume the fruit,
which was formerly gathered by local inhabitants. The fruit would
seem to vary in taste according to latitude, pawpaws grown in the
southern United States tasting the best. Some liken the taste of the
fruit to that of bananas, cream, apples, pineapples, cologne—even
turpentine.

G 522j

Black Tupelo

Black gum, pepperidge,
sourgum, tupelo

Nyssa sylvestre, gommier noir,
nyssa des forêts, tupélo, tupélo
de montagne

Nyssa sylvatica Marsh.

Nyssa family (Nyssaceae)

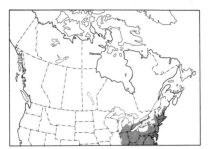

Rare in Ontario

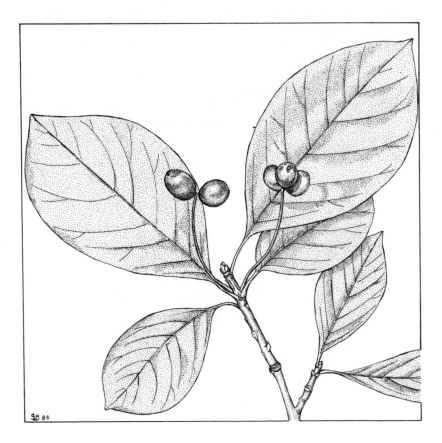

Distribution
Deciduous Forest Region.

Distinctive features
Leaves. 5-12 cm long; dark green and shiny above, and pale beneath with a light covering of hairs; tough. **Fruit.** 1 or 3 drupes with a ribbed stone, blue-black, at end of a long stalk; thin, oily, sour flesh. **Twigs.** Chambered pith. **Bark.** Roughly fissured, giving the appearance of a square pattern or alligator skin. **Size.** Height 12-15 m, diameter 10-20 cm.

Carl Linnaeus (1707-1778), the Swedish naturalist, probably chose the generic name *Nyssa* because of the habitat (low, wet ground) of tupelos in general. *Nyssa* comes from the Greek *nusa* (nymph), a minor divinity associated in Greek mythology with rivers and fountains. The specific name *sylvatica* (of the woods or trees) is from the Latin *silva* (forest). The name gum refers to the oily, gummy flesh of the fruit, and black refers to the colour of the fruit. The name pepperidge derives from the resemblance that the ridged stone of the fruit bears to the peppercorn.

The wood of the black gum is still used for panelling and for the manufacture of boxes and crates. In the United States, because of its hardness and heaviness, it is widely used to make objects in which resistance to wear is important. The black gum's handsome, shiny foliage turns golden and scarlet in autumn, making the tree much prized as an ornamental.

G 522k

Cucumbertree

Cucumber tree, cucumber magnolia, magnolia, pointed-leaved magnolia

Magnolier acuminé, magnolia à feuilles acuminées

Magnolia acuminata L.

Magnolia family (Magnoliaceae)

Rare in Ontario

Distribution
A few locations within the Deciduous Forest Region.

Distinctive features
Leaves. Long, narrow (18 cm long, 10 cm wide), with prominent veins. **Flowers.** Odourless, approximately 5 cm long; 3 sepals and 6 greenish-yellow petals; solitary; appearing after the leaves. **Fruit.** Compound, an aggregate of follicles resembling a cone or cumcumber when green; dark red, shiny, erect when ripe. **Size.** Height 18-24 m, diameter 30-60 cm.

The cucumbertree is the only species of its family to grow in Canada. This family is well known for its large, opulent flowers, which reach a width of 30 cm in some species. The flowers of this species make it much in demand as an ornamental for parks and gardens; they appear between mid April and mid June. The dull, greenish-yellow flower stands out clearly from the foliage. The cucumbertree has very resistant roots, and it can be used as a stock on which to graft the buds of exotic magnolias, so that they can survive our harsh winters.

The generic name is after Pierre Magnol (1638-1715), director of the botanical garden in Montpellier, France. The specific name *acuminata* comes from the Latin *acuminare* (to sharpen), referring to the pointed form of the leaf. The name cucumbertree refers to the shape of the fruit.

Rare in Canada, the cucumbertree and its varieties are of little economic importance. They are often planted as ornamentals, and horticulturalists have developed a number of varieties with quite showy flowers. They have cultivated several species with larger and more attractive flowers than the native magnolia. Among them is the *Magnolia* x *soulangiana* Soul., a hybrid resulting from the crossing of two Chinese species. It is tolerant of pollution and poor soils. Its large, tulip-shaped flowers may be seen in various horticultural varieties in different colours and sizes.

G 5221

Sassafras
Cinnamon wood, greenstick, mittentree, sassafrax, saxifrax

Sassafras officinal, laurier-sassafras

Sassafras albidum (Nutt.) Nees

Laurel family (Lauraceae)

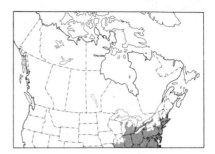

Distribution

Deciduous Forest Region, no further north than Toronto.

Distinctive features

Fragrant, spicy-smelling leaves, twigs and bark. **Leaves.** 10-25 cm long; 3 types of shapes on the same tree: unlobed, 1-lobed and 2-lobed. **Flowers.** Small, in loose clusters, greenish yellow; males and females on different trees (dioecious). **Fruit.** Dark blue drupes. **Size.** Shrub or small tree. Height 5-8 m, diameter 30-40 cm.

This tree can be recognized by the spicy fragrance of its leaves, twigs, bark and wood, and by the varying shapes of its leaves. During their explorations in Florida in the sixteenth century the Spaniards mistook its aroma for cinnamon; hence the name cinnamon wood. It was believed that the roots of this tree had extraordinary healing powers, and it was exported to Europe, where it was quickly learned that this was a mere superstition. The generic name *Sassafras*, used by the French and Spanish settlers in Florida, may have come from the Indians. The specific name *albidum* (whitish) refers to the colour of the leaves. Lobed leaves decrease in number as the tree grows older, becoming rare on old trees. The resemblance of the 2-lobed leaves to mittens has earned the sassafras the name mittentree.

The sassafras is often found as a shrub with brittle, crooked branches and a thicket of root sprouts surrounding its base. It grows under the cover of other trees and prefers loamy, sandy soils. Its capacity to multiply both by spreading its seeds and by sending up shoots from its roots enables it to rapidly take over abandoned fields—much as a weed does.

Its brittle wood has no commercial value. An oil derived from its roots is used to perfume soaps and to give rootbeer its distinctive flavour. Its bark can be boiled in water to obtain a tasty and invigorating tea; it also yields an orange dye. The dried bark is sold at natural food stores and gourmet food counters. The characteristic odour of the sassafras comes from safrol, a food additive banned in Canada and the United States because of its carcinogenic properties.

312

G 532a

American Beech
Beech, red beech

Hêtre à grandes feuilles, hêtre,
hêtre américain, hêtre rouge

Fagus grandifolia Ehrh.

Beech family (Fagaceae)

Distribution
Throughout the Deciduous and Great Lakes-St Lawrence forest regions and in the Acadian Forest Region.

Distinctive features
Leaves. 5-15 cm long; leathery, with parallel veins each ending in a tooth. **Twigs.** Slender, shiny; slender buds approximately 2 cm long. **Fruits.** 2 brown achenes or nuts, pyramidal and smooth, encased in a prickly husk, opening into 4 parts at maturity; edible and sweet. **Bark.** Smooth, silvery grey with dark markings. **Size.** Height 18-24 m, diameter 60-100 cm.

The American beech is easy to recognize at any time of year, owing to its smooth, silvery bark with dark, diamond-shaped markings. The leaves of young trees sometimes remain in place throughout the winter. Lovers carve a heart enclosing their initials and the date in the bark, believing that in so doing they are preserving their union for eternity—their testimonial lasts for 300 or 400 years. This practice of carving in the bark is not recommended; it injures the tree, making it vulnerable to disease and insect attacks. Black bears are fond of beechnuts and do not hesitate to climb the tree in order to gather them. The marks left by their claws expand as the circumference of the tree increases, giving rise to exaggerated claims regarding giant bears. The name of the family, Fagaceae, and the generic name, *Fagus*, come from the Greek *fagein* (to eat), in reference to the edible fruit of the beech and various members of its family, which includes the oaks and chestnuts. *Grandifolia* (large leaves) is the specific name, serving to distinguish this tree from the European beech (*Fagus sylvatica* L.), a smaller-leaved species frequently planted as an ornamental.

Its root system absorbs nutrients near the soil's surface, inhibiting the growth of other vegetation. Because of the dense shade produced by the foliage of a beech-dominated stand, green plants are almost absent at ground level.

Beechnuts, very rich in oil, are a major food source for small rodents, bears, muskrats and various birds (e.g., ruffed grouse and spruce grouse).

The beechnuts are gathered after the first October frosts, then dried, roasted and ground into meal or flour for making nutritious beverages. The meal can be used on its own as a coffee substitute, or can be mixed with coffee, milk or chocolate, with honey added to taste.

In areas where once the American beech grew in abundance, an oil not unlike olive was extracted from its fruit. Early settlers used the oil as a butter substitute and as lamp oil. Some twenty years ago beechnuts could be purchased in large markets. They are best eaten in moderation, as they are thought to cause enteritis.

The wood, which is rigid, hard and strong, is used for making turned articles, plywood, inexpensive furniture, flooring and utensils. It is also used as fuel and in the making of barrels and casks, and railroad ties.

The American beech has various enemies, including the porcupine, which eats its bark—sometimes all around the trunk, causing the death of the tree. Entire populations of this tree are sometimes infested with small sucking insects called beech scale (introduced into Canada via Nova Scotia in 1890), making the trees more vulnerable to canker (a tree disease). In addition, the roots of the American beech are often host to a parasitic plant called beechdrops (*Epifagus virginiana* (L.) Bart.). Beechdrops, which lacks chlorophyll, shares the same range as the American beech.

G 532b

Large-toothed Aspen

Bigtooth aspen, big-toothed poplar, largetooth poplar, poplar

Peuplier à grandes dents, grand tremble, tremble jaune

Populus grandidentata Michx.

Willow family (Salicaceae)

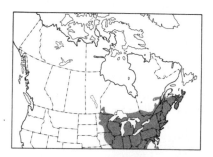

Rare in Manitoba

Distribution
Deciduous and Great Lakes-St Lawrence forest regions and Acadian Forest Region.

Distinctive features
Leaves. Blade 5-8 cm long; flattened stalk, generally shorter than blade. **Twigs.** Stout; bud covered with greyish down. **Bark.** Similar to that of the trembling aspen; has small, orange, diamond-shaped markings when young and deep furrows when mature. **Size.** Height 15-25 m, diameter 30-60 cm.

The large-toothed aspen is easily recognizable in springtime. As it begins to leaf out, its twigs and buds become covered with a whitish down, making its crown stand out against the vault of the other trees. The fact that in the slightest breeze, its leaves rustle and shake (the case with most members of the genus *Populus*) accounts for its French common name, *grand tremble.*

The name *Populus* (people) goes back to the time when this tree was planted in public squares reserved for the people. The specific name, *grandidentata* (large-toothed), describes the leaf. The large-toothed aspen is a pioneer species and prefers moist, fertile soils. It is often found in association with paper birch, trembling aspen and red maple. Like trembling aspen, it reproduces by sending up suckers from its roots and by dropping its seeds, which are viable for only a few days. Unlike the eastern cottonwood and the willows, it does not multiply vegetatively if one of its twigs or branches is planted in the ground.

Cultivation of the edible oyster mushroom (*Pleurotus*) is becoming increasingly popular. For this purpose, the mycelium of the mushroom is implanted in logs of aspen or poplar or other soft-wooded deciduous trees (willow, birch), or hardwoods (maple, ash, oak). A year or two later there is a fine harvest of fresh mushrooms. Conifers do not lend themselves to this type of cultivation.

Trembling aspen and large-toothed aspen are the favourite food of beavers. The wood of the large-toothed aspen is similar to that of the trembling aspen and is used for the same purposes.

G 532c

Wild Crab Apple

American crab apple, garland-tree, sweet crab apple, wild crab

Pommier odorant, pommettier, pommier coronaire, pommier sauvage

Malus coronaria (L.) P. Mill.
  syn. *Pyrus coronaria* L.

Rose family (Rosaceae)

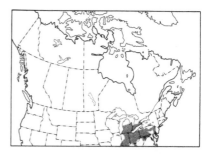

Distribution
Deciduous Forest Region.

Distinctive features
Leaves. Blade 5-10 cm long; shiny green above, almost hairless beneath, sometimes lobed at base. **Flowers.** Pink to white, fragrant, very showy, in clusters on short twigs. **Fruit.** An apple, almost round (3.5 cm in diameter); yellowish green at maturity; edible, sour. **Twigs.** Older twigs have thorn-like spurs; smooth, with bright red buds. **Size.** Shrub or small tree. Height 6-10 m, diameter 15-25 cm.

The generic name *Malus* is the Latin name for the apple tree; it comes from the Greek *melon* (apple, or fruit). Some authors group pears, mountain-ashes and apples under the genus *Pyrus*, while others separate them into three separate general: *Pyrus* for the pears; *Sorbus* for the mountain-ashes; and *Malus* for the apples. The leaves and flowers of apple and pear trees are quite similar, but their fruits are quite different. The specific name *coronaria* (crown-like, or suitable for a garland), refers to the tree's attractive flowers and is the basis of the name garlandtree.

The absence of hairs on the undersurface of its leaves and the presence of spurs make this tree easily distinguishable from the common apple. In the spring, the wild crab apple is adorned with delicate, fragrant fiowers. When the sour green fruit appears, it attracts birds, white-tailed deer and skunks. Humans are also fond of crab apples, cooking them to decrease their acidity. The flavour of the pectin-rich jelly blends pleasantly with the flavours of other wild or cultivated fruit, giving them a special aroma. The Indians gathered crab apples in autumn and kept them all winter. In spring they used them to make syrup or a delicious cider. They also exploited the qualities of the wood—its hardness, strength and flexibility—by using it to make harpoon shafts, handles of adzes and pickaxes and the working parts of grist mills. The wood is suitable for carving, and when turned on a lathe it reveals interesting shades of colour. The trunk is used as a stock, onto which various less hardy varieties of apples are grafted.

G 532d

Pacific Crab Apple
Oregon crab apple, western crab apple

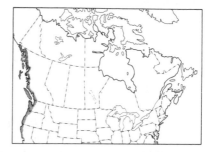

Pommier du Pacifique

Malus fusca (Raf.) Schneid.
    syn. *Malus diversifolia* (Bong.) M. Romer
    syn. *Pyrus fusca* Raf.

Rose family (Rosaceae)

Distribution
Coast Forest Region.

Distinctive features
The only apple tree with oval fruit native to the Pacific coast. **Leaves.**
Blade 5-10 cm long; dark green above, virtually hairless below; sometimes lobed at the base. **Flowers.** Range from pink to white, per-
fumed, very showy, in small bouquets on short twigs. **Fruits.** Apples,
oval or oblong (1.2-2 cm long); yellow or red when ripe; edible, sour.
Twigs. Old twigs have thorn-like spurs; bright red buds. **Size.** Shrub
or small tree. Height 6-8 m, diameter 20-30 cm.

The generic name *Malus* is the Latin name for the apple tree. Some
botanists group pear, mountain ash, and apple trees under the genus
Pyrus, others separate them into three different genera. The specific
name *diversifolia*, from the Latin *diversus* (separate) and *folium*
(leaf), refers to the leaves' various shapes. *Fusca*, from the Latin
fuscus (black), refers to the leaf's dull, dark green upper surface,
which differs from the shiny green leaf of wild crabapple. The Pacific
crab apple was first described in 1792 by Archibald Menzies, the Scottish physician-botanist who accompanied Captain George Vancouver
on his travels.
  Preferring moist soils, the riverine species, which has spurs, sometimes forms almost impenetrable thickets. Like its eastern counterpart
(wild crab apple), its very hard, durable wood is used to make parts
where resistance to wear and tear is important. It is used to make tool
handles, clubs and ball bearings. The Indians carved the wood to
make wood-splitting wedges, which they used on the western red cedar
to obtain planks.
  The very bitter fruit makes excellent jellies and jams. The Indians of
the coast ate the fruit raw, cooked, mixed with other fruit or kept it
for the winter. Like all species of plum, pear and cherry trees, the
seeds of apple trees contain substances which, when acted upon by
gastric acids, release prussic acid. Eating a few seeds is not dangerous
but large quantities can cause severe poisoning.

G 533

Red Mulberry

Mûrier rouge, mûrier rouge d'Amérique, mûrier sauvage

Morus rubra L.

Mulberry family (Moraceae)

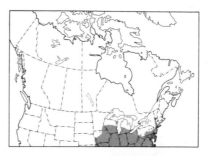

Rare in Ontario

Distribution

Deciduous Forest Region, planted as a fruit tree or an ornamental elsewhere in Canada; has escaped from cultivation.

Distinctive features

Leaves. Blade 7-13 cm long; unlobed or lobed (1-5 narrow lobes); undersurface hairy. **Twigs.** Reddish. **Fruit.** Compound, multiple drupes (like raspberries), 2.5 cm long; dark red to almost black at maturity; sweet, juicy and edible. **Bark.** Reddish brown, separating into scaly plates or strips like the bark of the hop-hornbeam. **Size.** Small tree. Height 6-10 m, diameter 10-20 cm.

The red mulberry belongs to a family that plays a significant economic role. The fig, grown for its fruit, and the Indian rubber-tree plant, widely used as a house plant, belong to this family. The generic name comes from the ancient Greek *morea* (mulberry), and the specific name *rubra* (red) describes the colour of the fruit. Scarce as a wild tree, the red mulberry is planted for its tasty fruit and its beauty. It is also used to lure birds away from other fruit or attract them to gardens.

If fully ripe, the sweet-tasting fruit can be eaten raw or in pies or cakes. Green mulberries can cause stomach disorders. A person with a very sensitive skin may get dermatitis after contact with the leaves or stems.

Also found in Canada is a species native to China: the white mulberry (*Morus alba* L.). This tree, cultivated throughout the world as a food source for silkworms, was introduced into the United States with the same intention. However, the project failed, and the white mulberry, long ago escaped from cultivation, and once acclimatized, returned to its wild state.

The white mulberry can be distinguished from the red by its leaf, which is hairless except along the midrib.

G 542a

Choke Cherry
Chuckley-plum, common choke
cherry, red choke cherry,
sloetree, wild cherry

Cerisier de Virginie, cerisier,
cerisier à grappes, cerisier
sauvage

Prunus virginiana L.

Rose family (Rosaceae)

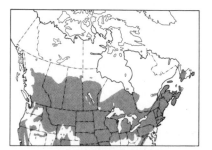

Rare in the N.W.T.

Distribution
Deciduous, Great Lakes-St Lawrence, Acadian and Boreal forest
regions; Grasslands.

Distinctive features
Leaves. Blade 4-12 cm long, thin; broadest in upper third of the blade; pair of glands on the leaf-stalk. **Fruit.** Drupe; dark red or black cherries in elongated clusters; very astringent but edible. **Bark.** Smooth, dark brown. **Size.** Shrub or small tree. Height 4-8 m, diameter 5-15 cm.

The odour of bitter almond, characteristically given off when the bark is broken, is a sure means of confirming the identity of this species of cherry. This odour reveals the presence of prussic acid, which, when acted upon by enzymes in the stomach, becomes an extremely dangerous poison for humans—these observations regarding poisoning apply to all cherry and plum trees.

The generic name *Prunus* is the Latin name for the plum or cherry. The specific name *virginiana* comes from the name Virginia. The common name choke cherry refers to the highly astringent fruit, which coats the mouth if eaten, especially when unripe. The fruit of the choke cherry is similar to that of the black cherry and is prepared in the same manner. Like all cherry trees, the choke cherry is an important food source for birds, which are the primary agents for seed dispersal. This is a light-loving species, commonly found on the edge of forests, maple stands and copses and along creeks and rivers, where it serves to stabilize soil against erosion. On the basis of differences in the leaf and the fruit, some botanists divide this variable species into three varieties, each with its own geographical range.

It is not uncommon to find caterpillar webs in the forks of cherry trees or other members of the rose family. These webs shelter vast numbers of larva known as tent caterpillars. Fortunately, the latter do not kill the tree, even when they completely strip its foliage. The tent caterpillars (*Malacosoma* sp.) become small moths that are classified as being among the six greatest enemies of the Canadian forests. In addition to the cherries, they attack birches, elms, poplars and willows. The twigs of the choke cherry are sometimes deformed by a black excrescence known as black knot. This condition, very widespread on cherry trees in North America, results from a disease caused by a fungus (*Apiosporina morbosa* (Fr.) Arx.).

Both the choke cherry and the black cherry have been used frequently in folk medicine, although today this practice is not considered advisable. The Indians and the first settlers used the leaves, bark or roots to prepare a tea for treating coughing, malaria, stomach aches, tuberculosis and intestinal worms. The roots and bark were also used as a sedative, a tonic to fortify the blood, and an appetite stimulant.

G 542b

Bitter Cherry

Bird cherry, quinine cherry, wild cherry

Cerisier amer

Prunus emarginata
(Dougl. ex Hook) Walpers

Rose family (Rosaceae)

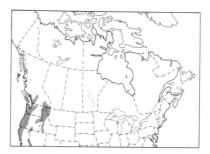

Distribution
Coast Forest Region, Columbia Forest Region, in moist sectors of the
Montane Forest Region and in southern British Columbia.

Distinctive features
Leaves. 3-10 cm long; thin and fragile, tapered at both ends, uneven-
sized teeth; broadest in middle of leaf-blade; dull on both surfaces;
presence (usually) of 1 or 2 pairs of glands on stalk. **Twigs.** Several
buds clustered at end of twig; shiny red; bitter taste. **Fruits.** Berry-like
bodies, dark red cherry, or wild cherry, attached to a short stalk; extremely bitter and astringent. **Bark.** Smooth, reddish brown, varnished appearance, conspicuous orange, powdery, horizontal markings
(lenticels); very bitter. **Size.** Shrub or small tree. Height 4-15 m,
diameter 10-30 cm.

There is no better name for this tree! One taste of its fruit, leaves or
bark will impress its flavour upon your memory. Although humans
find this fruit virtually inedible, many birds, bears and small rodents
eat it with alacrity.

The generic name *Prunus* is the Latin name for the prune or cherry
tree. The specific name refers to the slightly notched petals and sepals.

Like the pin cherry and choke cherry, the bitter cherry is a colonizing species of short duration. These species are soon replaced by
species that tolerate shade better. The bitter cherry is often used as a
"nurse tree" in plantations of conifer seedlings. It is very similar to
the pin cherry but differs in its leaves, which taper at both ends; in its
upper portion, which is often rounded; and in the short stalk of its
fruit. Some botanists divide this species into two varieties: var. *mollis*
(Dougl.) Brewer, usually a good-sized tree found along the coast, and
var. *emarginata*, an inland shrub.

Like the small cherry trees, the soft, not very durable wood of the
bitter cherry is used only as fuel. Its solid bark, which can be peeled
like the birch, was used by the Indians to make baskets and ropes, and
to decorate or reinforce bows, arrows and pipes. The bark, stuck on
with resin, served to dress wounds.

G 542c

Serviceberry

Chuckley-pear, Indian pear, juneberry, peartree, sarviceberry, sarvissberry, saskatoon, Scotch apple, servicetree, shadberry, shadbush, sugarplum, sweetpear, wild pear

Amélanchier, petites poires, poirier

Amelanchier Medik.

Rose family (Rosaceae)

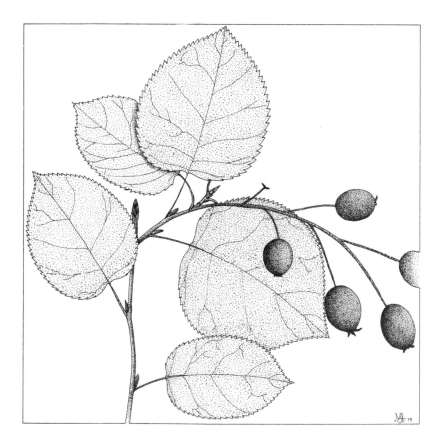

Distribution
From the Atlantic to the Pacific.

Distinctive features
Leaves. Less than 8 cm long; thin, dark green above, paler beneath.
Flowers. 5 dazzling white petals; appear before the leaves come out,
usually in clusters at the end of twigs. **Fruit.** Pome; dark purple,
sweet, juicy, with several large seeds; retains calyx of flower at top;
edible. **Bark.** Thin and smooth, greyish, with vertical strips, becoming
rough with age. **Size.** Shrub or small tree. Height 2-10 m, diameter
7-30 cm.

It is not difficult to identify the genus *Amelanchier*. Its dazzling white
flowers, appearing in early spring, and its small black pearlike fruit,
ripening in late July or early August, make it clearly distinguishable.
However, identifying the various species—all closely related—is a difficult task. Even the experts cannot agree. The problem stems from
hybridization, from reproduction by polyploidy (splitting of the genetic material) and by apomixis (reproduction of plants by seed, but
without fertilization), which take place between the different species
of serviceberry. The generic name is the common name of a European
species. The name serviceberry is a deformation of sarvissberry, from
the word sarviss, a transformation of the Latin *Sorbus*. The flowers
appear in June; hence the name juneberry. The word shad appears in
two of the common names, in reference to the fish of the same name;
a member of the herring family, which ascends rivers in Canada in the
spring at the time when the serviceberry is flowering. The city of
Saskatoon derives its name from a word used to designate the serviceberry, which formerly grew in abundance around the city. A number
of mammals eat its fruit and foliage. Birds such as the American robin
and the northern cardinal, which are fond of its fruit, often nest in its
branches.

The serviceberry provided the basic ingredients for the famous pemmican, a food made with dried meat and animal fat, which the Indians
ate or carried with them when they travelled in the winter. A person
could survive for quite a long time on this food if supplemented by
vitamin C (contained in wild rose hips or a spruce-based tea) to prevent scurvy.

The fruit of the serviceberry, very rich in iron and copper, can be
eaten raw or dried like raisins. It can also be made into jelly or jam or
added to pancakes, muffins and pies.

G 542d

Common Apple
Apple, common apple tree,
common domestic apple, wild
apple

Pommier commun, pommier,
pommier nain, pommier sauvage

Malus pumila P. Mill.
  syn. *Malus communis* Poir.
  syn. *Pyrus pumila* (P. Mill.) K. Koch ·

Rose family (Rosaceae)

Distribution
Native to Europe and Western Asia, planted widely as a fruit tree and an ornamental; has escaped from cultivation.

Distinctive features
Leaves. Blade 4-10 cm long; leaf stalk and undersurface of blade downy. **Fruit.** Pome; yellow-green, tart or sweet. **Twigs.** Lacking in spurs resembling thorns; end often covered with whitish down. **Size.** Height 9-12 m, diameter 30-60 cm.

The common apple is probably the ancestor of the apples cultivated today. Long ignored by the peoples of Asia Minor, it was quickly brought under cultivation by the Greeks. By the time of the Roman emperor Augustus there were already no fewer than thirty different varieties. Today there are several thousand varieties of cultivated apples originating from this species and from the Siberian crab apple (*Malus baccata* (L.) Borkh.). In Canada, the common apple can be distinguished from the wild crab apple by the pubescence of its leaf stalks and the undersurface of its leaves. The French word *pomme* (apple) comes from the Latin *pomum*, which means fruit (i.e., without distinction as to type). The generic name *Malus* is the Latin name for the apple tree, and the specific names are *pumila* (dwarf) and *communis* (common). *Pyrus* is the Latin name for the pear tree.

In appearance, the common apple is characterized by a short trunk, a low, dome-shaped crown and numerous crooked branches. It readily grows in a wide variety of environments, even in the forest. This phenomenon is undoubtedly the work of loggers, hunters and woodsmen who threw away apple cores during their excursions. The fruit of this tree is made into jelly and can be prepared in the same way as wild crab apple. Bear, deer and foxes eat the fruit in autumn.

The wood, which is reddish brown, hard, solid and fine-grained, is used for both turning and carving. It is an excellent fuel, and its sawdust is often used for the smoking of meat.

Aside from the qualities of its wood, the apple tree has a number of medicinal virtues. The apple is a good source of vitamins, sugars, essential acids and various minerals such as potassium, sodium and phosphorus. Eating too many apple seeds, however, can prove fatal. Of the various parts of the fruit, the skin contains the most nutrients. Unfortunately, nowadays a cultivated apple should be peeled, since modern arboriculture draws on an arsenal of pesticides and harmful products.

G 542e

Wild Plum
American plum, brown plum,
plum, red plum, yellow plum

Prunier d'Amérique, guignier,
prunier, prunier de La
Gallissonnière, prunier sauvage

Prunus americana Marsh.

Rose family (Rosaceae)

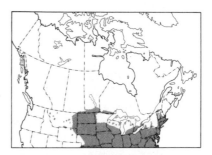

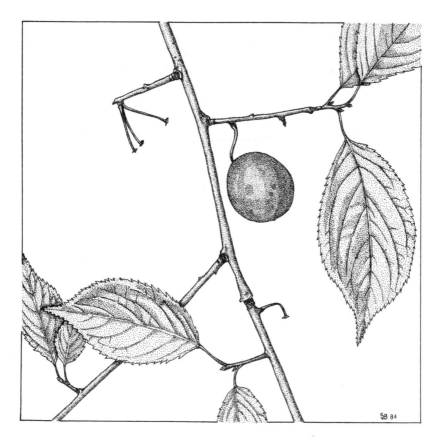

Distribution
Deciduous Forest Region; planted across Canada; has escaped from cultivation.

Distinctive features
Leaves. Blade 4-12 cm long; no small glands at the ends of the teeth; pair of glands present on leaf stalk. **Flowers.** Fragrant, dazzling white, appearing before or during foliation. **Fruit.** Drupe; red to yellow, coated with a waxy bloom; flesh juicy and acidic, edible. **Twigs.** Have spine-like projections. **Size.** Shrub or small tree. Height 6-8 m, diameter 12-20 cm.

The wild plum has often been planted beyond its natural range. Hundreds of large-flowered cultivars have been developed for ornamental purposes. This tree is found along streams, where it serves to stabilize the soil by containing erosion.

The colours of the fruit are indicated in several of its common names. This fruit can be prepared in the same ways as that of the Canada plum. Beware of the bark and leaves of this tree and of the stones of its fruit: when consumed, they produce prussic acid in the stomach. The wood, which is hard and strong, is of no commercial value because of its small dimensions.

G 542f

Cascara

Bayberry, bearberry, bearwood,
bitterbark, cascara buckthorn,
cascara sagrada, holybark,
Persian bark

Nerprun Cascara, cascara,
écorce sacrée, nerprun de pursh ·

Rhamnus purshiana DC.

Buckthorn family (Rhamnaceae)

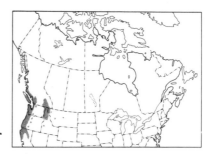

Distribution
Southern Coast and Columbia forest regions.

Distinctive features
Leaves. 6-15 cm long; 10-15 pairs of conspicuous parallel veins; often clustered at end of twigs, sometimes opposite on twig. **Fruit.** Small, red, berry-like bodies that turn black, containing 2 or 3 nutlets, slightly sweet. **Twigs.** Slender, reddish brown; small buds with no scales, covered with rust-coloured hair. **Bark.** Thin, smooth, grey or brown, split into small scales in older trees; yellow inner bark turns brown when exposed to air; extremely bitter. **Size.** Shrub or small tree. Height 5-12 m, diameter 15-40 cm.

The generic name *Rhamnus* is the Latin name for buckthorns and probably means spiny, referring to the thorny branches of certain buckthorn species, or is derived from the Greek *rhamnos*, the name for certain species of this genus. The specific name *purshiana* was attributed in honour of the German-American botanist, Fredrick Pursh (1774-1820), author of *Flora Americae septentrionalis*, who died in Montreal while preparing a book on the flora of Canada. The French name *nerprun* is a contraction of the Latin *niger prunus* (black plum tree).

Cascara sagrada means sacred bark in Spanish. Spanish settlers learned the medicinal properties of these trees from the North American Indians, who boiled the bark to obtain an extract used as a laxative and tonic. A strong dose sometimes caused poisoning and could be fatal. The fruit has a similar milder purging effect. The tannin-rich bark was also used to produce a green dye.

A product known in pharmaceutical circles as cascara sagrada (the dried, pulverized bark of the cascara) came onto the market in the 1880s. Since that time, it has been included in the American pharmacopoeia and is today listed in the Canadian Drug Identification Code. The prospect of this new market attracted cascara bark harvesters, or "barkers", seeking large specimens. The debarked tree is cut to stimulate the formation of rootsuckers for future harvesting. The harvester must wear rubber gloves; chemicals from fresh bark can be absorbed by the skin and have a laxative effect. The "CC pills" many soldiers came to know during World War II, are made from this bark. Although there are several man-made laxatives on the market, the demand for cascara bark continues. It is harvested commercially in Washington state and Oregon, in forests and in plantations established for exploiting the bark. In Canada, a license is required to cut cascara on Crown Lands. This natural laxative can be obtained from a pharmacist or a health food store; in its pure state, as liquid or as tablets, or mixed with other products. It is also used as a laxative in veterinary medicine.

The cascara's fruit appears towards the end of the summer. A number of authors write that the fruit of the cascara is edible while others state the contrary. The nutlets, and to a lesser degree the pulp, contain toxic substances. Nevertheless, birds, raccoons and bears eat the fruit; hence the name bearberry.

The cascara resembles a shrub of the same genus found throughout Canada—the alder-leaved buckthorn (*Rhamnus alnifolia* L'Her.). The leaves of the cascara differ in having 10-15 pairs of veins instead of the 5-7 pairs of the alder-leaved buckthorn. Two species of buckthorn introduced from Europe grow wild and have become naturalized in eastern Canada: the alder buckthorn (*Rhamnus frangula* L.), which can be identified by its oval, entire leaves; and the European buckthorn (*Rhamnus cathartica* L.), which has nearly round, finely toothed leaves, (mostly opposite along the twig) and spiny branches.

G 542g
Arbutus (*see* G 522h)

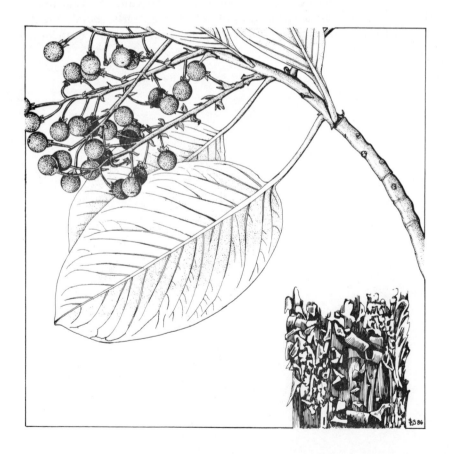

G 542h
Black Cherry (*see* G 442a)

G 552a

Hawthorn
May-apple, thorn

Aubépine, cenelle, cenellier,
pommetier, senelier, snellier

Crataegus L.

Rose family (Rosaceae)

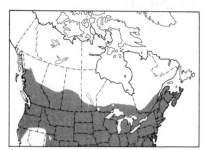

Distribution
Various locations across Canada.

Distinctive features
Leaves. Highly variable; variable on the same tree. **Flowers.** Resembling apple blossoms; white to pink; foul-smelling. **Fruit.** An apple-like "haw", red, orange, yellow, blue or black; edible, with a dry pulp. **Bark.** Usually armed with strong, smooth, shiny thorns. **Size.** Shrub or small tree. Height 5-10 m, diameter 20-40 cm.

Almost everyone is familiar with this tree, whose twigs with their long spines form almost impenetrable tangles. Birds find them an ideal nesting place. This genus, which cannot tolerate shade, is found in abandoned fields, along fences, on roadsides and by streams. In autumn its flowers give way to haws, to the great joy of cedar waxwings, fox sparrows, ruffed grouse and small rodents, all of which help to disperse the seeds. Humans often consider the hawthorn as a pest, although they themselves have helped to spread and diversify the genus.

Distinguishing between the various species of hawthorn can be difficult. Botanists themselves can only guess at the number of Canadian and American species. The genus *Crataegus*, however, is very characteristic and very stable. The great diversification that the hawthorn species has undergone seems to have been caused by the massive clearing of our virgin forests, which began even before the early settlers arrived in North America and resulted in the creation of new habitats formerly inaccessible. The invasion and colonization of these new habitats by the different species of hawthorn led to their hybridization. Two additional factors undoubtedly served to expand the range of variations: polyploidy, the splitting the genetic material; and apomixis, the reproduction of plants by seed but without fertilization.

The generic name *Crataegus* is the Latin name for hawthorn. It derives from the Greek *krataigos* (needle-tree) and *dratos* (strong), in reference to the hardness and strength of the wood. The latter is used in the manufacture of tool handles and mallets and for wood carving. The thorns are used as toothpicks, awls, pins and sometimes fishhooks. When used as a hedge, hawthorn forms an impassable barrier.

Widely known in Europe, its flowers when dried are used to make a tea that has a tonic effect on the heart and circulation. They contain substances with the same properties as digitalin. The bark is used against fever, and the haw against diarrhea.

The haws may be eaten, their taste varying greatly from one species to another. They contain several pits, making them less inviting to eat. They may be combined with other fruit to make jellies, jam and compotes. The Indians mixed them with dried meat to make a traditional food, namely pemmican.

G 552b

Speckled Alder

Alder, grey alder, hoary alder,
mountain alder, red alder, river
alder, rough alder, tag alder

Aulne rugueux, aulne blanc,
aulne à feuilles minces, aulne
blanchâtre, aulne commun,
vergne, verne

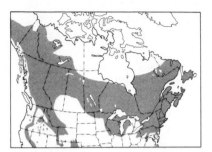

Alnus incana (L.) Moench
    ssp. *rugosa* (Du Roi) Clausen and
    ssp. *tenuifolia* (Nutt.) Breitung
    syn. *Alnus rugosa* (Du Roi) Spreng.
    syn. *Alnus tenuifolia* Nutt.

Birch family (Betulaceae)

Distribution
In almost all forest regions except the Coast Forest Region.

Distinctive features
Leaves. Blade 5-10 cm long; dull; 6-12 veins, straight, impressed above; veinlets form a ladder-like pattern. **Twigs.** In zigzag pattern; buds have distinct peduncle or stalk. **Fruit.** Resembles a small "cone" when mature; remains on tree throughout winter. **Bark.** Smooth, reddish brown, with prominent orange lenticels. **Size.** Shrub or small tree. Height 2-10 m, diameter 6-10 cm.

Incapable of growing in shade, the speckled alder is found in abundance along streams, in marshes and bogs and in thickets or copses.

The generic name *Alnus*, the Latin name for alder, comes from the Celtic and means neighbour of streams. The specific name *rugosa* (rough) and the common name speckled alder, denote the presence of prominent lenticels on the bark. *Incana*, (greyish, or whitish) refers to the hoary undersurface of the leaf (hoary alder and grey alder). *Tenuifolia* (thin-leaved) designates the subspecies found in the West.

The speckled alder is one of the first trees to come into flower in spring, and the bees seek it out for the pollen, which they use to nourish the eggs in the brood-comb. This tree differs from most deciduous trees in that its leaves do not change colour or fade, but fall green in late autumn.

Alders, like poplars, are pioneer species that invade an area after a forest fire or clearcutting. Like the paper birch and the poplars, the alder is a transitional species, since it can neither reproduce nor grow in the shade; it is quickly replaced by species that are much more shade-tolerant. However, it plays an important role in the different stages of succession. Its leaves enrich the litter, and like most leguminous plants, it fertilizes the soil by way of its roots, which bear nodules resulting in the tree's capacity to fix nitrogen from the air. When the leaves, roots and nodules decompose, they release the stored nitrogen.

Although it has no economic value, the speckled alder serves to protect banks from erosion. The Inuit stain cariboo hides with a substance extracted from its bark, and this dye, which is darker than the one obtained from Labrador tea (*Ledum groenlandicum* Retzius), was much used by early settlers.

The Indians treated rheumatism with a liquid prepared by boiling the alder bark, which, like that of willows, contains salicin, a product similar to aspirin (acetylsalicylic acid). The outer bark was also used as a poultice to stop the bleeding of wounds and to reduce swelling. Tea made from the bark has astringent qualities and was used to heal wounds and abrasions.

The black alder (*Alnus glutinosa* (L.) Gaertn.) was originally introduced for the production of charcoal. A European species, it is planted in Canada and the United States as a shade tree and an ornamental. It has become naturalized in some places. It is also used to improve the soil in conifer plantations. A tall-growing tree, it is characterized by sticky new shoots, and leaves that are wider at the top with an apex or tip that is truncated or indented.

Another alder, the American green alder (*Alnus viridis* (Villars) Lam. & DC. ssp. *crispa* (Ait.) Turril), sometimes reaches the size of a small tree. It differs from the speckled alder in having pointed, stalkless buds and leaves with finely toothed margins.

G 552c

Sitka Alder
Mountain alder, slide alder, wavyleaf alder

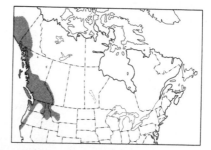

Aulne de Sitka

Alnus viridis (Chaix) DC. ssp. *sinuata* (Reg.) Love & Love
    syn. *Alnus crispa* (Ait.) Pursh ssp. *sinuata* (Reg.) Hult.
    syn. *Alnus sinuata* (Reg.) Rydb.
    syn. *Alnus sitchensis* (Reg.) Sarg.

Birch family (Betulaceae)

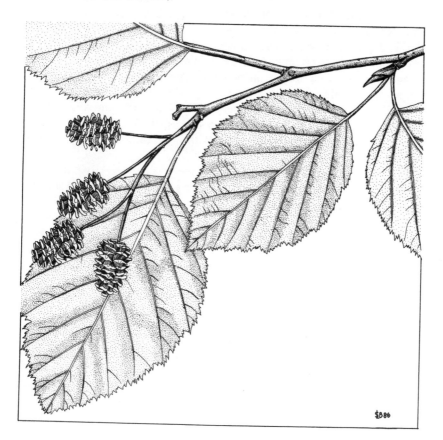

Distribution
Most of British Columbia excluding the northeastern part, and in some parts of the Rocky Mountains of Alberta.

Distinctive features
Leaves. 2-10 cm long; shiny on both surfaces, curly edges; gummy when young; 6-10 straight veins conspicuous above; veinlets do not occur in ladder-like patterns. **Twigs.** Buds without clearly distinct stalk. **Fruit.** Resembles a small "cone" when ripe; remains on twig all winter. **Bark.** Shrub or small tree. Height 8 m, diameter 20 cm.

Botanists have not yet answered the question of the similarities between the Sitka alder and other alders. Some consider it to be a distinct species whereas others view it as a variety of a species that is distributed across the continent, namely the American green alder (*Alnus viridis* (Villars) Lam. & DC. ssp. *crispa* (Ait.) Turril). The scientific names *sinuata* (wavy margined) and *crispa* (curled) refer to the leaf's curled edge. This characteristic also inspired the name wavyleaf alder. Its presence in Alaska gives it the name *sitchensis*, i.e., from Sitka (an area in the southeastern part of Alaska).

   The Sitka alder and the American green alder differ from other Canadian alders in several respects. They are the only mountain alders, and the only alders with shiny leaves, distinct, stalkless buds, and clusters flowering at foliation. Of the two only the Sitka reaches the size of a small tree.

   Like the other alders, the Sitka alder is an aggressive, pioneer species that invades moist soils exposed by sliding earth (slide alder), retreating glaciers, and burned-over areas. Its short life spans less than 50 years, but when dead it improves the soil, allowing other species of conifers to take root there. It thus plays an important role in countering the effect of soil erosion. Its soft, small-sized wood has no commercial value. Like the other alders, it is used locally for heating.

G 552d

Paper Birch

Canoe birch, white birch, silver birch (Maritimes), spool wood

Bouleau à papier, bouleau à canot, bouleau blanc

Betula papyrifera Marsh.

Birch family (Betulaceae)

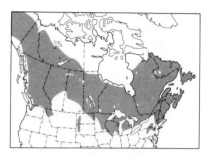

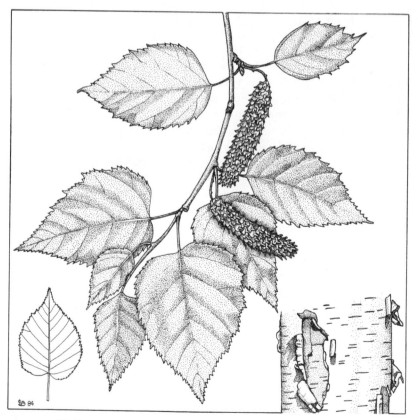

var. *cordifolia*

Distribution
Throughout most of Canada. Less abundant in the Deciduous Forest Region.

Distinctive features
Leaves. 5-10 cm long; 5-9 pairs of lateral veins. **Fruit.** "Cone", cylindrical and hanging; 4-5 cm long. **Twigs.** Smooth. **Bark.** Thin, smooth; reddish brown, turning creamy white with age; peels easily; horizontal lenticels. **Size.** Height 15-25 m, diameter 30-60 cm.

The generic name *Betula*, from the Celtic *betu* (tree) is the Latin name for birch; it means shine, in reference to the tree's white bark (also referred to in the name white birch). The specific name *papyrifera*, from the Greek *papuros*, or *papyros* (paper) and the Latin *ferre* (to bear), refers to the bark, which is as thin as paper and peels off easily. **Bark should never be stripped off the living tree,** as this can result in unsightly black rings or even **kill the tree.**

Birches are generally easy to recognize, but some species have a tendency to interbreed, making identification more difficult. In eastern Canada, from Ontario to the Maritimes, the paper birch can be confused with the heart-leaved birch (*Betula cordifolia* (Regel) Fern.), considered a distinct species by some, and a variety of the paper birch by others (*Betula papyrifera* var. *cordifolia* (Regel) Fern.). Their form and bark are similar but the heart-leaved birch is distinguished by the heart shape of its leaf-base—that of the paper birch is rounder.

The paper birch is an important element in the boreal forest. Found across the continent in our latitudes, it seeks full sun and is intolerant of the shade created by other trees. It is found in the company of other pioneer species such as pin cherry, willow and poplar.

The paper birch is more widespread today than in the early days of settlement, land clearing and forest fires having favoured its spread. Although forest fires create sites conducive to the propagation of this species, they are also fatal to it, since its thin bark is highly flammable.

The Indians used the bark of the paper birch to make the legendary birch-bark canoes, hence the name canoe birch. With a frame made of white cedar, the canoes were stitched together with spruce roots and waterproofed with fir or pine pitch.

The Indians also used strips of white birch bark to make their rudimentary dwellings known as wigwams, as well as for making baskets, mattresses and even message paper. So important was the paper birch to some Indian tribes that one might almost speak of civilization based upon the birch.

The bark is slow to rot, and for this reason it is not unusual to encounter dead trees with only the bark remaining. In an emergency, the bark can be used to make winter "sunglasses" to prevent the eye damage caused by sunlight reflecting off the snow: these are made of a strip of bark 4 or 5 cm wide, the natural openings (lenticels) serving as apertures for the eyes. The lenticels take the form of horizontal cracks or slits that allow for gaseous exchanges with internal tissues.

The wood of the paper birch is inferior in quality to that of the yellow birch. It does not stain easily but is suitable for turning, veneer stock and pulpwood. It is also used to make various everyday objects such as clothespins, toothpicks, popsicle sticks, spindles, spools and broomsticks. In areas where it is plentiful, it is used as firewood. It splits well and gives off considerable heat even when green, but tends to quickly coat chimneys with a layer of creosote. Like the sugar maple, it can be tapped in spring to make birch syrup. Its sap flows abundantly, but its sugar content is low. When exposed to sun, the sap quickly turns to vinegar.

G 552e

Yellow Birch

Black birch, cherry birch, curly birch, gold birch, hard birch, Newfoundland oak, red birch, silver birch, sweet birch, tall birch

Bouleau jaune, bouleau des Alleghanys, bouleau frisé, bouleau merisier, merisier, merisier blanc, merisier jaune, merisier ondé

Betula alleghaniensis Britt.
     syn. *Betula lutea* Michx. fil.

Birch family (Betulaceae)

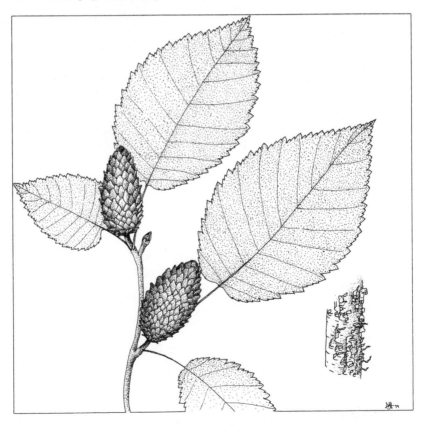

Distribution
Deciduous, Great Lakes-St Lawrence and Acadian forest regions, southeastern portion of Boreal Forest Region.

Distinctive features
An aromatic tree: the bark, twigs, buds and leaves smell and taste of wintergreen (*Gaultheria procumbens* L.) when broken. **Leaves.** 7-13 cm long, 9-11 pairs of lateral veins. **Fruit.** "Cone", oval and upright; 2-3 cm long. **Bark.** Thin, shiny, reddish, gradually turning yellowish or bronze; not peeling easily. **Size.** Height 15-25 m, diameter 60-100 cm.

The largest and most important of our birches, the yellow birch is also one of our main timber hardwoods. Too dense to float, its wood has not been used by the pulp and paper industry. Its generic name *Betula* is the Latin name for birch, and *alleghaniensis* refers to the Alleghany Mountains, which border the Appalachian plateau from Pennsylvania to Virginia. *Lutea*, referring to the golden yellow colour of the bark in mature specimens, derives from the Latin *lutens* or *lutum*, the name given by the Romans to Weld, or Dyer's Rocket (*Reseda luteola* L.), a plant cultivated in nineteenth-century France and which yielded a yellow dye.

Young paper birch and yellow birch trees bear a strong resemblance to each other, but the odour of wintergreen that is given off by a broken twig or the bark of the yellow birch serves to identify it with certainty. When the two are at the seedling stage, this is the only means of differentiating them. More tolerant of shade than the white birch and the trembling aspen, but less so than the sugar maple and the beech, the yellow birch is an important element in stands dominated by maple. Its light seeds are sometimes airborne over great distances, germinating in any moist place—even on partly rotted stumps and logs. Over the years the roots surround the stump or log, which in rotting away leaves the yellow birch standing on what look like stilts. This tree may live for up to 300 years but is highly vulnerable to forest fires. Even when wet, it has very flammable bark, like that of the white birch. A word of warning: **never tear the bark off a living tree**, since this will cause the formation of black rings and possibly even **kill the tree**.

The leaves and twigs of this highly aromatic tree can be used to make an excellent tea. Like all birches, it can be tapped in the spring. Its sap flows abundantly, but a great quantity is required in order to make even a little sugar. It can also be fermented to make beer. The bark, along with that of the cherry birch (*Betula lenta* L.), was formerly used to obtain what was commercially known as oil of wintergreen; this was added to various medicines to mask their flavour. Today the volatile essence known by this name is either extracted from the wintergreen or synthesized in a laboratory.

The wood—as hard as white oak but less hard than sugar maple—is strong, closed-grained, resistant and heavy, and it stains well. In the eighteenth century it was used in preference to oak for building the submerged parts of a ship. Today it is used for parquet flooring, fine furniture, panelling, plywood and veneer, as well as for railroad ties and pulpwood.

The cherry birch (*Betula lenta* L.), sometimes called mountain-mahogany or sweet birch, has the same characteristic odour as the yellow birch. It may be distinguished from the latter by its rarity: there are only about fifty mature trees on the shore of Lake Ontario, to the west of Port Dalhousie. Its presence in Ontario was not confirmed until 1967.

G 552f

Western Birch

Black birch, mountain birch, red birch, water birch, western white birch

Bouleau occidental, bouleau fontinal, merisier occidental, merisier rouge

Betula occidentalis Hook.
     syn. *Betula fontinalis* Sarg.

Birch family (Betulaceae)

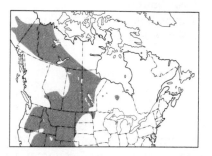

Distribution
Throughout most of the forested areas west of Ontario, except in the
Coast Forest Region.

Distinctive features
Leaves. Small, 2-5 cm long, with large teeth and less than 6 pairs of
lateral veins. **Fruit.** "Cones", cylindrical tending to hang, 2.5-4 cm
long. **Twigs.** Densely glandular. **Bark.** Thin, lustrous, reddish brown
to almost black, not coming off in thin sheets or peeling off readily;
long, conspicuous horizontal lenticels. **Size.** Shrub or small tree.
Height 3-10 m, diameter 15-35 cm.

The generic name *Betula* is the Latin name for birch. The specific
name *occidentalis* refers to the habitat of this tree, for it is found in
the western provinces; *fontinalis* suggests its resemblance to a fountain. The name water birch refers to its affinity for water, since it
grows almost exclusively along streams or around springs. Where its
range overlaps that of the white birch, it hybridizes, producing offspring with intermediate characteristics. Too small to be exploited
commercially, it is used locally for fence posts and fuel.

G 552g

American Hop-hornbeam

Deerwood, eastern
hop-hornbeam, hornbeam,
ironwood, leverwood,
rough-barked ironwood

Ostryer de Virginie, bois à
levier, bois dur, bois de fer

Ostrya virginiana (P. Mill.) K. Koch

Birch family (Betulaceae)

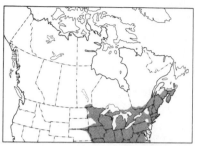

Rare in Manitoba

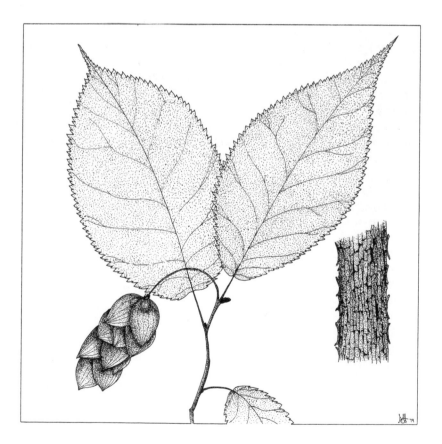

Distribution
Deciduous, Great Lakes-St Lawrence and Acadian forest regions. In the north, enters the southern fringe of the Boreal Forest Region and in the west, part of the Grasslands.

Distinctive features
Leaves. 6-13 cm long; lateral veins forking near margin. **Fruit.** Hanging clusters resembling hops, 4-5 cm long, consisting of groups of wrinkled white or greenish sacs each containing a small nut or nutlet. **Bark.** Dull greyish brown, broken into narrow rectangular strips, free at both ends. **Size.** Height 7-12 m, diameter 15-25 cm.

For anyone familiar with the woodlands of eastern Canada, the common names of the American hop-hornbeam are highly evocative. Its wood, one of the hardest and most resistant in the country, has earned it the name ironwood. The generic name *Ostrya* comes from the Greek *ostrua*, or *ostruoes*, which was the common name of a tree with very hard wood; *virginiana* means of Virginia, probably in reference to the place where this species was first identified.

Capable of tolerating the shade of tall trees, the American hop-hornbeam is frequently associated with sugar maple, American beech, yellow birch and basswood. It prefers well-drained slopes. Its leaves can be confused with those of white elm, paper birch and American hornbeam, but its bark, which peels off in much smaller longitudinal strips than the bark of the shagbark hickory, serves to identify it beyond all doubt. Because of its scattered occurrence and small size, this tree has not been exploited commercially.

Its wood is ideal for making tool handles, mallets and sleigh runners, and other articles in which resistance to wear is essential. It is a good fuel wood but is almost impossible to split.

G 552h

American Hornbeam

Blue-beech, hornbeam, ironwood, muscle-beech, smooth-
barked ironwood, water-beech

Charme de Caroline, bois de
fer, bois dur, charme bleu,
charme d'Amérique, charme de
la Caroline

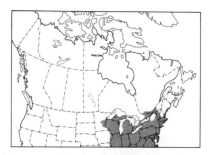

Carpinus caroliniana Walt.

Birch family (Betulaceae)

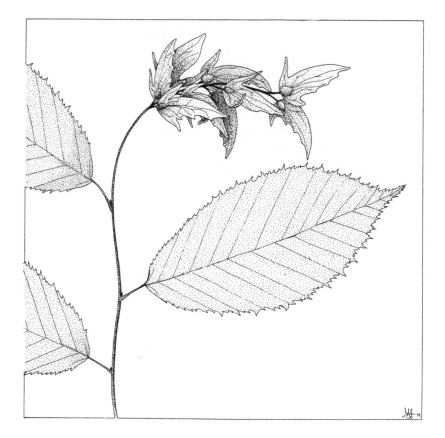

Distribution
Scattered throughout the southern part of the Great Lakes-St Lawrence Forest Region and the Deciduous Forest Region.

Distinctive features
Leaves. 5-10 cm long; lateral veins exhibit little or no forking. **Fruit.** In hanging clusters, consisting of a small nut at the base of a 3-lobed bract or leaf-like structure. **Bark.** Resembles that of the true beech; smooth, unbroken, bluish grey, but with conspicuous longitudinal ridges. **Trunk.** Short, crooked and fluted. **Size.** Large shrub or small tree. Height 4-9 m, diameter 10-20 cm.

The American hornbeam, like the American hop-hornbeam, is commonly called ironwood and has a heavy, strong wood and a great tolerance of shade. It is also called water-beech, because it is often found in maple-dominated stands on moist soils and in stands on alluvial deposits. It is often confused with beech (to which it is not related) because of the similarity of its bark, which, however, has conspicuous, muscle-like ridges (hence the name muscle beech). Furthermore, its leaves have intermediate teeth between the large teeth at the end of the lateral veins—not the case with the beech. The name hornbeam was originally given to a European relative, *Carpinus betulus* L., in reference to both its use in construction and its horn-like hardness. The generic name *Carpinus* comes from the Celtic *car* (wood) and *pen* or *pin* (head); it seems that this wood was used to make yokes for cattle. The specific name *caroliniana* means of Carolina. The wood of this tree (and that of the American hop-hornbeam) is so hard and strong that it was used to make wedges with which to split other types of wood. American hornbeam wood is used for the same purposes as the wood of the American hop-hornbeam, but it rots very quickly on contact with soil. Because of its slow growth and its scarlet fall foliage turning to gold, this is a fine ornamental that is, unfortunately, underutilized.

G 552i

American Elm (*see* G 952a)

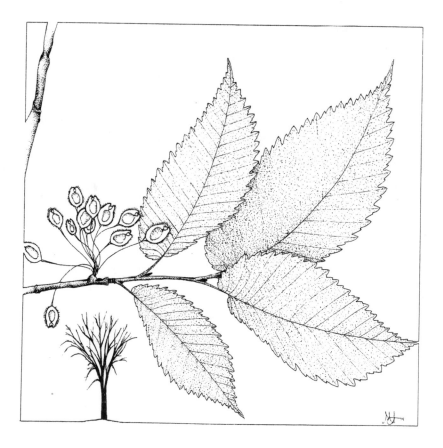

G 552j
Rock Elm (*see* G 952b)

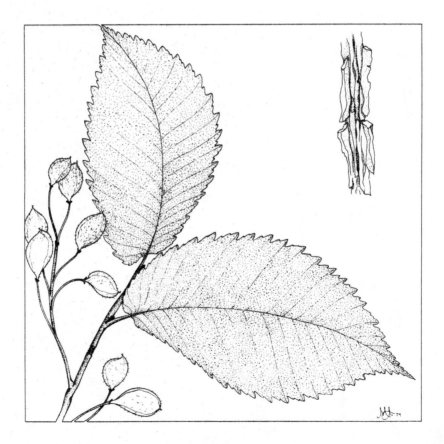

G 552k
Red Elm (*see* G 952c)

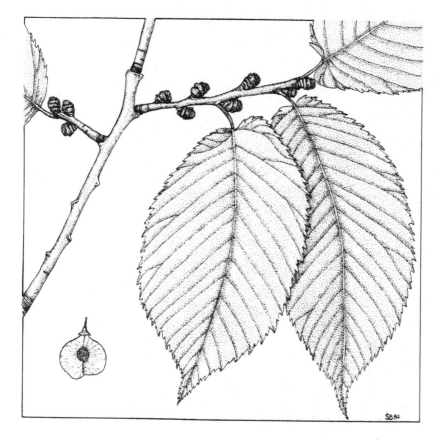

G 562a

Balsam Poplar

Balm tacamahac, balm poplar,
balm-of-Gilead, balsam
(Maritimes), bam, hamatack,
rough-barked poplar, tacamahac

Peuplier baumier, baumier,
liard, peuplier, peuplier noir

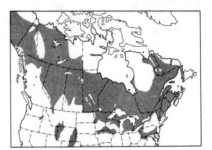

Populus balsamifera L. ssp. *balsamifera*
    syn. *Populus tacamahacca* P. Mill.

Willow family (Salicaceae)

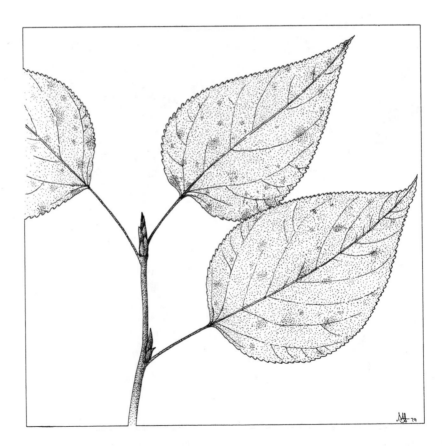

Distribution

All forest regions east of the Rockies.

Distinctive features

Leaves. 6-15 cm long; round petiole or leaf-stalk; undersurface often stained with brownish resin blotches; fragrant. **Twigs.** Lateral buds pressed against the twig; buds very gummy and fragrant. **Size.** Height 18-24 m, diameter 30-60 cm.

This fast-growing tree grows along river banks, dry stream beds, and in moist fields and bogs. It can be recognized by the balm-like fragrance given off by its buds, as is reflected in a number of its popular names in both English and French. Formerly the resin was used to make cough medicines, and ointments to stop bleeding. The Indians also used the resin to waterproof the seams of the canoes they made from the bark of the paper birch. The balsam poplar and the western balsam poplar are the only native poplars to have a leaf-stalk that is easy to roll between the thumb and the forefinger.

The specific name *balsamifera* (balsam-bearing) refers to the tree's fragrance. The name, *tacamahacca*, from the Aztec *tecomahiyac* (designating a highly resinous tropical plant), was given to the balsam poplar because of its very resinous buds. The generic name *Populus* evokes the period when poplar trees were planted in public squares reserved for the people.

It is the balm-of-Gilead (*Populus candicans* Ait.) whose buds are sold in stores marketing natural foods and other products, even though the buds of the two species have similar properties. Balm-of-Gilead, often planted as an ornamental, is seen by some as an introduced species, others consider it a female clone of a variety of the balsam poplar.

The wood of this tree is similar to that of the trembling aspen and is used for the same purposes. It is used on the Prairies as a roadside tree, forming screens along roads and property lines. Although not indigenous to Prince Edward Island, the balsam poplar was introduced there long ago. Its wood gives off a pleasant odour when burned, but it is hard to split when wet. When the temperature drops to − 12 °C or lower, and the wood is frozen, it splits readily.

G 562b

Western Balsam Poplar

Balm, California poplar,
northern black cottonwood,
black cottonwood

Peuplier occidental, peuplier
baumier de l'Ouest

Populus balsamifera L.
    ssp. *trichocarpa* (T. & G.) Brayshaw
    syn. *Populus trichocarpa* T. & G.

Willow family (Salicaceae)

Distribution
Most of British Columbia and western Alberta.

Distinctive features
Leaves. 6-15 cm long; round petiole or leaf-stalk; underside frequently stained with brownish resin blotches; fragrant. **Twigs.** Lateral buds pressed against the twig, diverging occasionally; very sticky and fragrant. **Size.** Height 18-40 m, diameter 30-150 cm.

The western balsam poplar is the largest poplar native to North America and the largest deciduous tree in British Columbia. In common with the balsam poplar, its leaves and gummy buds release a very characteristic balsam fragrance. This characteristic smell confirms the presence of one of these two poplars; however, it is difficult to distinguish between them. The two species are often considered as one, divided into two subspecies which integrate where their ranges overlap. The distinction between the two is based on the male flowers' number of stamens and the number of parts into which the fruit is split: the balsam poplar's male flowers have at least 20 stamens and its fruit is split into two parts, whereas the western balsam poplar has 30 to 60 stamens and 3-part fruit (hence the Latin name *trichocarpa*). Poplars have short-lived male and female flowers that bloom before the leaves unfold. Moreover, male and female flowers are found on different trees. These features make identification difficult. Like the fruit of the eastern cottonwood and balsam poplar, the fruit of the black cottonwood (covered with white silky hairs) resembles that of the cotton plant (black cottonwood).

The buds of western balsam poplar, like those of the balsam poplar, were collected for medicinal purposes. They were used as expectorants and stimulants.

The Indians of British Columbia and Alberta sought out the larger specimens of western balsam poplar and balsam poplar to make ceremonial canoes, particularly in regions where the giant arborvitae was absent; they also used the wood as fuel. They treated the ashes to produce a type of soap and made containers and temporary shelters with the bark. Like the Indians of the east, they harvested the gummy buds for use as a glue.

A sizable tree, the western balsam poplar yields large amounts of timber and a veneer free of knots. It is used to manufacture boxes, crates, containers for small fruit and pulpwood.

G 562c

Canada Plum
Red plum, wild plum, horse plum

Prunier noir, guignier, prunier sauvage, prunier canadien

Prunus nigra Ait.

Rose family (Rosaceae)

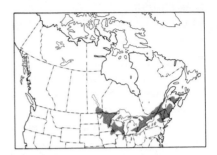

Distribution
Deciduous Forest Region and Great Lakes-St Lawrence Forest Region.

Distinctive features
Leaves. 8-14 cm long; small glands at ends of teeth; pair of glands on stalk. **Flowers.** Fragrant, white, often tinged with red. **Fruit.** Drupe; red-orange plum without bloom (light waxy coating); skin thick, tough and astringent; edible after first frosts. **Twigs.** Have spine-like projections. **Bark.** Greyish brown to black. **Size.** Shrub or small tree. Height 6-8 m, diameter 12-25 cm.

The Canada plum can be recognized by its round-toothed leaves, its spiny twigs and its bark marked with long, brownish lenticels. It may be confused with the wild plum, but the latter has leaves with pointed teeth.

The generic name *Prunus* is the Latin name for the plum tree, and the specific name *nigra* (black) refers to the colour of the bark. Well before its leaves come out, the Canada plum is adorned with 5-petalled white flowers. Along with the serviceberry, it is one of the first trees to announce its presence in the woods during the first warm days of spring. Its fruit is a source of food for deer, muskrats, foxes and small rodents. The delicious red plums are so enticing to bears that they often break off large branches trying to reach them. Unripe, the fruit is astringent and tough-skinned. Be patient and wait for the first frosts, which will make them soft to the touch and thoroughly delicious. They can be stewed or made into jelly, jam or juice, or they can be eaten raw.

There have been cases of poisoning and death among children who have eaten large quantities of plums without removing the stones. The stones contain prussic acid, an extremely dangerous poison (the same is true of cultivated plums). It is also inadvisable to plant potatoes near plum trees because of an aphid, which, although not dangerous to the plum, can cause disease in potatoes.

Because of its small size, the Canada plum is of no economic importance; however, it is often planted as a fruit tree or an ornamental, and horticulturists have developed a number of varieties with showy flowers.

G 562d

Red Alder
Oregon alder, western alder

Aulne rouge, aulne de l'Oregon

Alnus rubra Bong.
syn. *Alnus oregona* Nutt.

Birch family (Betulaceae)

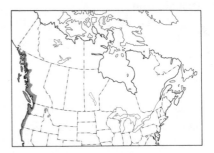

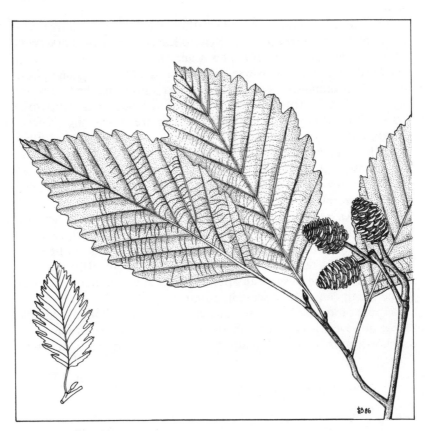

var. *pinnatisecta*

Distribution
Coast Forest Region.

Distinctive features
Leaves. 7-12 cm long; 10-15 very conspicuous straight veins on upper surface covered with rust-coloured hair; curled edge. **Twigs.** Green at the outset, becoming red later; red bud with clearly distinct stalk. **Fruit.** Resembles small "cone" at maturity, upright; remains on twigs throughout winter. **Bark.** Smooth, silvery-white; pale lenticels. **Size.** Height 12-25 m, diameter 30-75 cm.

It may seem strange for a tree with remarkably white bark to be called red alder. The specific name, *rubra* (red) in fact refers to the colour of its inner bark and wood: simply scratch the bark lightly with a finger-nail and it will turn a reddish colour. The generic name *Alnus*, the Latin name for the alder, derives from the Celtic word meaning bordering rivers.

The red alder, the easiest of the Canadian alders to recognize, can be identified by its whitish bark and round-toothed, curled-edge leaves. In winter the dark red twigs against a white background indi-cate its presence. One variety with very jagged leaves (var. *pinnatisecta* Starker) grows around Cowichan Lake and in the Nimpkish Valley of Vancouver Island as well as in some areas of Washington and Oregon states.

Like all Canadian alders, the red alder prefers fresh, moist areas, where it forms dense clumps. This pioneer species is intolerant of shade and rarely lives longer than a hundred years. The millions of seeds transported by the wind invade burned-over and cut-over areas, and within a few years the trees are several metres high. The decom-position of their leaves enriches the soil with a rich humus while their root nodules fertilize it, preparing it for the arrival of more tolerant species such as the Douglas fir, Sitka spruce and giant arborvitae. Today, the red alder is used to control river bank erosion and to reaf-forest roadsides.

A species very wide-spread along the British Columbia coast, the red alder is the largest alder native to North America. For a long time, lumberjacks and foresters considered it to be of little value and it was used only for charcoal and as fuel. Today, however, the red alder is one of the most important hardwoods in the Coast Forest Region. It grows quickly, reaching cutting size after 35 to 50 years. Its pale, light, uniformly-textured wood is used to make furniture, utensils, trinkets and paper. It is also valued as a fuel since it does not throw out sparks and leaves very few ashes. The red alder's freshly cut wood or its charcoal can be used to smoke salmon and other fish.

Like the other alders, the red alder played an important role in popular medicine among the pioneers and the Indians. Its bark contains salicin, a product similar to aspirin. An infusion of its bark was used to treat rheumatic pain and diarrhea.

The Indians used various techniques to obtain dyes, ranging from black or orange-red, from the alders. They coloured almost everything with these dyes, even tatooing the skin with it. The wood was carved to make spoons, bowls, masks and oars. They also used it for smoking salmon, cooking large pieces of meat, and as fuel. In Alaska, the Indians carved the trunks of alders into canoes.

G 562e

Bebb's Willow (*see* G 522a)

variation of leaf margin

G 562f

Pussy Willow (*see* G 522b)

G 572a

Bur Oak
Blue oak, mossy-cup oak, mossy oak, over-cup oak, scrubby oak

Chêne à gros fruits, chêne, chêne à gros glands, chênc blanc, chêne blanc frisé

Quercus macrocarpa Michx.

Beech family (Fagaceae)

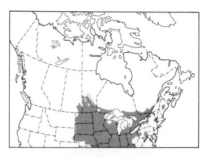

Distribution

Deciduous Forest Region, in scattered localities throughout the Great Lakes-St Lawrence Forest Region, in the central portion of the Acadian Forest Region, and in the zone of transition between the Grasslands and the Boreal Forest Region.

Distinctive features

Leaves. 10-25 cm long often broadest beyond the middle; undersurface covered with fine white hairs; 5-9 deep lobes. **Twigs.** Twigs often have conspicuous corky ridges by second year. **Fruit.** Acorn variable in shape, sweet-tasting kernel; 1.9-3.2 cm long, in a deep burlike cup with fringe along the rim; matures in autumn of first year. **Size.** Height 12-18 m, diameter 60-80 cm.

The bur oak is the most widely distributed of all oaks indigenous to Canada. The oak was the sacred tree of antiquity and represents power and strength. It was the proud symbol of Gaul, the tree of the gods from which was harvested mistletoe, the parasitic plant made famous by Panoramix in the French comic book *Astérix*. It was also under this tree that the Gauls rendered justice. Among the Romans, receiving a crown of oak leaves was a form of reward. To this day the oak is seen as a symbol of strength and durability.

The generic name *Quercus* is the common Latin name for oak; it is derived from Celtic and means "tree above all others". The generic name *macrocarpa*, from the Greek *makros* (large) and *karpos* (fruit), refers to the acorns of this tree—the largest of all our indigenous oaks. The French name *chêne à gros fruits* is the literal translation of the Latin. Some of the English names refer to the tree's fringed acorns.

The bur oak survives in dry environments such as on limestone-based soils, but grows best on deep, dry soils in bottomlands. Formerly sometimes found in pure oak stands, it now tends to be mixed with other hardwood species and with conifers.

Its wood, hard, strong, heavy and resistant, is like that of the white oak (under which name it is sold) and is used for the same purposes. Its sweet-tasting fruit is prepared in the same way as that of the white oak, and the caveat concerning tannins also applies to it (*see* White Oak). It is often planted as an ornamental, or a shade tree. It is used along streets and in parks mainly because of its tolerance of urban air pollution. However, it is difficult to transplant because of its taproot.

The ten species of oak in Canada fall into three distinct groups on the basis of their leaf shape, their bark, and the maturation time and taste of their fruit. The species in the "white oaks" group have leaves with deep, rounded lobes, sweet-tasting fruit that ripens in one season, and scaly bark. This group consists of the bur oak, the white oak and the garry oak (the only oak west of the Rockies in Canada). The species of the "chestnut oaks" group, namely the swamp white oak, and the chinquapin oak, resemble those in the white oaks group in terms of their fruit and their bark, but differ in their leaves, which instead of being lobed, have rounded or angular teeth. Finally, the "red or black oaks" group, represented by the red oak, the black oak, the pin oak, the northern pin oak and the shumard oak, have deeply lobed leaves with teeth that have pointed tips, non-scaly bark and bitter fruit with long maturation period, taking two years to ripen.

G 572b

White Oak
Stave oak

Chêne blanc, chêne de Québec

Quercus alba L.

Beech family (Fagaceae)

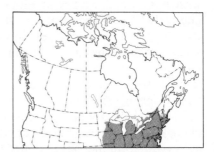

Rare in Quebec

Distribution
Deciduous Forest Region and southern parts of the Great Lakes-St Lawrence Region.

Distinctive features

Leaves. 12-22 cm long; downy only when unfolding, then become hairless, with 5-9 deeply-cut lobes. **Twigs.** With no corky ridges. **Fruit.** Elongated acorn, edible, and sweet-tasting kernel; 1.2-2 cm long, in a shallow, knoblike cup without fringe along rim; matures in autumn of first year. **Bark.** Pale grey and scaly. **Size.** Height 15-30 m, diameter 60-100 cm.

The white oak, one of our most valuable and perhaps most important hardwoods, is a characteristic tree of the Deciduous Forest Region. It grows slowly and has a life span of five or six centuries. It played a vital role in shipbuilding and mast construction until the advent of metal-hulled ships. In 1672 oak wood was set aside for the exclusive use of the Royal Navy, a practice later extended to include the eastern white pine.

The generic name *Quercus* is the Latin name for oak, and means "tree above all others". The specific name *alba* (white) denotes the pale grey colour of the bark. This tree may be confused with the bur oak, but its hairless leaves, twigs lacking corky bark and cups without fringe serve to make it easily distinguishable. Like the bur oak, it grows in a variety of soils, but prefers deep, moist soils with good drainage.

Its wood, hard, heavy, non-porous and strong, is considered to be the best of all native oaks. The watertight barrels made from this wood and that of the other species in the white oaks group are used to age liquor and to store other liquids; hence its common name, stave oak. Whisky, left to age for a number of years in these barrels, derives its flavour and colour from this wood. It is an excellent wood for use in barrel-making because of its impermeability and its surprising elasticity; indeed it can be bent at almost a right angle.

Because of its appearance and fine qualities, the wood of the white oak is used in cabinetmaking, flooring, fine panelling and boat building, as well as in the manufacture of veneer and plywood. It is also used in the making of caskets, tool handles, pianos and organs. Formerly it was used in the construction of automobile and airplane bodies, and ploughing implements.

The bark of trees in the white oaks group, being very rich in tannic acid, was used in tanning. It is now used to dye wool for craft purposes. If no mordant is used, it yields attractive brown colours: with alum as a mordant, it yields yellow; with chrome, a golden colour; and with pewter, a yellow-orange. But take note: **bark must not be removed from living trees.** The same results can be obtained by using galls—also very rich in tannin. These are tumours caused by multitudes of tiny insects that live as parasites on some plants, particularly oaks. The usual parasite affecting oaks, the cynips, is a tiny wasp.

In folk medicine, a decoction has long been made from the bark as a cure for diarrhea, inflammation of the digestive tract, burns, bleeding gums, etc, but this practice is inadvisable because of the high tannin content of the bark and leaves. A relationship has been noted between high consumption of tannin and certain types of cancers.

The sweet-tasting kernels of the white oaks group are good to eat, even on their own. Acorns were once a major food source for the Indians, who dried and ground them into a meal used to thicken soups or to make a type of pancake. Boiled and peeled, acorns were consumed as vegetables; mixed with suet or simply roasted on coals, they were eaten as a snack. Today, roasted and ground they make an excellent caffeine-free coffee substitute. They can also be made into flour and used with other flours in the making of bread, muffins and cakes, imparting a most interesting flavour.

Acorns are also valued by various mammals and birds; they form a basic part of the diet of animals such as chipmunks and squirrels, who play a vital role in the propagation of oaks. White-tailed deer and black bears are also fond of acorns.

G 572c

Garry Oak

Pacific post oak, Oregon white oak, western white oak

Chêne de Garry

Quercus garryana Dougl. ex Hook.

Beech family (Fagaceae)

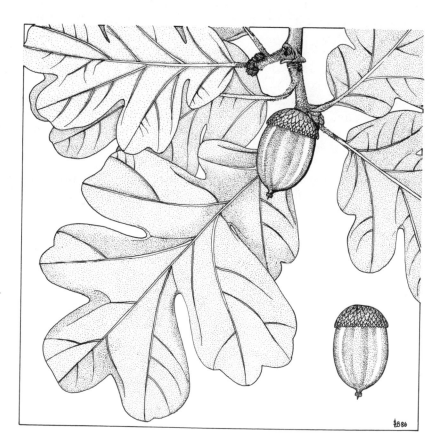

Distribution
Southeastern part of the Coast Forest Region of Vancouver Island and the adjacent islands, and inland to Yale and Abbotsford.

Distinctive features
The only oak native to Canada's Pacific coast. **Leaves.** 7-15 cm long; 5-9 cm deep, often notched lobes. **Twigs.** Covered with hair the first year; buds densely hairy. **Fruit.** Elongated acorn, edible sweet-tasting kernel; 2-3 cm long, in scaly thin saucer-like cup without fringe along rim; matures in autumn of first year. **Bark.** Pale grey, scaly. **Size.** Shrub 3 m in height in exposed areas. A tree 10-20 m in height, 30-80 cm in diameter.

Canada is the northernmost limit of the Garry oak's range. Its most beautiful stands are located near Victoria, where they are threatened by urban development. The botanist David Douglas discovered the Garry oak in 1820 and named it in honour of Nicholas Garry, a Hudson's Bay Company administrator, who helped him during his expeditions. Fort Garry, now Winnipeg, was named after the same person. The Garry oak is common in Oregon and belongs to the white oaks groups, hence the American name Oregon white oak. Since its wood is easy to split and its heartwood is decay-resistant, farmers used it for fence posts, thus the name Pacific post oak. As it is often twisted and crooked and not very abundant in Canada, the Garry oak has no real commercial value.

Like the white oak, its relatively sweet acorns can be eaten raw. The Indians ate them in this manner or soaked them in a stream or lake until winter before eating them.

The English oak (*Quercus robur* L.), cousin of Europe's white oak, is often planted in Canada. It can be recognized by its very short-stemmed leaves, its leaf-stalk with a series of small lobes at the base, and its acorn with its long, 4 to 8 centimetre stalk. Introduced at the time of the colonization of plants from England, it sometimes grows wild in the provinces of New Brunswick, Prince Edward Island and Nova Scotia.

G 572d

Swamp White Oak
Blue oak, swamp oak

Chêne bicolore, chêne bleu

Quercus bicolor Willd.

Beech family (Fagaceae)

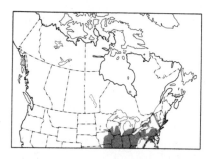

Rare in Quebec

Distribution
Deciduous Forest Region; in Great Lakes-St Lawrence Forest Region, confined to the Hochelaga archipelago and a few sites along the Richelieu River and the Quebec side of the Ottawa River.

Distinctive features
Leaves. 12-20 cm long; shallow lobes; undersurface pale green, covered with white down; top is shiny, dark green. **Fruit.** Nearly round, edible, sweet-tasting kernel; 2-3 cm long, generally on long stalk (2.5-7.6 cm); matures in autumn of first year. **Bark.** Scaly, reddish brown, becoming greyish brown with age. **Size.** Height 12-18 m, diameter 60-90 cm.

With a small population confined to a very small range, the swamp white oak is a rare tree in Canada. The use of its wood in construction has made it an endangered species in Quebec; in order to protect it, in August 1986 the Ministry of Environment of Quebec created the Marcel-Raymond Ecological Reserve on the Richelieu River. It prefers wooded sites on bottomlands and the edges of swamps, from which it draws its name. This species can be identified by the small, crooked twigs hanging from the branches, as well as by the bark on the branches, which peels off in layers to reveal the paler colour of its inner part. This tree is not self-pruning. The dead branches remain attached to the trunk for years, giving it a scraggy appearance.

The generic name *Quercus* is the Latin name for oak, meaning "tree above all others". The specific name *bicolor* (of two colours), refers to the leaf.

Its life span is comparable to that of the white oak (300 years or more) but it is considerably more vulnerable to forest fires, having much shallower roots. Its wood, similar to that of the white oak but of inferior quality because of its knottiness, is sold under the name of the white oak and used for the same purposes. Its acorns are a food source for wildlife, and can be prepared for human consumption in the same manner as those of the white oak.

G 582a

Red Oak

Grey oak, northern red oak

Chêne rouge, chêne boréal

Quercus rubra L.
 syn. *Quercus borealis* Michx. fil.

Beech family (Fagaceae)

variation of leaf margin

Distribution
Deciduous, Great Lakes-St Lawrence and Acadian forest regions.

Distinctive features
Leaves. 10-20 cm long; 7-11 divided lobes, bristle-tipped lobes. **Twigs.** Hairless; terminal buds shiny and hairless, reddish brown. **Fruit.** Ovoid acorn, bitter-tasting kernel; 1.5-2.8 cm long, ¼ to ⅓ enclosed in a generally shallow, saucer-shaped cup; matures in autumn of second year. **Bark.** Smooth, slate grey on young trees, becoming darker and vertically grooved. **Size.** Height 18-25 m, diameter 30-90 cm.

The most important and plentiful of its group, the red oak is generally found in sunny, rocky and dry places. It sometimes forms pure stands—referred to as red oak or northern red oak stands—on rocky uplands; it also mixes with other hardwoods and conifers such as trembling aspen and eastern white pine. It tolerates shade, probably to a greater extent than the other oaks but to a lesser extent than sugar maple and beech. A fast-growing species, it lives for about two or three centuries. It regenerates well after a fire, as it can send up shoots or suckers from its roots.

The generic name *Quercus*, the Latin name for oak, means "tree above all others". The specific name *borealis*, from Boreas, Greek god of the north wind, and from *boreal* (from the north), refers to the range of this species, which is the most northerly of the eastern oaks. *Rubra* (red) describes its autumn foliage and its reddish-brown wood.

The wood of the red oak is heavy, hard, resistant, strong and close-grained. It is highly valued for the making of furniture, for interior finishing and for flooring. However, it is less resistant to decay than the wood of the white oak. It is suitable for making barrels, but, because of its porosity, only for holding dry goods. Its porous quality can be demonstrated by dipping one end of a twig in soapy water and blowing on the other end: bubbles will form. (The vessels of the white oak are obstructed by gummy deposits or outgrowths extending across these vessels, making the wood impermeable.)

The kernels of the red oak are bitter and can be eaten raw only in small quantities. They must be soaked for several days to draw out the tannin, which is toxic in high concentrations. There are reports of cattle being poisoned, both in Europe and in the United States, as a result of ingesting raw acorns. All parts of oaks contain more of this substance than does any other plant. Although the fruit is unsuitable for humans, it is much prized by squirrels, chipmunks, white-tailed deer and various other small mammals and birds. In order to remove the bitterness from the acorns, the Indians buried them for an entire winter, plunged them into a river or brook, or boiled them in water with wood ash (lye). In Europe these acorns were once commonly used to fatten pigs.

It has been noted that the diameter of the acorn is related to the latitude and site conditions, trees that are further north having smaller acorns.

Introduced into Europe long ago (1724) for its ornamental value and the quality of its wood, the red oak has become naturalized there as a forest tree.

It is often planted as an ornamental or shade tree in parks and private gardens because of its handsome, dark red autumn colours, its rapid growth and its resistance to the shock of being transplanted. While largely invulnerable to insect infestations and disease, it is, like most oaks, often inhabited by small, parasitic insects that cause the formation of galls.

384

G 582b

Black Oak
Quercitron oak, yellow-barked oak, yellow oak

Chêne noir, chêne des teinturiers, chêne quercitron, chêne velouté, quercitron

Quercus velutina Lam.

Beech family (Fagaceae)

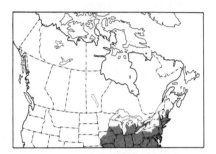

Distribution
Deciduous Forest Region and northeast of Lake Ontario.

Distinctive features
Leaves. 10-20 cm long; downy when unfolding, later hairless except along the veins on the undersurface; 5-7 lobes, oblique in relation to the midrib. **Twigs.** Hairy the first season, thereafter hairless; buds dull greyish brown, densely covered with hairs. **Fruit.** Ovoid acorn with bitter-tasting kernel; 1.3-1.8 cm long, ⅓ to ½ enclosed in a large, bowl-shaped cup; matures in autumn of second year. **Bark.** Smooth, dark grey on young trees, becoming almost black on older trees, deeply cracked into small squares; inner bark bright yellow to yellow-orange. **Size.** Height 15-20 m, diameter 30-100 cm.

Of all the northern oaks, the black oak is the most variable in its features. Furthermore, where their ranges overlap (i.e., in the southern-most part of Ontario) it hybridizes with the red oak and the pin oak, but can generally be distinguished from them by its leaves, its woolly buds and, especially, by its bitter, orange-coloured inner bark.

The generic name *Quercus* (tree above all others) is the Latin name for oak. The specific name *velutina* (velvet-like) from the Latin *vellus* (fleece) and *ina* (resembling), refers to the pubescence of the young leaves. The name black refers to the colour of the bark on older specimens. All the other names in both English and French refer to the inner bark containing a yellow pigment: quercitron, from which a dye is obtained.

Formerly the inner bark of the black oak had a number of uses: it was a source of tannin before the advent of synthetic products; it was valued for its astringent properties in folk medicine; and it was a natural source of colour for dyes. Oddly enough, it was not until it was introduced into Europe that quercitron became important, and it was sold commercially until the late 1940s.

Intolerant of competition, the black oak monopolizes poor, dry, sandy soils, where it sometimes forms pure stands. It is very common and widespread in the United States, with the northern edge of its range being in southern Ontario. While it is a poor producer of fruit, sometimes bearing none for a number of years, it vigorously regenerates itself by suckering, a process whereby new plants grow from aerial shoots coming up from the roots. Its wood, heavy, hard and strong, is sold as red oak and is used for similar purposes.

G 582c

Pin Oak
Swamp oak, water oak

Chêne palustre, chêne à épingles, chêne des marais

Quercus palustris Muenchh.

Beech family (Fagaceae)

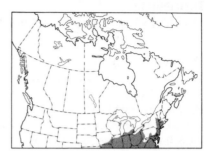

Rare in Ontario

Distribution

Confined to a small part of the Deciduous Forest Region.

Distinctive features

Leaves. 7-15 cm long; on the undersurface tufts of hairs present where principal veins join; 5 (sometimes 7) deeply cut lobes at right angles to the midrib. **Fruit.** Small, nearly round acorn with bitter-tasting kernel; less than 1.3 cm long, partially enclosed in a thin, saucer-shaped cup with fine hairs; matures in autumn of second year. **Bark.** Smooth in appearance and remaining so even in older specimens. **Size.** Height 15-20 m, diameter 30-60 cm.

The small population of pin oak is found in a very confined area on the northern edge of its American range. Some of its names in both English and French, as well as its specific name, *palustris*, from the Latin *palus* (swamp), refer to its preferred habitat: moist soils bordering swamps or streams, or places frequently flooded in spring. The name pin oak and its French equivalent, *chêne à épingles*, describe the tree's spiny appearance, which it owes to the many stiff, persistent twigs or branchlets that stand out from the trunk and larger branches. Because of this peculiarity its wood is knotty and of poor quality. Unlike most Canadian oaks, the pin oak has a shallow taproot, which makes it relatively easy to transplant.

Much appreciated by landscape gardeners for its ability to beautify streets and parks, it provides checkered shade because of the shape of its leaves. It has handsome, bright red foliage in autumn and a compact, conical or pyramidal crown. It is hardy outside its range.

Its wood is similar to that of the red oak, is sold commercially under its name and is used for the same purposes. The oak galls—small growths produced by tiny insects—yield a black ink when steeped in water. The acorn is a food source for wildfowl, white-tailed deer, and squirrels, chipmunks and other small rodents.

G 582d

Northern Pin Oak
Black oak, Hill oak, jack oak, upland pin oak

Chêne ellipsoïdal, chêne des marais du Nord, chêne Jack

Quercus ellipsoidalis E.J. Hill

Beech family (Fagaceae)

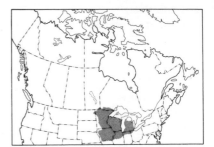

Rare in Ontario

Distribution
A species confined mainly to the United States, it is found in a small part of the Deciduous Forest Region.

Distinctive features
Leaves. Similar to the pin oak; 7-13 cm long. **Fruit.** Elliptical or almost round, bitter-tasting kernel, 1.2-1.8 cm long, enclosed in a scaly, deep bowl-shaped cup; matures in autumn of second year. **Bark.** Similar to the pin oak. **Size.** Height 15-20 m, diameter 30-60 cm.

Removed from the Canadian flora in the *Native Trees of Canada* (7th ed., 1978), the northern pin oak has since been restored to it. The National Herbarium, among others, has specimens of this species. Similar to the pin oak in a number of respects (hence its name), it can be distinguished from it by its habitat (dry, sandy or rocky soil, on higher ground than the pin oak) and its acorn. It may also be confused with the black oak (whose name it sometimes bears) but differs in its smaller leaves, its inner bark, which is not bright yellow, and its branchlets persisting on the trunk and larger branches.

The form of its fruit is indicated in the specific name, *ellipsoidalis*, and the French name, *ellipsoïdal* (elliptical in shape). The generic name *Quercus* is the Latin name. The common name Hill oak is sometimes used, in honour of the botanist Ellsworth Jerome Hill (1833-1917), who officially named it.

Northern pin oak is a rare species in Canada, where it is not exploited commercially. In the United States it is sometimes used as industrial or construction timber because of its hard, heavy and strong wood.

G 582e

Shumard Oak
Shumard red oak, spotted oak,
swamp oak, swamp red oak

Chêne de Shumard

Quercus shumardii Buckl.

Beech family (Fagaceae)

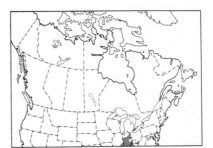

Rare in Ontario

Distribution
Confined to a small area in the southern part of the Deciduous Forest Region.

Distinctive features
Leaves. 10-20 cm long; like those of black oak, but with 7-11 deeply cut lobes. **Fruit.** Oval acorn, bitter-tasting kernel; 1.5-2.5 cm long, enclosed in a thick, shallow, saucer-shaped cup covered with hairs; matures in autumn of second year. **Size.** Height 15-30 m, diameter 30-60 cm.

The tendency of various oak species to hybridize is particularly well illustrated by the red or black oaks group, which includes red oak, pin oak, black oak, northern pin oak and Shumard oak. Long confused with the black oak or considered to be a hybrid of it, the Shumard oak was not known to be a member of the Canadian flora. Only in 1977 did botanists recognize it as a species native to Canada. It can be distinguished from the black oak and the red oak by its deeply indented leaves and its preference for moist, clayey soils. It bears a close resemblance to the pin oak. Both species are found in the same type of habitat, but the Shumard oak has larger leaves and much larger fruit.

The specific name *shumardii* was given in honour of a Texan geologist, Benjamin Franklin Shumard (1820-1869); the generic name is the Latin name for oak. Its wood is similar to that of the red oak and it is mixed freely with it and sold under the same name. The term Shumard is mainly used by botanists and by forestry personnel in order to distinguish this species from others in the red or black oaks group.

G 592a
Wild Crab Apple (*see* G 532c)

G 592b

Pacific Crab Apple (*see* G 532d)

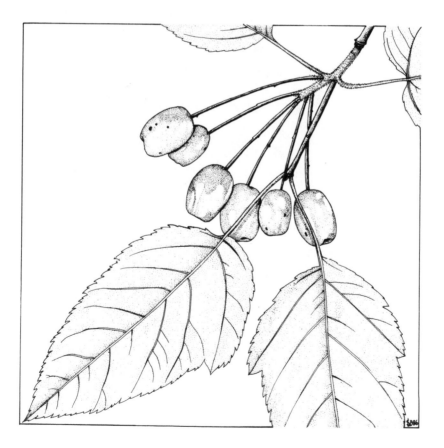

G 623

Redbud
Eastern redbud, Judas tree

Gainier rouge, arbre de Judée, bouton rouge, gainier du Canada

Cercis canadensis L.

Pea family (Leguminosae)

Rare in Ontario

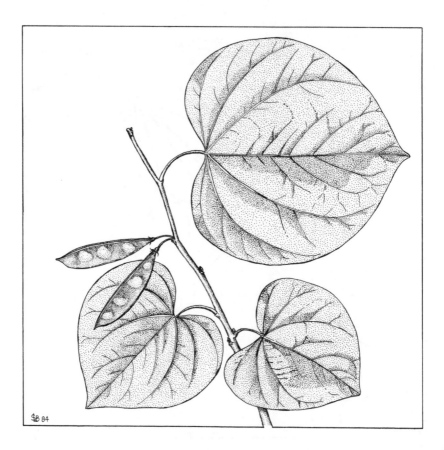

Distribution
Deciduous Forest Region, in the extreme southern part of Ontario.

Distinctive features
Leaves. Blade 7-12 cm long; top of leaf stalk swollen. **Flowers.** Pink or purple, somewhat resembling those of the pea; grow in clusters along twigs and branchlets, often appearing before the leaves. **Fruit.** Reddish-brown pods with large, flat seeds. **Size.** Small tree. Height 4-8 m, diameter 30 cm.

Situated on the extreme northern limit of its range in America, the redbud was recognized in 1892 as a native tree, on the basis of a specimen gathered by John Macoun on Pelee Island. For some time it was believed to have disappeared from this site, and was recently reintroduced. Elsewhere it is planted as an ornamental.

The redbud owes its name to its colourful spring flowers. These flowers are sometimes found on the larger branches and even on the trunk, giving the tree an unusual appearance. Its generic name *Cercis* derives from the Greek *kerkis*, the ancient name of the Judas tree. According to legend, Judas hanged himself on a species of Judas tree (*Cercis siliquastrum* L.) that is found in Asia and Europe. Its flowers are said to have turned red when the blood of shame flowed onto them. The redbud is one of only a few species in the Leguminosae family whose roots do not have nodules that store nitrogen fixed from the air.

G 632
Large-toothed Aspen (*see* **G 532b**)

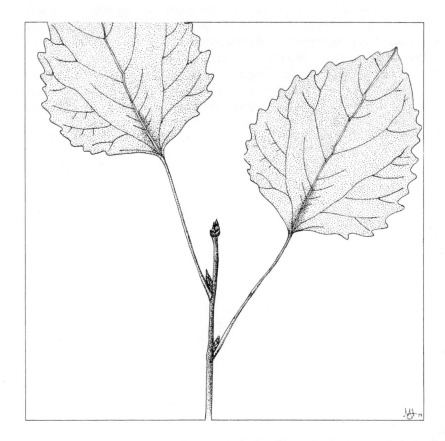

G 662

Trembling Aspen

Aspen, American aspen, aspen poplar, golden aspen, poplar, popple, quaking aspen, small-toothed aspen, smooth-bark poplar

Peuplier faux-tremble, faux-tremble, peuplier, peuplier tremble, tremble

Populus tremuloides Michx.

Willow family (Salicaceae)

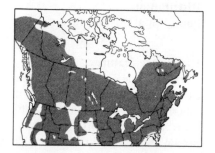

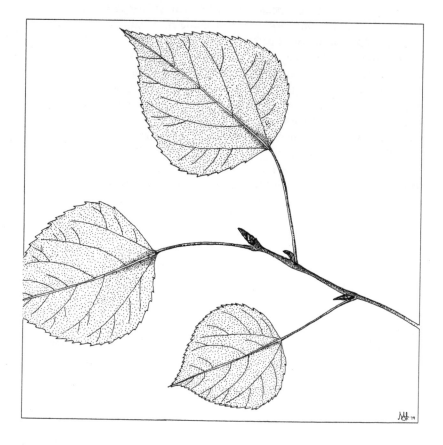

Distribution
Found in almost all forest regions in Canada.

Distinctive features
Leaves. Blade 4-6 cm long; flattened petiole or leaf stalk, often longer than blade. **Twigs.** Slender, smooth, shiny, greyish brown. **Bark.** Smooth, pale grey to almost white, covered with whitish powder that stains the hands; with age becoming rough and furrowed; from grey to brown. **Size.** Height 12-20 m, diameter 30-60 cm.

The trembling aspen is one of the most widely distributed tree in North America. It tolerates light, drought, wind and cold and accommodates itself to a wide variety of soils, but has little tolerance of strong competition and has difficulty reproducing in its own shade. Along with Bebb's willow, pin cherry and large-toothed aspen, it is considered as a pioneer species, invading forest sites destroyed by fire or clear-cutting. It thus provides the shade necessary for the development of other hardwoods or conifers.

Like the willows, the trembling aspen disperses its tiny seeds by wind or water. It can also reproduce by sending up suckers from its roots, a process often resulting in clones. A clone is a group of trees that have the same genetic material. In favourable conditions a clone can regenerate itself for centuries or even millenia. Unlike the willow, this tree cannot reproduce vegetatively if one of its twigs or branches is planted in the ground.

The generic name is the Latin name for poplar (people), in reference to the practice of planting this tree in public squares reserved for the people. The specific name *tremuloides* comes from the Latin *tremulus* (trembling) and the Greek *oides* (appearing like), in reference to this species' resemblance to the European aspen (*Populus tremula* L.). This resemblance is also reflected in the French name *peuplier faux-tremble* (false aspen). The leaf has a long, flattened leaf-stalk, and trembles or quakes in the slightest breeze, thus earning its name. French folklore has it that the True Cross was made of aspen, and that since that time aspens have never ceased to tremble. The Indians simply named this species the noisy tree.

The trembling aspen is found in a great variety of habitats over vast areas. It constitutes an important food source for deer and moose; beavers, which are very partial to the bark and leaves, often use the branches to construct their dams and lodges; snowshoe hares are also fond of the bark; grouse eat the winter buds. Like all members of the

Salicaceae family, the trembling aspen contains salicylic acid, the active ingredient in aspirin.

The soft, close-grained wood of this tree is important to the pulp and paper industry, but must be sent to the mill by land since it cannot be floated—when freshly cut the wood is very heavy, because its cells contain a great deal of water. When dried in the open, it becomes as light as red pine. It is also used for excelsior and for making boxes and crates. Wooden matches are made from wood of this tree by steaming the logs and peeling layers from them.

G 672a/G 682a

European White Poplar
Abele, white poplar, silver-leaved poplar, silver poplar

Peuplier blanc, abèle, érable argenté, peuplier argenté

Populus alba L.

Willow family (Salicaceae)

variation of leaf margin

Distribution
A native of Europe, frequently planted as an ornamental; escapes from cultivation in settled areas.

Distinctive features
Leaves. Blade 5-10 cm long; often maple like; undersurface covered with dense, white, woolly down; top surface dark green; leaf-stalk or petiole flattened. **Twigs.** Covered with white, woolly down; buds covered with white hairs. **Size.** Height 16-25 m, diameter 60-100 cm.

In the shape of its leaf the white poplar somewhat resembles the silver maple—indeed, in French it is sometimes mistakenly called *érable argenté* (silver maple)—but there the resemblance ends, for the leaves of our native maple have a smooth undersurface and are opposite (i.e., arranged opposite each other on the twig), whereas the white poplar is characterized by the pubescence of its leaves, buds and twigs, and its leaves are arranged in an alternating pattern on the twig.

The white poplar is a very fast-growing tree, and multiplies by sending up suckers from its roots at such a rate that it is often considered a pest. Like willows, it can be propagated vegetatively by planting a bud-bearing twig. In the slightest breeze, its leaves shake, exposing their silvery colour for which it was given its specific name, *alba* (white) and most of its English and French common names. Where its range overlaps those of the largetoothed aspen and the trembling aspen, it hybridizes with them.

The grey poplar (*Populus canescens* (Ait.) Sm.), a European hybrid or intermediary between the white poplar and the European aspen (*Populus tremula* L.), is also planted as an ornamental tree. Its bark can be used in treating burns and sciatica.

402

G 672b/G 682b

Tuliptree
Tulip-magnolia, tulip-poplar,
whitewood, yellow-poplar

Tulipier d'Amérique, bois
jaune, tulipier à tulipes, tulipier,
tulipier de Virginie

Liriodendron tulipifera L.

Magnolia family (Magnoliaceae)

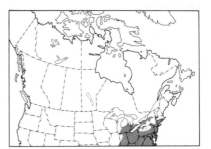

Rare in Ontario

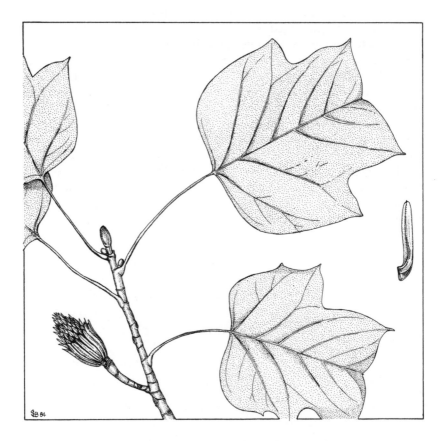

Distribution
Southern part of Deciduous Forest Region.

Distinctive features
Leaves. Blade 8-15 cm long; saddleshaped, appear cut off at top.
Flowers. Tulip or lily-shaped, with 6 petals, yellow green (orange at base), 4-5 cm in diameter. **Fruit.** Compound; aggregate of overlapping samaras, conelike appearance, some staying on tree all winter. **Twigs.** Flattened terminal bud. **Trunk.** Branch-free up to a considerable height (25 m or more). **Size.** Height 20-30 m, diameter 60-150 cm.

The flowers of this tree come out in May and June and resemble tulips or lilies; hence its name. It is one of the largest hardwoods in North America, sometimes called the "Apollo of the woods". The generic name, *Liriodendron*, from the Greek *leirion* (lily) and *dendron* (tree), refers to the very showy flowers. The specific name *tulipifera* derives from the Turkish word *tulbend* (turban) and the Latin *ferre* (to bear): a tree bearing tulips, or a lily tree bearing tulips. Even though some of the common names contain the word poplar, it is in no way related to trees of that name. Perhaps the reason for the name poplar in its common names is the soft and light quality of its wood—both characteristics of the poplar—and the fact that its leaves tremble in the wind like those of various poplars.

From its trunk, which is straight, tall and wide, the Indians built excellent canoes; solid and lightweight, and capable of carrying some twenty passengers. Its pungent-tasting roots have long been used to combat rheumatism and fever. Its wood has physical qualities similar to basswood, and for this reason it is mistakenly called white wood, another name for the basswood. The word yellow in the name yellow poplar refers to the pale yellow colour of the wood.

The tuliptree is not exploited commercially. In the United States, however, it is one of the most important timber trees. Its wood is pale and easily worked, and is used in cabinetmaking and the pulp and paper industry. It is also used for interior finishing, plywood and musical instruments, etc. Where it is hardy it is planted as an ornamental and a shade tree.

G 673
Sassafras (*see* G 5221)

G 683a

Sycamore

American sycamore, buttonball, buttonwood, planetree, American planetree

Platane occidental, boule de boutons, platane d'Occident, sycamore

Platanus occidentalis L.

Plane family (Platanaceae)

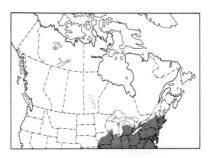

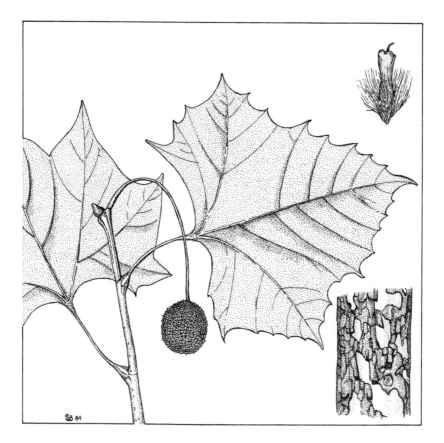

Distribution
Deciduous Forest Region. Planted as an ornamental outside its natural range.

Distinctive features
Leaves. Blade 10-20 cm long; leaf-stalk hollow at base, completely enclosing the bud; stipule present. **Fruit.** Compound; multiple akenes, solitary ball-like head on slender stem, staying on the tree almost all winter. **Twigs.** Shiny, growing in zigzag pattern, with single scale completely covering bud. **Bark.** Smooth when young, later peeling off in thin plates; brittle (like an old coat of paint peeling off), revealing pale inner layer beneath; greyish brown. **Size.** Height 18-30 m, diameter 60-120 cm.

The sycamore, along with the tuliptree, is one of the largest hardwoods in eastern North America, and probably has the largest diameter (4.6 metres). Its mottled bark and its massive, crooked branches make it easy to recognize, even at a distance. Early French settlers hollowed out the trunks of sycamores to make enormous barges capable of carrying several tons of goods.

The generic name *Platanus*, from the Greek *platys* (wide), refers to the large leaf; the specific name *occidentalis* (western, of the West) was given to differentiate this tree from the other species, which until then had all been native to the Orient. The name sycamore is the result of settlers mistaking this tree for the sycamore maple (*Acer pseudoplatanus* L.), a European species. The sycamore prefers moist, rich soils, growing best along streams and on lake shores.

It is sometimes planted as an ornamental or shade tree, but the London plane (probably a hybrid between *Platanus occidentalis* L. and *Platanus orientalis* L.) is often used in its place, since it is more resistant to pollution, readily accepts pruning and requires little root space. The London plane can be distinguished from our native trees by its leaf, which bears a strong resemblance to the maple leaf, and by its paired (instead of single) ball-like fruit on each stem.

The sycamore, being relatively scarce in Canada, is of little economic importance, but its wood is used in cabinetmaking. The massive chopping block in the butcher's shop is often made from the sycamore.

G 683b

Red Mulberry (*see* G 533)

G 723
Redbud (*see* G 623)

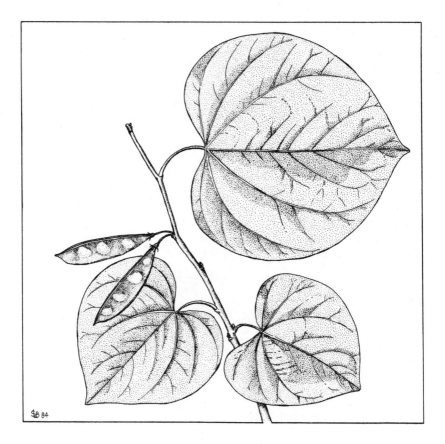

G 732a/G 733a

American Basswood

Basswood, American linden,
beetree, basttree, lime, limetree,
linden, spoonwood, whitewood

Tilleul d'Amérique, bois blanc

Tilia americana L.
  syn. *Tilia glabra* Vent.

Linden family (Tiliaceae)

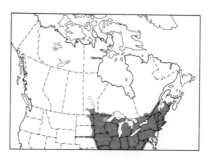

Distribution
Deciduous Forest Region, Great Lakes-St Lawrence Forest Region, western New Brunswick and along rivers in Manitoba.

Distinctive features
Leaves. Large, 12-15 cm wide. **Flowers.** 5 yellowish-white petals; drooping, fragrant, at end of a long stalk, attached to a membranous bract (leaflike structure); appear in summer. **Fruit.** Round, dry, hard capsule, pea-sized; hangs on tree into winter. **Twigs.** Smooth, in zigzag pattern; buds lopsided, large, often reddish or greenish. **Bark.** Smooth, becoming scaly, forming long, narrow and almost parallel ridges. **Size.** Height 18-22 m, diameter 40-80 cm.

The basswood has the longest leaves of any member of its family. Its slender, regular silhouette looks as if it were drawn by an artist. In summer its many nectar-rich flowers perfume the air around. Bees and other insects visit the basswood continually during this season—hence one of its names, beetree—even in the rain, and indeed its leaves do serve to protect the flowers from bad weather. Basswood honey, with its delicious flavour, is highly appreciated.

In North America, there are several species of basswood, sometimes quite difficult to distinguish. Many specimens interbreed, producing natural hybrids with intermediate characteristics; classification thus becomes a challenge. In Canada, there is only one indigenous species.

The generic name *Tilia* is the Latin name, probably deriving from the Greek *ptilon* (wing), in reference to the large floral bract. In French, the word *tille*, or *teille*, is derived from the Latin name for the bark of the Basswood, it also applies to other fibre-yielding plants such as flax and hemp. It designates the inner bark (phloem), used to make rope, matting and fibre. Jute belongs to the same family as the basswood. The latter takes its name from the word bass, or bast, which, like the word *teille*, refers to the phloem.

The Indians and early settlers made strong rope by separating the fibres of the stem or bark after soaking it in water. They also used these fibres to make nets, mats, shoes and clothing. The name whitewood refers to the colour of the wood; the name spoonwood comes from the utensils made from it. The Americans call this tree basswood in a forest context and linden in horticulture. The names linden and lime probably derive from the Anglo-Saxon word *linde*. *Linde* is the common name in both German and Dutch.

The American basswood is often found on the edge of streams and lakes and in maple-dominated stands in association with yellow birch,

American beech, ash, walnut and hickory. It reproduces by seeds, which take two years to germinate. Once established, the young seedlings are highly shade-tolerant. When cut back to a stump, American basswood sends up suckers from the base, giving it a characteristic clump-like appearance.

The wood is one of the lightest and softest, but is nevertheless very strong. Because of these qualities it is an excellent wood for turning and carving. The Indians carved ritual masks in the sapwood of a living tree, then tore them off the tree to dry the other side. If the tree survived, the mask was considered to have supernatural properties. Like white spruce and elms, American basswood is odourless and bland-tasting, making an excellent material in which to preserve or store foodstuffs. Our grandparents' bread bins and butter coolers were made of basswood. It is still used today in the pulp and paper industry, in cabinetmaking, and in the manufacture of interior trim, musical instruments, measuring sticks and plywood.

Linden tea, well-known in North America and Europe, has sedative, antispasmodic and sweat-inducing properties. A bath to which linden flowers are added, followed by an infusion made from the flowers, will alleviate a cold, and in particular it will provide a good night of restful sleep. All species of linden or basswood have the same virtues. In addition, the flowers are used in beauty products and bath products.

Its fragrant flowers, delicate shape, handsome foliage and favourable response to pruning make this a fine ornamental or shade tree. A species recommended by landscape designers is the European or small-leaved lime (*Tilia cordata* P. Mill.). It is the dried flowers of the latter that are used commercially. It can be recognized by its roundish and much smaller leaves (5 cm in diameter), with their symmetrical base, although, like the native species, it may also have heart-shaped leaves, as its specific name *cordata* indicates.

412

G 732b/G 733b

Hackberry

Bastard-elm, common or
northern hackberry, nettletree,
sugarberry

Micocoulier occidental, bois
connu, bois inconnu,
micocoulier de Virginie,
micocoulier d'Amérique

Celtis occidentalis L.

Elm family (Ulmaceae)

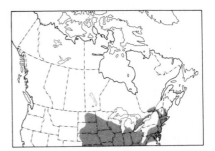

Rare in Quebec and Manitoba

Distribution
Deciduous Forest Region and part of Great Lakes-St Lawrence Forest
Region.

Distinctive features
Leaves. 6-9 cm long; rough above, hairy on lateral veins beneath;
blade often not indented at base; 3 prominent veins, with the others
forming intricate network. **Fruit.** Edible drupe with sweet-tasting
flesh, dark purple; ovoid, single on stalk; stone-pitted like a golf ball;
maturing September to October. **Twigs.** Chambered pith, as on
walnut trees. **Bark.** Greyish brown, corky and warty; thin; prominent
corky ridges. **Size.** Height 12-18 m, diameter 30-60 cm.

The early French settlers, not recognizing this tree, gave it the name
Bois inconnu (unknown wood). It is mentioned in the writings of the
botanist and traveller, André Michaud (1746-1802). The generic name
Celtis was given by Carl Linnaeus (1707-1778), the Swedish naturalist
and founder of the system of binomial nomenclature; it derives from
the word *celthis*, used by Pliny to designate a species of lotus with
sweet fruit. The specific name *occidentalis* means of the west. At first
glance this tree may be taken for an elm because of the appearance of
its leaf, hence its common name bastard-elm. The name sugarberry
refers to its sweet-tasting, edible fruit.
   A tree most often found at the edge of streams and lakes, it has a
fruit resembling a cherry, and the Irish dubbed it hagberry, a name
they commonly used for certain cherries. This name is probably the
origin of the present name hackberry. It is also called nettletree,
because its leaves resemble those of the herbaceous Canada nettle.
   A fungus disease, combined with the actions of mites, gives this tree
an odd and striking growth formation known as witch's broom; an
abnormal proliferation of buds and twigs on the trunk and main
branches.
   Formerly the most abundant of all trees on Ile Sainte-Hélène in
Montreal, the hackberry is now sparsely distributed throughout its
range. Its light yellow wood, heavy and weak, has no commercial
value. French settlers in Illinois extracted a substance from it, used in
treating jaundice. It is very easy to transplant and readily sends up
suckers after cutting or a fire. Some varieties of hackberry are used as
an ornamental in parks and small gardens. Various birds feed on its
sweet fruit, thereby greatly helping to spread the species.
   In the extreme southern part of Ontario grows a shrubby species
rare in Canada: the dwarf hackberry (*Celtis tenuifolia* Nutt.). Long

considered to be a variety of *Celtis occidentalis*, it is a shrub 1-4 m in height, with almost symmetrical oval leaves and brownish-orange fruit. Since 1974 it has been recognized as a separate species.

G 752
Paper Birch (*see* G 552d)

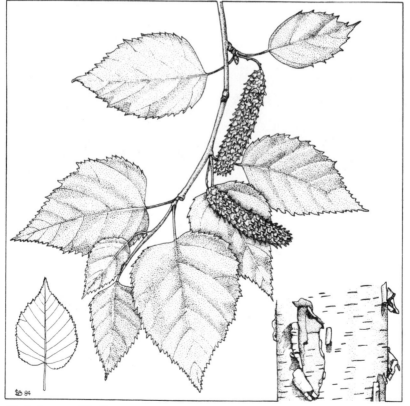

Betula cordifolia

416

G 852a

Grey Birch

Fire birch, gray birch, old field
birch, swamp birch, water birch,
white birch, wire birch

Bouleau gris, bouleau à feuilles
de peuplier, bouleau rouge

Betula populifolia Marsh.

Birch family (Betulaceae)

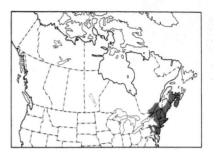

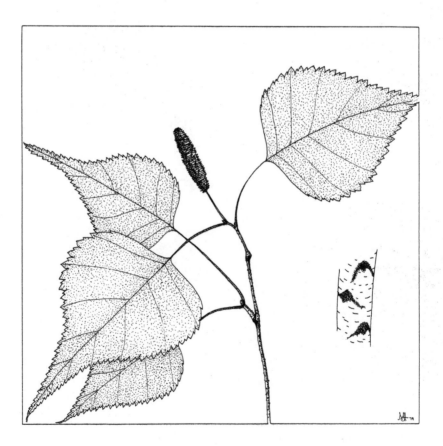

Distribution
Acadian Forest Region and parts of Great Lakes-St Lawrence Forest Region.

Distinctive features
Leaves. 7-11 cm long; fewer than 9 pairs of lateral veins, with long pointed tip; tremble in the slightest breeze. **Fruit.** "Cone", cylindrical and hanging; 2-3 cm long. **Twigs.** Somewhat resinous; speckled with glands; buds are gummy. **Bark.** Thin, chalky white, with triangular black patches below bases of branches; does not peel off in layers like bark of paper birch. **Size.** Small tree. Height 4-8 m, diameter 10-15 cm.

The grey birch, a light-loving pioneer species, grows very well on dry, sandy soils. It is considered a nuisance tree because it multiplies quickly, either by seed or by shoots from the base. It readily invades fallow, exhausted or abandoned fields—hence its common name old field birch—as well as burned-over or clearcut areas, where it frequently forms pure stands. It often grows along fences and on roadsides. As it rarely survives for more than 50 years, it is quickly replaced by other, more shade tolerant species. Like the hawthorn and the paper birch, the grey birch (favoured by human activity and the increasing number of sites conducive to its spread) is extending its range.

Its generic name *Betula* is the Latin name for birch, and is derived from the Celtic word *betu* (tree). Its specific name *populifolia* (with leaves like Populus) refers to the resemblance between its thin-stalked leaves and those of the trembling aspen, which tremble in the slightest breeze. The name grey birch refers to the chalky-white colour of the bark.

At first glance easy to confuse with the paper birch, it can be distinguished by its bark, which does not peel, its more prominent triangular black patches, its twigs speckled with glands, and its gummy buds.

The small size of the grey birch limits its economic value. It is sometimes planted in clumps as an ornamental. It may also be used as a "nurse tree": to form a cover under which a pine plantation can become established; it must, however, be cut very early, for later it will hinder the growth of pines. Ruffed grouse, squirrels, chipmunks and small rodents eat its seeds, and white-tailed deer nibble its leaves and twigs in late winter and early spring.

G 852b

Alaska Birch
Alaska paper birch

Bouleau d'Alaska

Betula neoalaskana Sarg.

Birch family (Betulaceae)

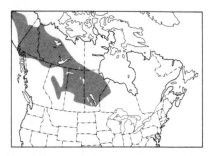

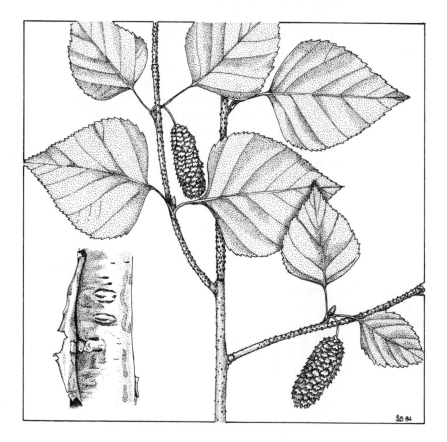

Distribution
Throughout the western area of the Boreal Forest Region.

Distinctive features
Leaves. 2-7 cm long; fewer than 7 pairs of lateral veins; no teeth near base of blade. **Fruit.** "Cone", cylindrical and hanging; 2-3 cm long. **Twigs.** Covered with multitude of resin glands that may entirely conceal twig surface. **Bark.** Thin, reddish brown, becoming creamy white; peels off in papery layers but not as freely as paper birch. **Size.** Small tree. Height 7-15 m, diameter 10-15 cm.

The Alaska Birch is basically a northern species. Its bark resembles that of the paper birch, of which species some consider it to be a variety. Still poorly understood, it appears to interbreed with the paper birch to produce specimens that are a mixture of the two, making identification difficult.

It is too small to be exploited commercially.

G 852c

European White Birch

European birch, European
weeping birch, silver birch

Bouleau blanc d'Europe,
bouleau verruqueux, bouleau
commun, bouleau pleureur

Betula pendula Roth
   syn. *Betula verrucosa* Ehrh.

Birch family (Betulaceae)

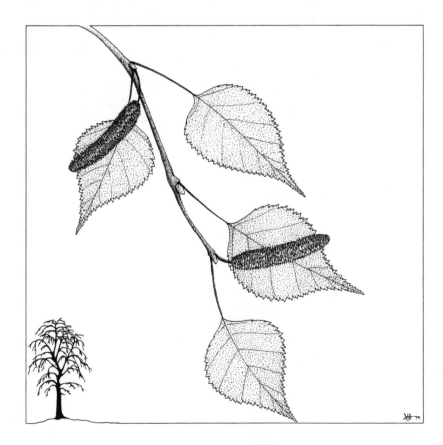

Distribution
Native to Europe, frequently used as an ornamental in Canada and the United States.

Distinctive features
Leaves. Small, 3-7 cm long, with long drawn-out tip; 6-9 pairs of lateral veins. **Fruit.** "Cone", cylindrical and hanging; 2-3 cm long. **Twigs.** Spindly, hanging, verrucose; covered with tiny resin glands. **Bark.** Thin, smooth, red-brown becoming pinkish white; covered with pale grey, horizontal lenticels and a scattering of black patches, later cracking and peeling off in papery sheets as with paper birch. **Size.** Rarely over 15 m in height and 30 cm in diameter.

This tree owes both its specific name (*pendula*) and its popular name (weeping birch) to the drooping appearance of its young twigs. Its French name, *bouleau verruqueux*, denotes the presence of small, whitish resin glands (*verrucosa*) on its twigs. The generic name *Betula* is the Latin name for birch and comes from the Celtic word *betu* (tree).

Its yellowish-white wood is a good fuel and, being durable, it can be used for making skis, clogs, turned objects and cellulose. The sweet-tasting sap, which flows in the spring, can be used to make a kind of beer or vinegar.

The European white birch is a light-loving species. In Europe it is often used to form a cover to help establish a plantation of beech or other species. Some Europeans know it as "the nephritic tree", since a diuretic tea made from its leaves was used to cure infections of the urinary tract and dissolve kidney stones. The resin glands are still harvested for use in a hair lotion.

Frequently used to embellish parks, avenues and small gardens, this tree is more graceful than the paper birch and makes an attractive display whether as a single specimen or in a group. The cultivars most often planted are "*Fastigiata*", which is slender like the Lombardy poplar, "*Pupurea*", with its curly, twisted leaves, and "*Gracilis*", one of the most beautiful of cultivars, with laciniate leaves and delicate, drooping twigs. Like most birches, the European white birch is vulnerable to attack by the birch leafminer.

G 862a

Eastern Cottonwood

Big cottonwood, common cottonwood, cottontree, necklace poplar, plains cottonwood

Peuplier deltoïde, liard, cotonnier, peuplier à feuilles deltoïdes, peuplier du Canada

Populus deltoides Bartr. ex Marsh.

Willow family (Salicaceae)

Distribution
Deciduous Forest Region, southern and eastern parts of Great Lakes-St Lawrence Forest Region.

Distinctive features
Leaves. 7-17 cm long; flattened petiole or leaf stalk; often with glands at base of blade. **Twigs.** Stout, yellowish green; lateral buds stand out from twig. **Bark.** Smooth and yellowish grey at first, later becoming deeply furrowed. **Size.** Height 20-30 m, diameter 60-120 cm.

The specific name of this tree, *deltoides*, delta (the Greek letter), refers to the shape of the leaf, which resembles an equilateral triangle with rounded corners. The generic name *Populus* (people) dates back to the time when these trees were planted in public squares reserved for the people. The name cottonwood refers to the resemblance of the fruit (covered with silky white hairs) to that of the cotton plant.

One of Canada's most attractive trees, and one of the largest poplars (up to 7 metres in circumference at the base), the eastern cottonwood can be easily recognized by its large branches forming an angle of roughly 45 degrees with the trunk. It is a very fast-growing species that occurs naturally on the banks of streams and lakes and on alluvial plains. Its lightweight seeds require considerable moisture throughout the germination period. The tree, however, grows very well when planted in much drier locations. A bud-bearing twig or branch will take root when planted in moist soil.

Early settlers to the Prairies brought the eastern cottonwood with them. Today it may be found almost anywhere there is a small stream. The plains cottonwood (*Populus sargentii* Dode), classified as a separate species by some and as a subspecies of the eastern cottonwood (ssp. *monilifera* (Ait.) Ecknwalder) by others, is also found on the Prairies.

The eastern cottonwood was introduced into Europe during the eighteenth century, and interbreeding with the black poplar (*Populus nigra* L.) produced numerous hybrids. These male hybrids (*Populus* × *canadensis* Moench) are called Carolina poplar: fast-growing trees, they are widely planted along streets and increasingly in plantations; in general appearance and the shape of their leaves they resemble the eastern cottonwood, whereas their buds and twigs resemble those of the lombardy poplar.

The protein-rich leaves of the poplar have a greater amino-acid content than wheat, corn, rice and barley. They are popular with cattle and sheep. A concentrate made from them is as nourishing as meat but can be produced faster and more cheaply. Some believe that the hybrid poplar will become a food source for humans and farm animals, as well as a source of energy (methanol). Tests are currently being conducted on the use of ground poplar foliage as chicken feed. One day it may be possible to enter a chic restaurant and order a dish based on protein obtained from poplar leaves, and, after the meal, fill the tank of one's car with a mixture of gasoline and methanol derived from poplar wood! Poplar wood will also be used increasingly as construction timber, and for chipboard and plywood.

G 862b

Lombardy Poplar

Peuplier de Lombardie, peuplier
d'Italie, peuplier noir d'Italie

Populus nigra var. *italica* Du Roi

Willow family (Salicaceae)

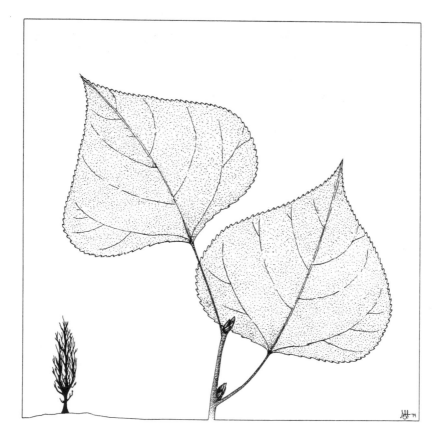

Distribution
Origin uncertain; believed to be a variety of the black poplar originating in the province of Lombardy, Italy. Widely planted as an ornamental in North America.

Distinctive features
A pyramidal crown in a narrow column, with almost vertical branches. **Leaves.** 7-12 cm long; flattened petiole or leaf stalk almost as long as leaf blade; absence of glands at base of blade. **Twigs.** Shiny, yellowish brown; buds flat against twigs. **Size.** Height 10-20 m, diameter 30-60 cm.

This large, narrow tree has branches almost parallel to its very straight trunk. It cannot be confused with any other tree. It is generally used as an ornamental, shade tree or a windbreak. Such uses are inappropriate, however, because it is a fragile tree, vulnerable to disease and insects, and lives only 15-20 years. The inside branches die quickly, owing to a lack of air circulation and light, and are easily damaged by hail and ice. This cultivar, or clone, of the black poplar occurs only as a male tree and thus can only be propagated by vegetative multiplication, cuttings, or suckers occurring naturally.

In Greek mythology, Phaëthon, son of Helios, god of the sun, was one day allowed, after receiving much advice, to drive his father's chariot. Because of his inexperience he was frightened and, when he beheld the monster Scorpion, lost control of the chariot, causing the world to catch fire. Earth complained to Zeus, who then struck Phaëthon with a thunderbolt and hurled him into the river Po, in Italy. Phaëthon's three sisters wept so much that they were changed into poplars standing along the river bank.

G 932a

American Basswood (*see* G 732a)

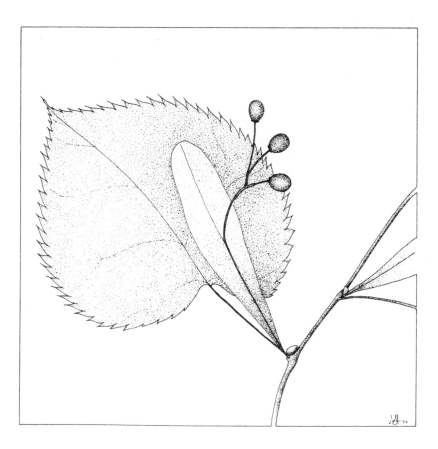

G 932b

Hackberry (*see* G 732b)

G 952a

American Elm

Elm, grey elm, soft elm, swamp elm, water elm, white elm

Orme d'Amérique, orme, orme blanc

Ulmus americana L.

Elm family (Ulmaceae)

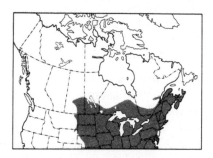

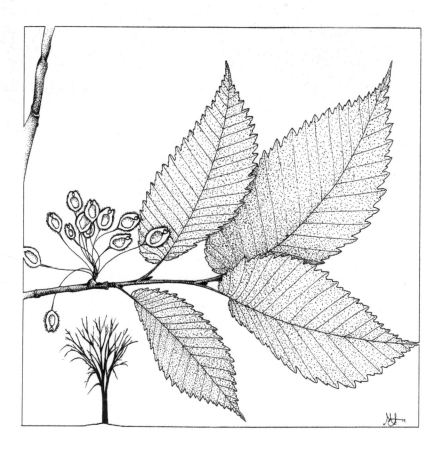

Distribution
Acadian, Great Lakes-St Lawrence, Deciduous and Boreal forest regions.

Distinctive features
Leaves. 10-15 cm long; slightly rough above; lateral veins rarely fork. **Twigs.** Hairless or slightly hairy; not corky; bud almost hairless, lying close to the twig. **Fruit.** Oval samara, fringed with hairs, in clusters; ripens and falls when leaves appear. **Bark.** Ashen grey, with deep intersecting ridges, or often scaly; when cut, reveals thin, paler layers alternating with thicker, reddish brown layers. **Shape.** Fan-shaped. **Size.** Height 18-24 m, diameter 60-80 cm.

The American elm is one of the most majestic trees, owing to the delicate, drooping branches that give it the appearance of a huge fountain. The European elms were long honoured by the Greeks, who considered them to be dream trees, dedicated to the goddess of sleep.

Because they are fast-growing and long-lived, American elms were planted as shade trees or as ornamentals in parks and along roads. Most of them have been destroyed by an extremely serious disease: Dutch elm disease, so named because the earliest research on the disease was carried out by the Dutch.

In the last century, the disease was unknown. It first appeared in the Netherlands and northern France in 1917. The infection was detected for the first time in North America in 1930, in Ohio, and was probably introduced via contaminated logs imported for the making of plywood. As with chestnut blight and white pine blister rust, Dutch elm disease spread very quickly in North America. Its first inroad into Canada was in 1944, at Saint-Ours, Quebec. This time the disease was transmitted by way of wooden crates. In less than 15 years, it destroyed from 600 000 to 700 000 trees. Newfoundland was spared until 1969, but today the disease extends from the Atlantic to southeastern Manitoba.

It consists of a fungus infection that spreads by spores disseminated by an insect, the elm beetle, a parasitic insect that breeds under elm bark. The infection kills trees by preventing the functioning of the system of water-carrying tissues. This accounts for the withering and yellowing of the leaves that lead to premature leaf drop. It is often difficult to identify the disease with certainty, especially at the end of the summer; furthermore, several other elm diseases have the same symptoms. Unfortunately, the treatments are not only quite limited but also very costly.

While the white elm is not currently an endangered species, or even a rare species in Canada, its survival may eventually be threatened by the disease. Its future depends on disease prevention, more effective treatments, and research to develop resistant varieties.

The American elm is found in wet places such as the edges of rivers, lakes and creeks (hence the common names water and swamp elm), but prefers rich soils such as occur on alluvial plains. The generic name *Ulmus* is the Latin name for elm. The specific name *Americana* serves to distinguish this species from the European white elm (*Ulmus laevis* Pall). The term white in the common name refers to the ashen-grey colour of the bark.

The Indians were well acquainted with this useful tree. From its bark (as with that of the red elm) they could, in less than a day, make a very solid emergency canoe. They fashioned strong rope from strips of the bark, which they used to secure the structure of their houses, subsequently covering them with more bark. They also used the bark to make various containers, including those used for gathering maple sap. The bark has various medicinal properties. It was used in the preparation of infusions, decoctions and poultices for treating bad coughs, influenza, dysentery, eye infections and diarrhea. **Under no circumstances must the bark be removed from the living tree**, as this will disfigure or even **kill it.**

Early settlers also used strips of American elm bark, soaked in water, to cane chair seats. They used the wood, which is heavy, hard and strong, to make the hubs and spokes of cart wheels, tool handles and other objects requiring resistant material. Odourless and mild tasting, it was used to make cheese containers and fruit and vegetable crates, and in slack cooperage, where the barrels do not have to be water-tight.

Today it is mainly used for making furniture and panelling and as pulpwood. It tends to be difficult to split, so is little used as firewood. Because it keeps well under water, it is used in maritime construction and in wharves. Even though vulnerable to Dutch elm disease, the tree is still planted as an ornamental.

G 952b

Rock Elm
Cork elm, winged elm

Orme liège, orme à grappes,
orme de Thomas

Ulmus thomasii Sarg.

Elm family (Ulmaceae)

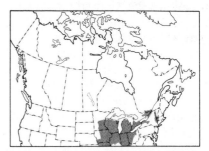

Rare in Quebec

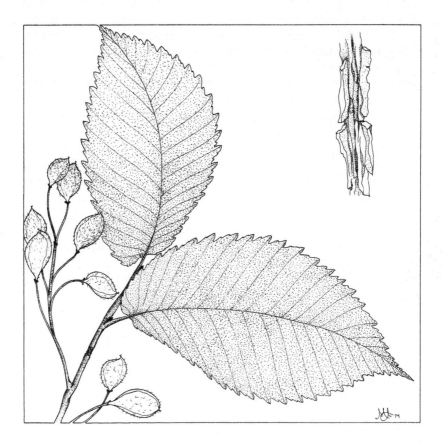

Distribution
Deciduous Forest Region, central portion of Great Lakes-St Lawrence Forest Region.

Distinctive features
Leaves. 5-15 cm long; smooth, dark green and shiny above; many closely-spaced lateral veins that rarely fork. **Twigs.** Hairy, becoming strongly ridged with corky bark after a year or two; buds finely pubescent, pointing away from twig. **Fruit.** Samara; oval, in clusters; hairy all over; maturing in spring. **Bark.** Ashen grey, similar to that of American elm. **Shape.** Undivided trunk. **Size.** Height 15-20 m, diameter 60-80 cm.

This tree grows on limestone ridges, on cliff tops, bordering rivers, and in rocky, dry, mountainous locations. In shape it bears no resemblance to any other native elm species, looking much more like an ash. Its single, undivided trunk is supported by numerous, almost horizontal branches.

The generic name *Ulmus* was given by the Romans. The specific name *thomasii*, from the name Thomas, was given in honour of David Thomas (1776-1859), an American civil engineer and horticulturist. The corky ridges that appear on the twigs and branchlets are the origin of the name cork elm; the French name *orme à grappes* (cluster elm) refers to the arrangement of the flowers.

The wood is hard, strong, resistant, close-grained and difficult to split—hence the name rock elm—and is in fact the most solid of all the American species. In the nineteenth century the Americans exported this wood to England for use in shipbuilding, and it was used for automobile chassis and ploughing implements before being replaced by steel.

In addition to being used for the same purposes as the wood of other elms, the wood of the rock elm is used to make piano frames and all types of tool handles. Being highly flexible, it is the main wood used in the manufacture of hockey sticks.

The fruit of all elms is an important food source for birds and for squirrels, chipmunks and other small rodents. Beavers and muskrats sometimes eat its bark.

Like other elms, the rock elm is vulnerable to Dutch elm disease.

434

G 952c

Red Elm
Budded elm, moose elm,
slippery-barked elm, slippery
elm, soft elm, sweet elm

Orme rouge, orme gras, orme
roux

Ulmus rubra Mühl.
  syn: *Ulmus fulva* Michx.

Elm family (Ulmaceae)

Distribution
Deciduous Forest Region and southern portion of the Great Lakes-St Lawrence Region.

Distinctive features
Leaves. 8-16 cm long; covered with hairs above and beneath: very rough above, sufficiently abrasive when dry to scratch surface of a fingernail; lateral veins often forked; aromatic. **Twigs.** Hairy, not corky; buds dark brown, covered with thick coat of reddish-brown hairs. **Fruit.** Samara, almost circular; only hairy over the seed; matures in spring. **Bark.** Reddish brown, shallowly furrowed, scaly; when cut reveals uniform dark brown colour rather than alternating light and dark colours seen in American elm and rock elm; inner bark gluey or slippery. **Size.** Height 15-22 m, diameter 30-50 cm.

Similar in appearance to the American elm but less elegant, the red elm can be distinguished by its longer trunk and its ascending, rather than drooping, branches. The generic name *Ulmus* is the Latin name for elm, and the specific name *rubra* (red) describes the bark and buds, which are reddish brown. The whitish, aromatic inner bark is easily distinguishable from that of American elm and rock elm in that it is quite slippery to the touch and gluey (hence the names slippery elm and slippery-barked elm). The wood, although marketed as American elm and used for the same purposes, is weaker than the wood of both the American elm and the rock elm, and for this reason is sometimes called soft elm. It grows in habitats similar to those of the American elm, but never forms pure stands and seems to prefer lime soils.

As with the American elm, but to a lesser extent, a number of fine specimens fall victim each year to Dutch elm disease (*see* American elm). The medicinal properties of this tree, similar to those of the American elm, were well known to the coureurs de bois, who chewed the gluey inner bark in order to quench or lessen their thirst. Still commercially available is a powder prepared from the inner bark, which has been boiled in water, then dried and ground. An infusion made from this powder was used as a highly effective remedy for fever, sore throat and various urinary problems. The bark was used to make poultices.

G 962

Witch-hazel

Snapping-hazel, spotted-alder,
striped-alder, winterbloom

Hamamélis de Virginie, café du
diable

Hamamelis virginiana L.
  syn. *Hamamelis macrophylla* Pursh.

Witch-hazel family (Hamamelidaceae)

Rare in Quebec and
P.E.I.

Distribution

Deciduous Forest Region and scattered locations in the Acadian Forest Region and in Great Lakes-St Lawrence Region.

Distinctive features

Leaves. 7-15 cm long; slightly aromatic. **Flowers.** 4 golden yellow petals, quite showy, strap-like; appear in autumn, before or just after leaves have fallen. **Fruit.** Capsules containing 2 black seeds 7-10 mm long. **Twigs.** Zigzag; yellowish; reddish-brown buds are hairy and have no scales. **Bark.** Smooth, mottled, with lenticels. **Size.** A large shrub or small tree. Height 4-8 m, diameter 10-15 cm.

The witch-hazel's intriguing common name suggests special powers. Water diviners used its forked branches to locate underground springs or mineral deposits. The genus *Hamamelis* comes from the Greek name for the medlar (*Mespilus germanica* L.), a tree from the rose family or some similar tree with apple-like fruit, and the species name *virginiana* is derived from the state Virginia.

This species produces lovely fragrant yellow flowers that blossom just before or immediately after the tree drops its leaves. Sometimes the flowers do not appear until snow covers the ground, a peculiarity that has given rise to its alternate name, winterbloom. No other Canadian tree or shrub blooms in the autumn.

The flowers develop into fruit that ripens the following autumn. As the fruit capsule dries, it splits, shooting two shiny, black seeds up to 12 m from the plant. The name snapping-hazel refers to this characteristic. The empty capsules remain on the tree throughout winter, making it easy to identify this species.

The leaves and fruit resemble those of a true hazel shrub, hence the common names witch-hazel and snapping-hazel. Spotted-alder and striped-alder refer to the smooth, pale brown or greyish bark, which bears horizontal markings (lenticels) and resembles alder bark.

Witch-hazel can be found in moist, shaded areas such as ravines, but it thrives in dry, sandy soil in clearings, thickets and forests.

Its wood is of no commercial use, but a volatile oil, sold as witch-hazel oil, is extracted from the leaves, bark and twigs. This oil has several medicinal properties; it can be used as an astringent, a sedative and to stop bleeding. It is an ingredient in after-shave and rubbing lotions. It is also used to soothe insect bites, burns, and itching caused by poison ivy.

List of Rare Trees of Canada

N.B. The species must be rare in all provinces and territories of its distribution in order to be part of this list.

Ohio buckeye	*Aesculus glabra*
Cherry birch	*Betula lenta*
Pignut hickory	*Carya glabra*
Big shellbark hickory	*Carya laciniosa*
American chestnut	*Castanea dentata*
Redbud	*Cercis canadensis*
Oregon ash	*Fraxinus latifolia*
Blue ash	*Fraxinus quadrangulata*
Honey-locust	*Gleditsia triacanthos*
Kentucky coffee tree	*Gymnocladus dioicus*
Cucumbertree	*Magnolia acuminata*
Black tupelo	*Nyssa sylvatica*
Pitch pine	*Pinus rigida*
Hoptree	*Ptelea trifoliata*
Northern pin oak	*Quercus ellipsoidalis*
Pin oak	*Quercus palustris*
Shumard oak	*Quercus shumardii*
Northwest willow	*Salix sessilifolia*

List of Rare Trees of Canada by Province

N.B.: The lists of rare plants for Prince Edward Island, Northwest Territories and Newfoundland are only temporary. There are no rare trees in the Yukon.

Northwest Territories

Alpine fir	*Abies lasiocarpa*
Choke cherry	*Prunus virginiana*
Lodgepole pine	*Pinus contorta* var. *latifolia*
Pin cherry	*Prunus pensylvanica*
Pussy willow	*Salix discolor*
Slender willow	*Salix petiolaris*

Newfoundland

Alternate-leaved dogwood	*Cornus alternifolia*
Black ash	*Fraxinus nigra*
Red pine	*Pinus resinosa*

Prince Edward Island

White ash	*Fraxinus americana*
Witch-hazel	*Hamamelis virginiana*
Jack pine	*Pinus banksiana*
Red pine	*Pinus resinosa*

New Brunswick

Nannyberry	*Viburnum lentago*

Nova Scotia

Northern red ash	*Fraxinus pennsylvanica* var. *austini*
Eastern arborvitae	*Thuja occidentalis*

Quebec

Black maple	*Acer nigrum*
Hackberry	*Celtis occidentalis*
Witch-hazel	*Hamamelis virginiana*

440

Pitch pine	*Pinus rigida*
White oak	*Quercus alba*
Swamp white oak	*Quercus bicolor*
Poison sumac	*Rhus vernix*
Rock elm	*Ulmus thomasii*

Ontario

Ohio buckeye	*Aesculus glabra*
Pawpaw	*Asimina triloba*
Cherry birch	*Betula lenta*
Pignut hickory	*Carya glabra*
Big shellbark hickory	*Carya laciniosa*
American chestnut	*Castanea dentata*
Redbud	*Cercis canadensis*
Blue ash	*Fraxinus quadrangulata*
Honey-locust	*Gleditsia triacanthos*
Kentucky coffee tree	*Gymnocladus dioicus*
Tuliptree	*Liriodendron tulipifera*
Cucumbertree	*Magnolia acuminata*
Red mulberry	*Morus rubra*
Black tupelo	*Nyssa sylvatica*
Hoptree	*Ptelea trifoliata*
Pitch pine	*Pinus rigida*
Northern pin oak	*Quercus ellipsoidalis*
Pin oak	*Quercus palustris*
Shumard oak	*Quercus shumardii*
Shrubby willow	*Salix arbusculoides*

Manitoba

Hackberry	*Celtis occidentalis*
American hop-hornbeam	*Ostrya virginiana*
Red pine	*Pinus resinosa*
Eastern white pine	*Pinus strobus*
Large-toothed aspen	*Populus grandidentata*

Saskatchewan

Narrowleaf cottonwood	*Populus angustifolia*
Nannyberry	*Viburnum lentago*

Alberta

Western larch	*Larix occidentalis*
Western yew	*Taxus brevifolia*

Western white pine	*Pinus monticola*
Western hemlock	*Tsuga heterophylla*
Alaska willow	*Salix alaxensis*
Sitka willow	*Salix sitchensis*

British Columbia

Oregon ash	*Fraxinus latifolia*
Jack pine	*Pinus banksiana*
Limber pine	*Pinus flexilis*
Northwest willow	*Salix sessilifolia*

List of Trees by Family

I. Conifers or Gymnosperms
  A. Yew family (Taxaceae)

Western yew	C 211 i

  B. Cypress family (Cupressaceae)

Eastern arborvitae	A 111 a
Giant arborvitae	A 111 b
Nootka false cypress	A 111 c
Red juniper	A 111 d
Rocky Mountain juniper	A 111 e

  C. Pine family (Pinaceae)

Alpine fir	C 211 b
Amabilis fir	C 211 c
Balsam fir	C 211 a
Grand fir	C 211 d
Douglas fir	C 211 h
Eastern hemlock	C 211 e
Mountain hemlock	C 211 g
Western hemlock	C 211 f
Alpine larch	B 211 c
Eastern larch	B 211 a
Western larch	B 211 b
Jack pine	B 211 k
Limber pine	B 211 g
Lodgepole pine	B 211 l
Pitch pine	B 211 h
Ponderosa pine	B 211 i
Red pine	B 211 j
* Scots pine	B 211 m
Eastern white pine	B 211 d
Western white pine	B 211 e
Whitebark pine	B 211 f
Black spruce	C 211 l
* Blue spruce	C 211 o
Engelmann spruce	C 211 k
* Norway spruce	C 211 p
Red spruce	C 211 m

	Sitka spruce	C 211 n
	White spruce	C 211 j

II. Deciduous Trees or Angiosperms
  A. Willow family (Salicaceae)

	Large-toothed aspen	G 532 b
	Trembling aspen	G 662
	Eastern cottonwood	G 862 a
	Narrowleaf cottonwood	G 442 c
*	Lombardy poplar	G 862 b
	Balsam poplar	G 562 a
	Western balsam poplar	G 562 b
*	European white poplar	G 672 a/G 682 a
	Alaska willow	G 522 f
	Bebb's willow	G 522 a
	Black willow	G 442 d
*	Crack willow	G 442 n
	Heart-leaved willow	G 442 h
	Hooker willow	G 522 e
	Pacific willow	G 442 g
	Peachleaf willow	G 442 e
	Pussy willow	G 522 b
	Sandbar willow	G 442 k
	Scouler willow	G 522 d
	Shining willow	G 442 f
	Shrubby willow	G 442 i
	Silky willow	G 422
	Slender willow	G 442 j
	Sitka willow	G 522 c
*	Weeping willow	G 442 l
*	White willow	G 442 m

  B. Walnut family (Juglandaceae)

Black walnut	F 432 e/F 442 e
Bitternut hickory	F 432 f/F 442 f
Butternut	F 432 d/F 442 d
Mockernut hickory	F 432 g/F 442 g
Pignut hickory	F 542 c
Shagbark hickory	F 542 a
Big shellbark hickory	F 542 b

  C. Birch family (Betulaceae)

Sitka alder	G 552 c
Red alder	G 562 d
Speckled alder	G 552 b
Alaska birch	G 852 b

	Grey birch	G 852 a
	Paper birch	G 552 d
*	European white birch	G 852 c
	Yellow birch	G 552 e
	Western birch	G 552 f
	American hornbeam	G 552 h
	American hop-hornbeam	G 552 g
D.	Beech family (Fagaceae)	
	American beech	G 532 a
	American chestnut	G 432 a
	Black oak	G 582 b
	Bur oak	G 572 a
	Chinquapin oak	G 432 b
	Garry oak	G 572 c
	Northern pin oak	G 582 d
	Pin oak	G 582 c
	Red oak	G 582 a
	Shumard oak	G 582 e
	Swamp white oak	G 572 d
	White oak	G 572 b
E.	Elm family (Ulmaceae)	
	Red elm	G 952 c
	Rock elm	G 952 b
	American elm	G 952 a
	Hackberry	G 732 b/G 733 b
F.	Mulberry family (Moraceae)	
	Red mulberry	G 533
G.	Magnolia family (Magnoliaceae)	
	Cucumbertree	G 522 k
	Tuliptree	G 672 b/G 682 b
H.	Custard-apple family (Annonaceae)	
	Pawpaw	G 522 i
I.	Laurel family (Lauraceae)	
	Sassafras	G 522 l
J.	Witch-hazel family (Hamamelidaceae)	
	Witch-hazel	G 962
K.	Plane family (Platanaceae)	
	Sycamore	G 683 a
L.	Rose family (Rosaceae)	
*	Common apple	G 542 d
	Bitter cherry	G 542 b
	Black cherry	G 442 a

Choke cherry	G 542 a
Pin cherry	G 442 b
Pacific crab apple	G 532 d
Wild crab apple	G 532 c
Hawthorn	G 552 a
American mountain-ash	F 432 b/F 442 b
Showy mountain-ash	F 432 c/F 442 c
Canada plum	G 562 c
Wild plum	G 542 e
Serviceberry	G 542 c

M. Pea family (Leguminosae)

Kentucky coffee tree	F 522 b
* Black locust	F 522 c
Honey-locust	F 522 a
Redbud	G 623

N. Citrus family (Rutaceae)

Hoptree	F 522 d

O. Quassia family (Simaroubaceae)

* Ailanthus	F 422

P. Cashew family (Anacardiaceae)

Poison sumac	F 522 e
Staghorn sumac	F 432 a/F 442 a

Q. Maple family (Aceraceae)

Bigleaf maple	E 683 c
Black maple	E 683 b
Douglas maple	E 693 e
Manitoba maple	D 572
Mountain maple	E 693 d
* Norway maple	E 683 d
Red maple	E 693 a
Silver maple	E 693 b
Striped maple	E 693 c
Sugar maple	E 683 a
Vine maple	E 693 f

R. Horsechestnut family (Hippocastanaceae)

* Horsechestnut	D 532

S. Buckthorn family (Rhamnaceae)

Cascara	G 542 f

T. Linden family (Tiliaceae)

American basswood	G 732 a/G 733 a

U. Nyssa family (Nyssaceae)

Black tupelo	G 522 j

V. Dogwood family (Cornaceae)
    Alternate-leaved dogwood   G 522 g
    Eastern flowering dogwood   E 522 a
    Western flowering dogwood   E 522 b
W. Heath family (Ericaceae)
    Arbutus   G 522 h
X. Olive family (Oleaceae)
    Black ash   D 542 b
    Blue ash   D 542 a
  * European ash   D 542 c
    Red ash   D 522 b
    White ash   D 522 a
Y. Bignonia family (Bignoniaceae)
  * Northern catalpa   E 723
Z. Honeysuckle family (Caprifoliaceae)
    Blue elder   D 432
    Nannyberry   E 542 a

Note: * = species that have been introduced

Bibliography

Abbreviations

NMC   National Museums of Canada
NMNS National Museums of Natural Sciences

Agriculture Québec. 1985. *Journée d'information sur l'acériculture; dépérissement des érablières.* Quebec.
Agriculture Québec. 1976. *Guide du botaniste amateur.* Quebec.
Anderson, J.R. 1925. *Trees and shrubs, food, medicinal, and poisonous plants of British Columbia.* B.C., Dept. of Education, Victoria.
Angier, B. 1974. *Field guide to edible wild plants.* Stackpole Books, Harrisburg.
Argus, G.W. and D.J. White. 1977. *The rare vascular plants of Ontario.* Syllogeus 14. NMNS, Ottawa.
Argus, G.W. and D.J. White. 1978. *The rare vascular plants of Alberta.* Syllogeus 17. NMNS, Ottawa.
Argus, G.W. and D.J. White. 1982-6. *Atlas of the rare vascular plants of Ontario.* Parts 1-4. NMNS, Ottawa.
Argus, G.W. 1986. Studies of the Salix lucida and Salix reticulata complexes in North America, *Can. J. Botany,* **64** (3), 541-51.
Argus, G.W. 1986. *The genus Salix (Salicaceae) in the southeastern United States.* Systematic Botany Mons 9, Amer. Soc. Plant Taxonimists. Ann Arbor.
Argus, G.W. and K.M. Pryer. 1987. Rare plants of Canada. Unpubld. NMNS, Ottawa.
Arno, S.F. 1977. *Northwest trees.* The Mountaineers, Seattle.
Assiniwi, B. 1972. *Indian recipes.* Copp Clark, Toronto.

Banfield, A.W.F. 1974. *The mammals of Canada.* University of Toronto Press, Toronto.
Barnes, Y.B., H. Warren and J.R. Warren. 1981. *Michigan trees.* University of Michigan Press, Ann Arbor.

448

Bëïgue, R. and G. Bonneau. 1979. *Les principaux insectes défoliateurs des arbres du Québec*. Ministère de l'énergie et des ressources, Service d'entomologie et de pathologie. Quebec.

Bélanger, M. 1975. *La culture de l'érablière pour la production de sucre*. Ministère des terres et forêts du Québec. Quebec.

Benedit, W.V. 1967. *Important forest insects and diseases of mutual concern to Canada, the United States, and Mexico*. Can. Dept. For. Rural Develop., Publn. 1180. Ottawa.

Benoît, P. 1975. *Noms français d'insectes au Canada*. Agriculture Québec. Quebec.

Berglund, B. and C.E. Bolsby. 1974. *The edible wild*. Pagunan Press Ltd, Toronto.

Boivin, B. 1967-72. *Flora of the prairie provinces: a handbook of the flora of the provinces of Manitoba, Saskatchewan and Alberta*. Parts 1-3, continuing Provancheria 2-4, Université Laval. Quebec.

Borror, D.J. and R.E. White. 1970. *A field guide to the insects of America, north of Mexico*. Peterson Field Guide Series, Houghton Mifflin, Boston.

Bouchard, A., D. Barabé, M. Dumais and S. Hay. 1983. *The rare vascular plants of Quebec*. Syllogeus 48. NMNS, Ottawa.

Bouchard, A. 1986. *Plantes rares de Terre-Neuve et du Labrador*. Unpubld. Jardin botanique de la ville de Montréal. Montreal.

Boudreault, M. 1983. *Guide pratique des plantes médicinales du Québec*. Editions Marcel Broquet, La Prairie, Quebec.

Braun, E.L. 1950. *Deciduous forests of eastern North America*. Blakiston, Philadelphia.

Brayshaw, T.C. 1976. *Catkin bearing plants of British Columbia*. B.C. Provincial Museum, Victoria.

Bretaudeau, J. 1981. *Le guide familier des arbres*. La Boétie. Editions des Deux Coqs d'or, Paris.

Brockman, C.F. 1968. *Trees of North America*. Golden Press, New York.

Brouk, B. 1975. *Plants consumed by man*. Academic Press, London.

Budd, A.C. 1979. *Budd's flora of the Canadian prairie provinces*. Revd and enlgd by J. Looman and K.F. Best., Research Branch, Agri. Can., Hull, Quebec.

Calder, J.A. and R.L. Taylor. 1968. *Flora of the Queen Charlotte Islands*. Part 1. Agri. Can., Research Branch, Mon. 4. Ottawa.

Canada, 1974. *Flore du Canada*. Secrétariat d'Etat. Bureau des traductions, Bulletin de terminologie 156. Ottawa.

Canada, 1975, *Douglas-fir*. (Brochure) Environment Canada, Ottawa.

Carrier, L. 1986. *Decline in Quebec's forests, assessment of the situation*. Ministère de l'Energie et des Ressources. Quebec.

Catling, P.M. 1986. *Rare vascular plants of Prince Edward Island*. Unpubld. Agri. Can., Ottawa.

Ceska, A., O. Ceska and W. Van Dieren. 1984. Oregon ash in British Columbia. *B.C. Natur.*, December (winter): **17**.

Chinery, M. 1976. *Les insectes d'Europe*. Elsevier Séguoia, Paris.

Cody, W.J. 1979. *Vascular plants of restricted range in the continental Northwest Territories, Canada*. Syllogeus 23. NMNS, Ottawa.

Cole, T.J. 1980. *A checklist of ornamental trees for Canada*. Ottawa.

Cole, T.J. 1981. *Growing trees in Canadian gardens*. Agri. Can., Ottawa.

Core, E.L. and N.P. Ammons. 1958. *Woody plants in winter*. Boxwood Press, Pacific Grove, Calif.

Couillard, L. and P. Grondin. 1983. *Les îles de Mingan, des siècles à raconter*. Gouvernement du Québec, Minstère de l'environnement. Quebec.

Craig, D.L. 1979. *La culture du sureau dans l'est du Canada*. Agri. Can., Ottawa.

Crockett, J.U. 1972. *Trees*. Time-Life Books, Alexandria, Va.

Cumming, W.A. 1979. *Hardy Fruits and ornamentals from Morden, Manitoba*. Agri. Can., Ottawa.

Darbyshire, S.J. and M.J. Oldham. 1985. Ohio buckeye, Aesculus glabra on Walpole Island, Lambton County, Ontario. *Can. Field Natur.* **99**: 370-2.

Daubenmire, R.F. 1968. *Plant communities*. Harper & Row, New York.

Daubenmire, R.F. 1974. *Plants and environment; a textbook on plant autecology*. 3rd edn. Wiley, New York.

Dawson, R. 1985. *Nature bound, pocket field quide*. Omnigraphics, Boise, Idaho.

Debot, L. 1960. *Calendrier nature*. 3rd edn. Patrimoine de l'Institut Royal des Sciences Naturelles de Belgique. Brussels.

Delisle, A. 1981. Une longuer d'avance pour le peuplier. *Québec Science* **19**, (8): 42-7.

Dept Health and Welfare Canada. 1986. *Canadian drug identification code*. 12th edn. Gov. Can., Ottawa.

Douglas, G.W., G.W. Argus, et al. 1981. *The rare vascular plants of Yukon*. Syllogeus 28. NMNS, Ottawa.

Driver, H.E. 1961. *Indians of North America*. University of Chicago Press, Chicago.

Duvigneaud, P. 1974. *La synthèse écologique*. Doin, Paris.

Ecole national du génie rural des eaux et des forêts. 1979. *La Forêt au Québec*. Quebec.

Eldin. H.L. 1979. *The tree key*. Charles Scribner's Sons, New York.

Elias, T.S. 1980. *The complete trees of North America. Field guide and natural history*. Van Nostrand Reinhold, New York.

Erichsen-Brown, C. 1979. *Use of plants for the past 500 years*. Breezy Creeks Press, Aurora, Ontario.

Erskine, D.S. 1985. *The plants of Prince Edward Island*. Research Branch, Agri. Can., Ottawa.

Erskine, J.S. 1976. *In forest and field*. The Nova Scotia Museum, Halifax.

Fernald, M.L. 1970. *Gray's manual of botany*. 8th edn. Van Nostrand, New York.

Fleurbec, 1981. *Plantes sauvages comestibles*. Le groupe Fleurbec, Saint-Cuthbert, Quebec.

Fleurbec, 1981. *Plantes sauvages au menu, guide culinaire*. Le groupe Fleurbec, Saint-Cuthbert, Quebec.

Fox, W.S. and J.H. Soper. The distribution of some trees and shrubs of the Carolinian Zone of Southern Ontario.
1952. Part 1. *Trans. Royal Can. Inst.* **29**: 65-84.
1953. Part 2. *Trans. Royal Can. Inst.* **30**: 3-32.
1954. Part 3. *Trans. Royal Can. Inst.* **30**: 99-130.

Frohne, D. and H.J. Pfander. 1984. *A colour atlas of poisonous plants*. Wolfe Publications Ltd., London.

Garman, E.H. 1973. *The trees and shrubs of British Columbia*. 5th edn, revd. B.C. Provincial Museum, Handbook 31. Victoria.

Gaudet, J.F. 1973. *Native trees of Prince Edward Island, and the more common woodland shrubs*. Dept Agri. For., Charlottetown.

Gibbons, E. 1972. *Stalking the healthful herbs*. D. McKay Co., New York.

Gillett, J.M. and D.J. White. 1978. *Checklist of vascular plants of the Ottawa-Hull Region, Canada*. NMNS, Ottawa.

Gingras, P. 1982. Le papillon bohémien menace encore. *Québec Science*, **20**, (10): 8-9.

Gleason, H.A. and A. Cronquist. 1963. *Manual of vascular plants*. Van Nostrand, New York.

Gleason, H.A. 1965. *New Britton and Brown illustrated flora of north-eastern United States and adjacent Canada*. New York Botanical Garden, New York.

Glendenning, R. 1944. The Garry Oak in British Columbia. *Can. Field Natur.*, **58**: 61-5.

Godfrey, W.E. 1986. *The birds of Canada*. Revd. Editn. NMNS, Ottawa.

Grandtner, M.M. 1966. *La végétation forestière du Québec méridional*. Presses de l'Université Laval, Quebec.

Griffith, B.G. 1934. *A pocket guide to the trees and shrubs of British Columbia*. B.C. Dept Lands, Victoria.

Grimm, W.C. 1966. *The book of trees for positive identification*. Hawthorn Books, New York.

Gross, H.L. and C.E. Dorworth. *Gremmeniella (Sclerodermis) disease of conifers*. (Brochure) Dept Environment, Can. For. Serv., Great Lakes Forest Research Centre. Sault Ste Marie, Ontario.

Guenther. E. 1969. *The essential oils*. Vol. 6. D. Van Nostrand, Toronto.

Guyot, L. and P. Gibassier. 1960. *Les noms des arbres*. Presses universitaires de France, Paris.

Harlow, W.M. and E.S. Harrar. 1968. *Textbook of dendrology covering the important forest trees of the United States and Canada*. 5th edn., McGraw-Hill, New York.

Hermann, M. 1973. *Le monde merveilleux des fleurs et plantes médicinales*. Solar, Paris.

Hinds, H.R. 1983. *The rare vascular plants of New Brunswick*. Syllogeus 50. NMNS, Ottawa.

Hinds. H.R. 1986. *Flora of New Brunswick*. Primrose Press, Fredericton.

Hitchcock, C.L. et al. 1959-69. *Vascular plants of the Pacific Northwest*. 5 vols. University of Washington Press, Seattle.

Hitchcock, C.L. and A. Cronquist. 1973. *Flora of the Pacific Northwest*. University of Washington Press, Seattle.

Hlava, B. and D. Lanska. 1979. *Les plantes saveur qui ensoleillent votre cuisine*. Elsevier Séquoia, Paris.

452

Hoadley, R.B. 1980. *Understanding wood*. The Taunton Press, Newtown, Conn.

Holmes, S. 1975. *Les arbres du monde*. Delachaux et Niestlé, Neuchâtel, Switzerland.

Hosie, R.C. 1979. *Native trees of Canada*. 8th edn. Fitzhenry & Whiteside, Don Mills, Ontario.

Hultén, E. 1968. *Flora of Alaska and neighboring Territories*. Stanford University Press, Stanford, Calif.

Huxley, A.J. 1985. *Green inheritance*. Collins, London.

Johnson, H. 1973. *The international book of trees*. Mitchell-Beasley Publishers Ltd, New York.

Kartesz J.T. and R. Kartesz. 1980. *A synonymized checklist of the vascular flora of the United States, Canada, and Greenland*. Vol. 2. University of North Carolina Press, Châpel Hill.

Keeler, H. 1969. *Our northern shrubs and how to identify them*. Dover Publications, New York.

Kingsbury, J.M. 1964. *Poisonous plants of the United States and Canada*. Prentice-Hall, Englewood Cliffs, New Jersey.

Kirk, D.R. 1975. *Wild edible plants of the western United States*. Naturegraph Publishers, Headsburg, Calif.

Knobel, E. 1972. *Identify trees and shrubs by their leaves*. Dover Publications, New York.

Knowles, R.H. 1975. *Woody ornamentals for the prairie provinces*. University of Alberta, Edmonton.

Kormondy, E. 1969. *Concepts of ecology*. Prentice-Hall, Englewood Cliffs, New Jersey.

Krochmal, A. and C. Krochmal. 1984. *A field guide to medicinal plants*. Times Books, New York.

Küchler. A.W. 1964. *Potential natural vegetation of the conterminous United States: map and manual to accompany the map*. Special Publication 36, Amer. Geog. Soc. New York.

Laforge M., L. Rail and V. Sicard. 1985. *La forêt derrière les arbres*. Broquet, La Prairie, Quebec.

Lamoureux, G. 1975. *Les plantes sauvages printanières*. Editeur Officiel du Québec, Quebec.

Lanzara, P. 1978. *L'univers inconnu des plantes en couleurs*. Elsevier-Sequoia, Paris.

Lewis, W.H. and Memory P.F. Elvin-Lewis. 1977. *Medical botany*. John Wiley, New York.

Li, H.L. 1963. *The origin and cultivation of shade and ornamental trees*. University of Pennsylvania Press, Philadelphia.

Little, E.L. 1980. *The Audubon Society field guide to North American trees, eastern region*. Chanticleer Press ed. Knopf, New York.

Little, E.L. 1980. *The Audubon Society field guide to North American trees, western region*. Chanticleer Press ed. Knopf, New York.

Little, E.L. 1971. *Atlas of United-States trees*. Vol. 1. *Conifers and important hardwoods*. For. Serv., United States, Washington, D.C.

Little, E.L. 1976a. *Atlas of United-States trees*. Vol. 3. *Minor western hardwoods*. For. Serv., United States, Washington, D.C.

Little, E.L. 1976b. *Atlas of United-States trees*. Vol. 4. *Minor eastern hardwoods*. For. Serv., United States, Washington, D.C.

Lortie, M. 1979. *Arbres, forêts et perturbations naturelles au Québec*. Presses de l'Université Laval, Quebec.

Loucks, O.L. 1961. *A forest classification for the Maritime Provinces*. Forest Research Branch, New Brunswick Dept Forestry, Fredericton.

Louis-Marie, R.P. 1967. *Flore-manuel de la Province de Québec, Canada*. Centre de Psychologie et Pédagogie, Montreal.

Lust, J. 1974. *The herb book*. Bantam Books, Toronto.

Lyons, C.P. 1965. *Trees, shrubs and flowers to know in British Columbia*, 2nd revd edn. Dent, Vancouver.

Maher, R.V., G.W. Argus et al. 1979. *The rare vascular plants of Saskatchewan*. Syllogeus 20. NMNS, Ottawa.

Maher, R.V., D.J. White, et al. 1978. *The rare vascular plants of Nova Scotia*. Syllogeus 18. NMNS, Ottawa.

Margulis, L. and K.V. Schwartz. 1982. *Five kingdoms*. W.H. Freeman. San Francisco.

Marie-Victorin, Fr. 1964. *Flore laurentienne*. 2nd edn. Presses de l'Université de Montréal, Montreal.

Marie-Victorin, Fr. and Fr. Roland-Germain. 1969. *Flore de l'Anticosti-Minganie*. Presses de l'Université de Montréal. Montreal.

Martin, 1979. *Les arbres*. Éditions Solar, Italy.

Martineau, R. 1984. *Insects harmful to forest trees*. Multiscience Publication. Montreal.

McAllister, D.E. and E.J. Crossman. 1973. *A guide to the freshwater sport fishes of Canada*. NMC, Ottawa.

454

McKay, S.M. and P.M. Catling. 1979. *Trees, shrubs and flowers to know in Ontario*. J.M. Dent & Sons, Don Mills, Ont.

MERCK Index. 1976. *An encyclopedia of chemicals and drugs*. 9th edn. Merck, Rahway, New Jersey.

Mességué, M. 1975. *Mon herbier de santé*. Laffont/Tchou, Paris.

Miller, H.A. and H.E. Jaques. 1978. *How to know the trees*. 3rd edn. W.C. Brown Co., Dubuque, Iowa.

Ministère des terres et forêts. 1974. *Petite flore forestière du Québec*. Quebec.

Ministère de l'Energie et des Ressources. 1981. *Les principaux arbres du Québec*. Quebec.

Mirov, N.T. 1967. *The genus pinus*. Roland Press, New York.

Mitchell, A.F. 1979. *Spotter's guide to trees of North America*. Mayflower Books, New York.

Mitchell, A. 1977. *Tous les arbres de nos forêts*. Elsevier Sequoia, Paris.

Montgomery, F.H. 1977. *Trees of Canada and the northern United States*. McGraw-Hill Ryerson, Toronto.

Morton, J.K. and J.M. Venn. 1984. *The flora of Manitoulin island*. 2nd revd edn. University of Waterloo, Waterloo, Ont.

Moss, E.H. 1983. *Flora of Alberta*. 2nd edn, revd John G. Packer, University of Toronto Press, Toronto.

Mullins, E.J. and T.S. McKnight. 1981. *Les bois du Canada*, 3rd edn. Editions du Pélican, Quebec.

Newcomb, L. 1983. *Guide des fleurs sauvages de l'est de l'Amérique du Nord*. Broquet, La Prairie, Quebec.

Nossert, E. 1975. *Guide des arbres*. Tardy, Kinkajou-Gallimard, Paris.

Ola'h, G.M. 1975. *Le pleurote Québécois*. Presses de l'Université Laval, Quebec.

Oliver, R.W. 1970. *Arbres d'ornement*. Agri. Can., Ottawa.

Otto, J.H. and A. Towle. 1969. *Modern biology*. Holt, Rinehart & Winston, Toronto.

Packer, J.G. and C.E. Bradley. 1984. *A checklist of the rare vascular plants in Alberta*. Provincial Museum of Alberta, Natur. Hist. Occ. Pap. 5. Alberta Culture, Edmonton.

Peattie, D.C. 1966. *A natural history of trees of eastern and central North America*. 2nd edn. Houghton Mifflin, Boston.

Peattie, D.C. 1980. *A natural history of western trees.* University of Nebraska Press, Lincoln.

Pendergast, J.F. 1982. *The origin of maple sugar.* Syllogeus 36. NMNS, Ottawa.

Peterson, L. 1978. *A field guide to edible wild plants of eastern and central North America.* Houghton Mifflin, Boston.

Petrides, G.A. 1972. *A field guide to trees and shrubs.* 2nd edn. Peterson Field Guide Series, Houghton Mifflin, Boston.

Phillips, R. 1978. *Trees in Britain. Europe and North America.* Ward Lock, London.

Porsild, A.E. 1964. 2nd edn revd. *Illustrated flora of the Canadian Arctic Archipelago.* NMC, Queen's printer, Ottawa.

Porsild, A.E. and W.J. Cody. 1980. *Vascular plants of continental Northwest Territories, Canada,* NMNS, Ottawa.

Porter, C.L. 1967. *Taxonomy of flowering plants.* W.H. Freeman, San Francisco.

Potterton D. 1983. *Culpeper's color herbal.* Sterling, New York.

Potvin, A. 1975. *A panorama Canadian forests.* Dept Environment, Can. For. Serv., Ottawa.

Pouliot, P. 1976. *Arbres, haies et arbustes.* Editions de l'Homme, Montreal.

Pryer, K.M. and G.W., Argus, 1987. *Vascular plants of restricted range in the continental Northwest Territories, Canada.* Unpubld. NMNS Ottawa.

Quartier, A.A. 1973. *Guide des arbres et arbustes d'Europe.* Delachaux-Niestlé, Neuchâtel, Switzerland.

Ringius, G.S. 1979. Thuja occidentalis in western Nova Scotia. *Can. Field Natur.* **93** (3): 326-8.

Robertson, S.M. 1973. *Dyes from plants.* Van Nostrand Reinhold, New York.

Rogers, J.E. 1920. *The tree book.* Doubleday, New York.

Roland, A.E. and E.C. Smith. 1969. *The flora of Nova Scotia.* Nova Scotia Museum, Halifax.

Roland, J.C. and F. Roland. 1980. *Atlas de biologie végétale.* Vol. 2, *Organisation des plantes à fleurs.* Masson, Paris.

Rose, A.H. and O.H. Linduist. 1977. *Insects of eastern spruces, fir and hemlock.* Dept Environment, Can. For. Serv., Ottawa.

Rouleau, Ernest. 1978. *List of the vascular plants of the province of Newfoundland (Canada).* Oxen Pond Botanic Park, St John's, Newfoundland.

Rousseau, C. 1974. *Géographie floristique du Québec/Labrador*. Presses de l'Université Laval, Quebec.

Rowe, J.S. 1972. *Forest regions of Canada*. For. Serv., Ottawa.

Ryan, A.G. 1978. *Native trees and shrubs of Newfoundland and Labrador*, Parks Div., Dept Tourism, St John's, Newfoundland.

Sargent, C.S. 1965. *Manual of trees of North America*. 2 vols, Dover Publications, New York.

Saunders, G.L. 1973. *Trees of Nova Scotia*. Dept Lands Forests, Truro, Nova Scotia.

Sauvé, P.M. 1977. *La teinture naturelle au Québec*. L'Aurore, Montreal.

Savile, D.B.O. 1962. *Collection and care of botanical specimens*. Publn. 1113, Can. Dept Agri., Ottawa.

Schuler, S. (ed.). 1978. *Simon and Schuster's guide to trees*. Simon & Schuster, New York.

Schweitzer, R. 1977. *Je fais mon herbier*. 2nd edn. André Lerson, Paris.

Scoggan, H.J. 1957. *Flora of Manitoba*. Dept Northern Affairs and National Resources. NMC, Bulletin 140, Ottawa.

Scoggan, H.J. 1978-9. *The Flora of Canada*. 4 vols. NMNS, NMC, Ottawa.

Scott, P.J. 1974. *Conifers of Newfoundland*. Oxen Pond Botanic Park, Memorial University of Newfoundland, St John's.

Sénécal, S.J. 1975. *L'herbier*. Les feuillets du club, No 67, Editions des Jeunes Naturalistes, Montreal.

Sherk, L.C. and A.R. Buckley. 1979. *Ornamental shrubs for Canada*. Supply and Services Canada, Ottawa.

Sherk, L.C. 1971. *Checklist of ornamental trees for Canada*. Dept Agri., Ottawa.

Smith, J. and L. Parrot. 1984. *Arbres, arbustes, arbrisseaux du Québec*. 8th edn. Ministère de l'Energie et des ressources, Quebec.

Smith, J.P. Jr. 1977. *Vascular plant families*. Mad River Press, Eureka, Calif.

Soper, J.H. and M.L. Heimburger. 1982. *Shrubs of Ontario*. Royal Ontario Museum, Toronto.

Soucy, R. 1976. *Récits de foresteries*. Presses de l'Université du Québec, Montreal.

Stanton, C.R. 1976. *Canadian forestry: the view beyond the trees*. Macmillan, Toronto.

Stewart, D. 1977. *Point Pelee: Canada's deep south.* Burns & MacEachern, Toronto.

Straley, B.G., R.L. Taylor and G.W. Douglas. 1985. *The rare vascular plants of British Columbia.* Syllogeus 59. NMNS, Ottawa.

Street, H.E. and H. Opik. 1970. *The physiology of flowering plants.* Edward Arnold, London.

Strobel, G.A. and G.N. Lanier. 1981. Dutch Elm disease. *Scien. Amer.*, **245** (3): 56-66.

Taylor, T.M.C. 1973. *The rose family (Rosaceae) of British Columbia.* B.C. Provincial Museum, Handbook 30, Victoria.

Taylor, R.L. and B. MacBryde. 1977. *Vascular plants of British Columbia.* University of British Columbia Press, Vancouver.

Thurzona, L. 1978. *Les plantes-santé qui poussent autour de nous.* Elsevier-Séquoia, Paris.

Turner, N.J. and A.F. Szczawinski. 1978. *Edible garden weeds of Canada.* NMNS, Ottawa.

Turner, N.J. 1979. *Plants of British Columbia Indians technology.* B.C. Provincial Museum, Handbook 38, Victoria.

Turner, N.J. 1975. *Food plants of British Columbia Indians.* B.C. Provincial Museum, Handbook 34, Victoria.

Turner, N.J. 1978. *Food plants of British Columbia Indians.* B.C. Provincial Museum. Handbook 36, Victoria.

Turner, N.J. and A.F. Szczawinski. 1979. *Edible wild fruits and nuts of Canada.* NMNS, Ottawa.

Underhill, J.E. 1967. *The plants of Manning Park, British Columbia.* B.C., Parks Branch, Victoria.

Underhill, J.E. and C.C. Chuang. 1976. *Wildflowers of Manning Park.* B.C. Provincial Museum, British Columbia Provincial Parks Branch, Victoria.

Uphof, J.C.Th. 1968. *Dictionary of economic plants.* 2nd edn. J. Cramer, Lehre.

Ursing B. 1975. *Les plantes sauvages d' Europe en couleurs.* Elsevier-Séquoia, Paris.

van Barneveld, J.W., M. Rafig, et al. 1980. *An illustrated key to gymnosperms of British Columbia.* B.C. Provincial Museum, Victoria.

Voss, E.G. 1972. *Michigan flora.* Pt I. Cranbrook Inst. Sci., Bloomfield Hills, Michigan.

458

Wagner, W.H., Jr. 1974. Dwarf hackberry (Ulmaceae: Celtis tenuifolia) in the Great Lakes Region. *Michigan Botanist*, **13**: 73-99.

Wharton, M.E. and R.W. Barbour. 1973. *Trees and shrubs of Kentucky*. University Press of Kentucky, Lexington.

White, D.J. and K.L. Johnson. 1980. *The rare vascular plants of
Manitoba*. Syllogeus 27. NMNS, Ottawa.

White, J.H. 1973. *The forest trees of Ontario and the more commonly
planted foreign trees*. 5th edn. Ministry of Natural Resources,
Toronto.

Zavitz, E.J. 1973. *Hardwood trees of Ontario with bark characteristics*. Ministry of Natural Resources, Toronto.

Ziller, W.G. 1974. *The tree rusts of western Canada*. Environment
Canada, For. Serv., Ottawa.

Zim, H.S. and A.C. Martin. 1956. *Trees: a guide to familiar American trees*. Golden Press, New York.

INDEX

Page number in **bold-face type** indicates recommended English or scientific name and that the species is illustrated and described.

459

460

474

478

NOTES

NOTES

NOTES

NOTES

NOTES

NOTES

NOTES

NOTES

NOTES

NOTES

NOTES

NOTES

NOTES

NOTES

NOTES